BACK TO SOURCES:

Essays Métis from the Outaouais

Pange lingua . . . .

Tommaso d'Aquino

Rather than saying that the soul is in the body,
we should say that the body is in the soul.

Albertus Magnus

To my father
Camille Augustin La Bossière
(d. Perth, Ontario), Manitoba métis, soldier,
homesteader at Lac du Bonnet, who had tales of
wonder to tell from
a boyhood in the Great Depression:
of skidding out pulpwood logs, sawing tamarack for
firewood, training sleighdogs, bringing home rabbits,
grouse, pike, deer, sturgeon,
and of being transfixed by a vision of
the Northern Lights;

et à Pépé Albert Jean-Marie Mainguy de Saint-
Aignan, Val de Loire
(d. Victoria, Colombie-britannique):
boulanger extraordinaire, soldat, homme de poids,
navigateur à la voile, jardinier et viticulteur,
grand chasseur et pêcheur,
qui lui aussi a su faire de son mieux pour assurer
le bien-être de sa famille.

BACK TO SOURCES: Essays Métis From the Outaouais

by

Camille La Bossière

The Tecumseh Press Ltd.
Ottawa, Canada
2003

Canadä

We acknowledge the financial assistance of the Government of Canada through the Book Publishing Program (BPIDP) for our publishing activities.

National Library of Canada Cataloguing in Publication Data

La Bossière, Camille R.
Back to sources : essays Métis from the Outaouais / Camille La Bossière

Includes bibliographical references.
ISBN 1-896133-35-5 (pbk.)

1. Métis. I. Title.

FC109.L32 2003 971'.00497 C2003-900490-2
E99.M47L32 2003

Cover: design by Bull's Eye Design, Ottawa, Canada.

Photographs on cover courtesy the author. Front—Pépé Mainguy, with his children, Jacqueline, Bebert and Mimi, next to her husband, Camille "Jackie" La Bossière, with their firstborn, the Critic (near Lac du Bonnet, Manitoba, in 1944); Back—Author with "Hercules," near their home, "Arborealis," in Ontario's Renfrew County, 2000

Printed and bound in Canada on acid free paper

Table of Contents

Preface v

Introduction, by G.W. Stephen Brodsky ix

I. Coyote Agape 1

II. Of Words and Understanding in Grove's *Settlers of the Marsh* 18

III. Le Silence chez Félix-Antoine Savard 42

IV. Compass of the Catopric Past: John Glassco, Translator 47

V. Du pain, du papier, et des cannibales: M. Carlyle et sa Révolution 66

VI. Nietzsche 77

VII. Of Acedia, Romantic Imagination and Irony Revisited: A Supplementary Context for *Under the Volcano* 89

VIII. Of Politics and *Irony's Edge* 118

IX. Montaigne's Unknown God and Melville's Confidence-Man 122

X. Of Huxley and Davies 142

Back to Sources

XI. Past and Present: Neobaroque Novels
from French Canada 149

XII. Of Montaigne, Dostoevsky and Gide: A *Sotie* . . 174

XIII. Of MacLennan or Conrad 190

XIV. Pop Conrad and Child's Play 202

XV. Of Bells, Nonsense, Words and Trees:
A Note on Conrad's *The Rover* 226

XVI. Péguy 238

Recursus/Excursus 260

Preface

Tanni, cher Lecteur.

The "Outaouais" in the title may need some explanation.

My first memories date from 1946 in Ottawa's Basse-Ville, where my sister Michelle Marie was born and baptized. In 1947, we returned to "all our relations" *au Manitoba.*[1] Some two decades later, after studies at Iona College, N.Y. (in medieval philosophy and theology, the Bible and "literary greats" from Britain, France and the Mediterranean), and these followed up by teaching French, English and Religion at St. Pius X High School in Montreal North and a stint of readings in Italian at McGill, I returned to the Outaouais to take my first graduate course: though on Renaissance poetry in English, it depended on a medieval rational psychology as revised by Jacques Maritain and still more or less consistent with a Chaucerian, even Thomistic, sense of the human condition.

Fortune smiled again in the 1970s, when after many shuttlings between Victoria and the Memorial University of Newfoundland, I was given a chance to renew acquaintance with W.A. Sinclair's *The Traditional Formal Logic* and to lecture on British, European and comparative Canadian literature in the Department of English and Philosophy at the bilingual Royal Roads Military College (in my native province of B.C.). Then nine years passed before I returned to the University of Ottawa. Moving it was to clap my eyes again on the bust of Thomas Aquinas at the entrance to the Pavillon Simard, headquarters for the Faculty of Arts. Words chiselled on the stand: *Sapientis est ordinare et judi-*

care. A homecoming, of sorts.

I should add this note. Necessarily different from Clara Thomas' *All My Sisters: Essays on the Work of Canadian Women Writers* in a number of ways, most of the pieces collected in *Back to Sources* do "represent duty-writing."[2] All of them were done in the performance, so to speak, of various duties. It goes without saying, though, that jumping through hoops and hoop-dancing, like working to put food on the table and following a profession or vocation, need not be mutually exclusive in practice or principle or intention. As Professor Thomas implies in her Introduction, among the many things that many a dutiful teacher/scholar/critic and many a dutiful literary artist have in common is the need to make a living. Readers will then have occasion, I hope, to find some respite in the fact that a number of the essays in *Back to Sources* (particularly those of a patently childrenly character) also represent "celebrations," perhaps even "show-casing[s]."[3]

An almost last word by way of prefacing. As its title in all seriousness suggests, *Back to Sources* means to be spiritual, full of hops, skips and jumps forwards and backwards as it is. All of which is to say in a roundabout way that the thing is intended to be "funny," in the multiple senses of that word.

* * *

Cher Lecteur, please indulge me for just a little while longer. I am compelled at this juncture to pay my respects to Soeur Marie-André du Sacré Coeur, who taught me something of ships at l'École du Précieux-Sang in Saint-Boniface, Manitoba; and to Father A.F. Tisdale, SJ, who introduced me, at St. Paul's College, across the Red River, to Gerard Manley Hopkins, Graham Greene and Charles Dickens, and had the knack of asking just the right question at just the right time.

And yet again to beg the reader's forbearance: "nomads," so Tante Jeanne d'Arc-Lilliane La Bossière (aka Marie-Jeanne) used to call us. And justifiably so. But the fact remains that Diane and I and our son Paul have lived more years in the Ottawa Valley than anywhere else. We are now in place, within sight of the Bonnechere River and Hills, with fine fishing and hunting just minutes away.

CRL
Douglas, Ontario
24.vi.MMII

ENDNOTES

1. As Thomas King explains by way of introduction to *All My Relations: An Anthology of Contemporary Canadian Fiction* (Norman and London: U of Oklahoma P / Toronto: M&S, 1990), "'All my relations' is the English equivalent of a phrase familiar to most Native Peoples in North America. It may begin or end a prayer or a speech or a story

[. . .] 'All my relations' is at first a reminder of who we are and of our relationship with both our family and our relatives. It also reminds us of the extended relationship we share with all human beings and . . . to the animate and inanimate forms that can be seen or imagined" (ix). I would add our communion in relationship with Being, or Manitou, the timeless Spirit of all life, everywhere.

2. Clara Thomas, *All My Sisters: Essays on the Work of Canadian Women Writers* (Ottawa: Tecumseh, 1994) xi.

3. Thomas xi.

INTRODUCTION:
Of Coincidental Sources and Nothing in Particular

by

G.W. Stephen Brodsky

> "The principal pain of existence is that from the beginning I am in contradiction with myself, that a person's true being comes through opposition." Kierkegaard, *Johannes Climacus* (1843)

> "Life . . . may be nothing but a joke in bad taste, but there is no reason not to enjoy a good laugh over it in the meantime." George Gabori, *When Evils Were Most Free* (1981)

1

The Introduction as Source

> *My way is to begin with the beginning; / The regularity of my design / Forbids all wandering as the worst of sinning. . . .* Byron, *Don Juan*

The Introduction to the epic critical achievement in the following pages embodies a contradiction worthy of Lyly's Euphues, who could not say yes without saying no. Coming at the beginning, it is a summing-up written at the end, a record of what has gone before. So the reader also begins with the Introduction as an anatomy of its author's wit for a chart; and if perseverant, the reader reaches the end of the critical epic's achievement, which, *Odyssey*-like, returns precisely where it began.

Not much perseverance is asked of the reader of *Back to Sources*. Camille La Bossière (whom I alternatively call the Critic) is in some ways Byronic, sincerely satirical, and divinely demonic in wit, imitating the irony of the mortal paradox plagued by dualities, expressed through a savagely exquisite laughter, at times hopefully joyful, at other times despairingly mocking, of authors who spin out the tragicomedy of contradictory existence. The media are as diverse as Canadian First Nations fiction, a *Québécois* priest's *ars poetica* and a dialogue between Carlyle and Emerson. The prospects are as varied as Teufeldröckh's arctic Weissnichtwo, the Melvillean analogical seascape and a Manitoban marsh. For the Critic's "sources" are richly diverse: his roots in the Canadian soil and beyond, the people, ideas and literature at the origins of his intellectual life–all the "accidents" that attached to the "substantial," unique Self which here reflects on being as darkly mirrored in works of literary art and criticism.

The title *Back to Sources* is apt for a collection of essays that celebrates beginnings. The essays are "catoptric," if one may borrow from Chapter IV, "'Compass of the Catroptic Past': John Glassco, Translator," the Critic's puckishly chosen sci-babble-term for Glassco's reconciliations of remembered past and present living, the "home," he says, that is always with him. The essays mirror the reflections from the Critic's understanding, refracting images on azimuths leading to a single focal point: the coincidence of vexatious opposites in sources abstract or material: being and non-being, sense and nonsense, silence and babble, light and dark, divine and diabolical, knowledge and ignorance, wisdom and folly, self and other, comedy and tragedy, native Canadian and native European, French and English language (in which the Critic is equally fluent) – all seen through the lens of art, and vicariously scanned by the Critic's imaginative, analytical savvy.

La Bossière is a joyous version of Dostoevsky's Man from Underground, the drearily passive wit who cautions his audience, "Gentlemen, of course I'm joking, and I know I am not doing it very successfully; but you know you musn't take everything I say for a joke. I may be joking through clenched teeth. Gentlemen, there are some questions that torment me. . . ." The sneer, like "the wee drop of irony" that Dostoevsky added to his distillations for Christ (as in *The Idiot*), expresses the futility of explanation, the invincible inadequacy of words for the veiled truth of a Monad, as it were, wherein the subterranean personage's doubleness is one, known only through eloquent silence beyond the reach of finite reason in a world where armies of individuated beings clash by night. The metaphor also has literal aptness. One need only think of the annual two minutes in Canada at the eleventh hour or of the eleventh day of the eleventh month, the day of remembrance when the roar of traffic around cenotaphs, the shouting and tumult die, even the rattle of a newspaper muted. Only a cough, perhaps, deepening the silence. At that moment, such a stillness, more profoundly eloquent than the myriad words written on war since Armistice Day, 1918.

Likewise the silence of a truth expressed but not explained is in a hubub of literary voices. Having begun at the end with this Introduction, the reader traverses a parabolic curve of sorts, drawn on by the sheer charm and elegance of the Virgil-guide Critic's wording and thought until, circling to his point of departure where Alpha and Omega join, he sees the disparate and contradictory parts coming together in a substantial integration. The "circle," it turns out, is a double gyre spiralling downward through Dantesque levels of mortal torment, finally to return on its own axis to its Alpha. However, unlike the author of epic criticism, the writer of the Introduction has no constraint to begin at the beginning.

2

Sources of the Critic's Intellectual Life

A Historian is a prophet looking backwards. Sybil Marshall, *Strip the Willow* (1996)

It seems obvious, *pace* Kierkegaard, that life is contradictory, having to be lived forwards, but understood only when read backwards. So, I assert my liberty, in defiance of Lord Byron, to "plunge '*in medias res*'," explaining (as it were, to make ends meet) the Critic himself as far as finite wit permits, starting with his intellectual life beyond his biological beginnings (which we shall come to at the end) and charting (I mean to evoke the cant term with due precision) "where he's coming from," his inspirational sources. Then, perhaps, the unity of the Critic's own explanations will be apparent as themselves comprising a work of art, and, therefore, of a certain unity.

In his Preface, Professor La Bossière "explains" that, in the early 1970s, he taught Literature at a military college. More important for meaning here, but unsaid, is his labouring over a doctoral dissertation at the same time. Its subject was the oeuvre of Joseph Conrad, an author bedevilled by the conflicting claims of Existence made on a humankind bearing the blessed curse of consciousness like a double mark of Cain. The most vital thing for a band of convicts cast up on a remote shore of a merely spectacular universe (so Conrad announced stonily in *Lord Jim*) is "how to be." The droll irony with which he faced the paradox of Being was a muted mirth, inspired by a rather too chilling intellectual love for the Divine Comedy. In his Abel-and-Cain tale "The Duel," a musical surgeon's disinterested amusement imputedly shields him from psychic wounding as he tends to the wounds of a suicidally bellicose duellist.

Then as now, La Bossière could share Conrad's silent laughter. But contrariwise, as befitted his sensibility and his training in Dominican scholarly tradition, the aspirant doctoral scholar's surgical tools were the metaphysics of a theology evincing a faith in an ethical, if enigmatic, cosmos. Salient among the works that influenced him was *De docta ignorantia* (1440), by Cardinal Nicholas of Cusa, an ecumenist a little ahead of Copernicus in his revolutionary thought. With the universal handicap of language as his only means of explicating the author's expressions of the mortal paradox, La Bossière explored an Orgoglio's Cavern of Conrad's knowing ignorance, his silent abysses of Self and Other as "truth manifold and one," and masked contrarily in *Heart of Darkness*, for instance, as the spoken "name" of the Intended. "Grac'd with Doctor's name," La Bossière went on to write *Joseph Conrad and the Science of Unknowing*, the first of a lifetime of scholarly achievements in print on related themes.

The Neoplatonists, from Christian scholars who left their mark on Cusa to mountebank magi, had this in common: their philosophy posited a Unity at the Source of Being, what Cusa called a *coincidentia oppositorum*, a coincidence of opposites. Finite existence is dyadic; and birth from the soul's home in the noumenal All into the realm of the finite is a tearing-away of the individual soul from the *nous* into alien sense experience and fragmented reason. Knowledge of Wholeness is perforce unspeakable, expressible only in the silences of knowing ignorance. Not coincidentally, the gods of most polytheistic religions are represented masked, two of the great monotheistic religions proscribing the utterance of the true name of God, and the other, the neoplatonized Christianity of "the Hidden God," the *Deus absconditus* and therefore unnammeable, having perforce lost sight of the Word in the Darkness (*in tenebra)* which was and is Divine. The babble bequeathed humankind as language only masks truth. That is a theme of the Critic's amused, ironic treatment of Thomas Carlyle's *The French Revolution* in Chapter V, "Du pain, du papier, et des cannibales." To a people starved of authentic material and spiritual sustenance, this is the response registered in a volume of a thousand pages and more: "Let them eat paper"

. . . and each other.

We may agree with Marlowe's Doctor Faustus that the problem with knowing "how to be," of finding some way of resolving the ambiguities of finite existence, how to reconconcile all that lies between the silent poles, can be a devilishly self-negating exercise. In Conrad, characters who seem to know how to be, such as Stein and a phlegmatic French Lieutenant (*Lord Jim*), emulate their cosmos. They are mere spectators at a point of equilibrium suspended between life's conflicting claims, onlookers reduced to a steely indolence at a still point of indisturbance, indifference. Just getting on with it suffices. For Conrad the trick was how to be, yet to remain immersed in being, to endure the curse of contradiction with equanimity. Taken to its *reductio ad absurdum*, this theory of knowing leads only to the grave. In *Nostromo*, Hirsch the dealer in hides is interrogated with questions for which he cannot know the answers. He finds the courage of contempt for his tormentor only when the rope by which he is suspended from a rafter ends its pendulum-oscillations. With every illusory hope of mortal salvation stripped away, he transcends hope, as it were at one terminus of his swing, and fear at the other. He is found still hanging (and hanging still), at last at peace, having achieved in the death of hope the unspeakable knowledge of "how to be." Not a very practical resolution of the human predicament, but (given Conrad's knack for macabre symbols) perhaps not to be wondered at in the case of a trader in the empty skins of dead creatures.

La Bossière wrote of such notions in another idiom in *The Victorian* Fol Sage (1989), wherein he reveals the "suicidal" nature of Montaigne's sceptical wisdom and sifts the abiding connection of folly with human art as expressed in writings from Carlyle, Emerson, Melville and Conrad. For better or for worse, art is to do. And to do is to be. But, contradictorily, to know how to be abides in the silence of not doing. The Critic shows a modicum of wisdom in not attempting the futile business of cutting that existential Gordian knot at the Source. Rather, he simply shows how others have faced (or not faced) Existential perplexity: with bitter laughter, stoic acceptance, amused disinterest, anger, love, hope, despair. Subsuming the whole (and, it is to be wished, the vision of every author in this book), is the unspoken Conradian precept that "the spectacle" is *never* "for despair." Implicit in the Critic's meaning is that the enigma of Being is for celebration, because it is all that we have this side of the Infinite. With exceptions notable but not always obvious, he finds celebration in the authors' silent laughter.

3

Sources in a Landscape

Suppose the stolen offspring of some mountain tribe brought up in a city of the plain . . . the spell-bound habit of their inherited frames . . . quivering throughout in uneasy mysterious meanings. . . . George Eliot, *Daniel Deronda*

In his Preface, La Bossière offers biographical facts to explain why "Outaouais" is in the title of his book. He "explains" that he lived in Ottawa as a child, returned, left, returned again. All of which is to say that he gives a factual *source,* a *reason* logical enough for his choice of a word. But a relation of facts *explains* nothing. A disappointing start, one may say. He has begun a book that should require exquisite scholarly precision with incondite *im*precision. Surely he owes it to us to explain himself? But by the time the reader has reached the end of this book of critical essays, s/he may have come to the realization that the book itself is the explanation we have sought where no explanation suffices and none is possible. The medium expresses its message. We have come to an intimate knowledge of the author/critic; not of facts of themselves, but of the workings of a mind.

La Bossière's first autobiographical "explanation" takes its meaning from a playfully expressive silence about the "Outaouais" itself, a site close to the spirit, heart, and mind of the Critic. If the reader isn't deaf to the sound of silence, the rush of the Ottawa River's rapids will be heard in these pages. With its headwaters in a mazed source of lakes in western Québec, the watercourse meanders absent-mindedly westward, recollects itself in Lake Temiskaming; then debouching southward and east, its waters plunge out of the Canadian Shield's rocky highlands, slice determinedly between the nation's Ontario capital and Québec's city of Hull, and float sedately onto a coastal plain, where at Montréal they join the waters of the St Lawrence on their southwesterly journey to fill the Great Lakes.

Since the days before Canada was a political fact, throughout its length from Lake Temiskaming to Montréal, the Ottawa River was taken by early European Canadians as the border between English and French, Upper and Lower Canada, and in due course, Canada and Québec. The imposition of a political and linguistic boundary on a landscape and an aboriginal people that knew no other than earth and sky seemed (and still seems) reasonable to politicians. No matter that the river's fertile trench, the Ottawa Valley, had already marked for the Algonquin people a rough limit of the region they had known as Outaouais from time out of mind. Not having need of maps, they knew the Outaouais. It stretched from where the rolling Laurentian Mountains met the rising sun, and to the river lit by sunset; then upstream through the valley's narrowing towards the Pole Star, and beyond Lake Temiskaming to another lake, the one they called Abitibi. Today the Algonquin who still have treaty rights live on a couple of reserves, and the rest of the region has been carved up into four districts, 79 municipalities, and three large urban centres.

Of all the areas of the Outaouais, the Ottawa Valley on its southern and western edges is uniquely situated where Canada's two "founding" European peoples rub shoulders, mingle, and have children with each other, and with the people of the First Nations, for whom the Outaouais had no paper boundaries. The Ottawa Valley's towns and villages, of Wilno, Douglas, Arnprior, Renfrew, Eaganville, Fort Coulonge, Waltham, and Mattawa, among many others, are like little United Nations. Algonkian gutturals are heard only rarely now, but one often hears *joual*, the endearing and oft-comically affected "Franglais," the patois no legislation can erase, and a special brand of English phonemes called the "Ottawa Valley twang" (a sound derived from a confluence of English, French and Canal Irish). There are bilingual folk, some not quite fluent in either of the 'official' languages, and immigrants or descendants from other sources entirely, who call the Ottawa Valley home. In all, a confluence or reconciliation of differences, even oppositions–racial, national, linguistic, cultural–made originally by a need for survival in an unforgiving frontier, into a distinct people, the Canadians of the Ottawa Valley. Of Métis stock, Camille La Bossière bodies forth that little world called the Outaouais.

4

Sources in Literature

Rejoice in the world, warts and all, because it's all you've got, and rejoicing and despair are therefore interchangeable terms. Salman Rushdie's Dubdub, in *Fury* (2001)

How to live with the paradox of self and world is the great human challenge. For a La Bossière writing in the Christian tradition, the answer is a loving laughter at the *comédie humaine*, making of it a Divine Comedy. The Critic in high good humour passes by the billboard posted at the entrance, "*LASCIATE OGNI SPERANZA VOI CH' ENTRATE!*," so to make life a little less infernal. Each essay, then, is a constituent of a whole, the sum of *Back to Sources* a Dantesque anagoge mocking the Greak Mocker.

For the Critic, this laughing love or loving laughter (take your pick) isn't an abstracted Universal Love of Existence or humankind-in-general, reconciling opposites by mere idealism. In Chapter III, "Le Silence chez Félix-Antoine Savard," the Critic describes the poetic imagination evoked by Msgr Savard in his *Journal et Souvenirs* as mediator between the finite and the Infinite, committed "à exprimer cet inexprimable d'une façon positive et concrète," the silent symbols of poetry offering objective correlatives to express but not explain "'l'ordre, la beauté du monde.'" The Critic's sympathy with the Québécois divine who grew up in Chicoutimi and thrived among loggers along the Saguenay and the inland sailors he frequently met when holidaying on the coast of the St Lawrence is apparent enough.

But the Critic's expression of sympathy has in it more than a touch of indulgence. He passes no judgment on an *ars poetica* grounded in a negative contemplative tradition; but one senses his wry smile in paraphrasing Msgr Savard's metaphor, which, like Robbe-Grillet's images of eloquent absences, approaches the mysticism of the East: "La blancheur silencieuse du papier dit plus que les mots noirs." Significantly, he credits Savard with finding "l'unité dans la poésie," but stands mute before the question of the efficacy of such a poetic *sacrum silentium*. While the poetic La Bossière respects imagination, his own silence is rather eloquent testimony that he is not entirely of a mind with Savard. There is precious little human warmth in the poetic love of the unity of all things that the Critic attributes to Savard's poetic imagination: "*la lune, la terre, la truite, l'arbre, l'eau,*" *etcétéra, etcétéra, etcétéra. . . .* The list is notable for its absences: People; flesh-and-blood folk, men, women, and children. Msgr Savard, so it would seem, believes that he has reconciled the irreconcilable to his own satisfaction. In Dostoevsky's *The Brothers Karamazov*, Mrs Khokhlakov confesses to Father Zosima, "The more I hate individual people, the more ardent is my general love for mankind." It would be a bit extreme to say that the Critic's silence is suggestive of Msgr Savard's omission showing him at one with her; but if there is silent laughter here, perhaps it is indeed La Bossière's, at a likeness that is merely a matter of degree for a divine who sees a substantial order primarily in the diversity of *things*.

5

Despair of Sources and the Sound Silence

Life cannot be explained to people; either you see it or you don't. Myrtle Brodsky, "Celia in England"

There is precious little to laugh about, however, when love, not even a generalized, abstracted, intellectual love informs the everyday lives of unphilosophic souls confronting the immensity of the silent void inside and outside themselves. The universals of Carlyle and Savard are behind us already, though predicted, still ahead in Chapters III and IV of the Critic's text. In Chapter II, on the matter of words and understading in Grove's *Settlers of the Marsh*, he finds characters who, if they had even a chord of music in their etiolated spirits, might hum along with the Beatles (to the accompaniment of the surgeon flotist in "The

Duel," a short story from Conrad's *Set of Six)*: "I can't live in a world without love." We find in *Settlers* the particulars of a certain place, where Grove's drear characters, Niels, Lars and Ellen, each unknowing in his and her own ways, face the silent immensity of northern Manitoba bushland that La Bossière has himself known. Incomprehension of language is an analogue of their vaster incomprehension. Unable to communicate with each other at any level, and without the warmth of affection, they suffer a "privation beyond remedy." The Critic imputes to Grove as "governing theme" the proposition that "the obscurity of the innermost life and the powerlessness of words to grasp and communicate the truth of that life." Incapacities of language are analogues for helpless passivity before the horror of "the inscrutable syntax of life." Void of love and faced with monstrously opaque facts that will not yield to reason, Niels and Ellen are outsiders, alien to each other and homeless in the vastness, until Niels learns the saving grace of laughter. The Critic concludes that "the semantics of privation is [basic] . . . to the articulation of Grove's thought." The "privatives" that figure so abundantly in Grove's "language of negation" express a "bafflement" remedied, perhaps, by "imagination, a faculty beyond reason, for the perception of essential, inscrutable truth." Msgr Savard's dictum that the poetic imagination is the mediator between finitude and Infinity, image and object made whole and one at the Source, is fine (so the Critic's silence seems to say) for poets and divines. But what about the rest of us, the simple folk who don't breathe such rarified air, but have only each other?

6

No Sources

'I must know the real truth,
the truth beyond magic.'
'There is no truth beyond magic,' said the king.
John Fowles, *The Magus* (1965)

Worse still than breathing the thin 'philosophical' air, do we suffocate in a void, there being no matter or substance, no objective truth, for anyone? The thought perishes in Chapter VI, the Critic's essay on the self-murdering thought of Friedrich Wilhelm Nietzsche. The chapter, though short and not quite celebratory in its irony, is not altogether without a certain deadpan sense of humour. Perhaps, that is because the essay was initially written as an encyclopaedia entry. The Critic finds nothing much to embrace with any joy in the Nietzschean twilight gloom, made lambent only in the reflected glow of other chapters. Implicit in his treatment of Nietzsche's fiercely vigorous rejection of "Christian faith" and its "grammar of the *Logos*" is the emptiness of non-being, the opposite of Being's silent spaces to be expressed and materially felt, but not, by nature, fully explicable. Nietzsche, the Critic implies, does not attempt to explain the inexplicable, or even to acknowledge that there is anything worthy of human articulation, however partial. Rather, he explains that there is *nothing* to be explained. The *sotto voce* Critic's unstated contempt for Nietzschean grand pessimism is implicit in its context. The pathetic figures in *Settlers of the Marsh* are dwarfed, impotent, and baffled through continual recourse to a positivist reason as they ask an uncomprehending "why?" in a vast landscape of unknowing. Frustrated in their inarticulate attempts to grasp the nature of things, they would (by Nietzsche's fiat) be simply deluded "slaves" if they were to come to an accommodation with an imputedly chimerical Existence, accepting it on its own terms of non-being without even so much as a modicum of objective truth or meaning.

Superficially, Nietzsche's notion of God as "the father of evil"–and its logical extension (in the Critic's paraphrase) of "the sublime as the artistic conquest of the horrible"–elides with Msgr Savard's *ars poetica*, in which a poetic imagination working through a love of the vexatious particulars of nature, transcends and unifies them in a harmonious and ordered Whole. However, whereas Msgr Savard finds his still point (a kind of *barachois*) in his exercise of a negative capability, Nietzsche jettisons the restraint implicit in harmony and order, the "Apollinian principle," and exults in "Dionysian" abandon to nature and impulse, by which his *Ubermensch*, "the conqueror of God," creates, and thus destroys, himself. The Critic invokes a phrase from *Ecce Homo*, as if he sees in Nietzsche the anarchist Professor in Conrad's *The Secret Agent*, who stalks the streets of London in a perpetual state of potential self-annihilation: "'I am no man; I am dynamite.'" The Critic's derision is apparent in his reference to "grammarless" (no God, no grammar) "theothanatology"; rather, he evokes for sanity's sake Gabriel Marcel's "unambiguous characterization of Nietzschean unreason as "suicidal, for theology and philosophy alike." While, as the Critic shows, the philosophies of Montaigne, Carlyle and even Savard bear that self-destructive seed, the reflexively self-destroying "anti-nihilist" Nietzsche is alone in intentionality, his bleak rejoicing in a "divine hell" taking his grammarless logic of the Eternal Yea-saying Nay relentlessly to its contradictorily nihilist conclusion.

7

Infernal Sources

This is hell, nor am I out of it.
Marlowe, *Doctor Faustus*

When the chapters of *Back to Sources* are read sequentially, one may gain an impression of rhetorical design, whereby the Critic advances responses to the enigma of Existence one after another, and lets each in turn demolish itself. Reason has proven inadequate for Grove's characters to resolve the ambiguities of Being, so perhaps the answer is in imagination, the poetic art that Msgr Savard finds satisfying. Yet, after Savard comes Glassco, for whom memory and the present offer only the irreconcilable paradox of image and object; then Carlyle's paradox of paper Babel-knowledge, and Nietzsche's exultant nihilism which threatens to render the Critic's entire endeavour as empty as Camus' Algerian sky. Beyond these, in Chapter VII, the reader is borne downwards to the Dantean circle (bearing, fittingly enough, the same such number), to find *Under the*

Volcano, where the spellbound Malcolm Lowry's drink-sodden paper self Geoffrey Firmin, in his burning-freezing infirmity, straddles hell's fiery seventh and icy ninth circles in an equilibrium-induced paralysis of ethical choice and will. The tragically self-reflexive Firmin/Lowry, author and persona in one, is ignorant of how to be. Rather, so the Critic avers, he is quite knowingly impotent, his ennui shaped as a philosophy founded on self-cancelling acedia, which vice/virtue liberates him to create himself through his art. Here the Critic discerns a nineteenth-century Teutonic romantic idealism that subverts the traditionally Christian critical view of self-creation as a destructive act of despair, the same which informed his muted derision of Nietzsche. In the Critic's interpretation of *Under the Volcano*, self-creation through a reconciliation of opposites in the artistic process seems its own vindication; indeed, in this instance acedia has been the necessary condition of Lowry's expression of his inner hell. The corollary is a life-denying paradox: the necessary condition for the creation of art is the destruction of life, a proposition worthy of Thomas Mann's *Death in Venice* or Conrad's "Il Conde." *Vidi Napoli e mori*.

8

Doubt about Sources

I deny nothing. Joseph Conrad, "An Anarchist"

After Lowry, at the furthest reach of this readerly experience, one may begin to suspect that our apparently non-judgmental Critic has been playful. It may occur that his mode is itself the matter: there is no rhetorical design, no linear movement towards an even partial resolution such as reason dictates should logically emerge as he proceeds. Instead, the Critic/Virgil has led the hungrily hopeful reader down a hellish *cul de sac*, reading forward, but all the while backward, retracing the trail of critical rice as far as the entrance to Lowry's modernly artistic, romantically ironic, and viciously circular inferno. With his commentary on Linda Hutcheon's *Irony's Edge: The Theory and Politics of Irony*, the circumspect Critic as educator leads the reader into a purgatory of doubt. Mentioning its "some thousand" scholarly sources and "aesthetic cultivation," yet regarding its achievement as "quite modest," the Critic is generously silent on the possible indiscrimination of an audience which has found it "influential." Traversing a path now well-trodden by acolytes of Stanley Fish, Hutcheon moves outside the single self to "reader response" in advancing her assertion of a complicity of "reader" with "author" in a consensus of values in "discursive community." Only with such "common sense," as neoclassical satirists sensibly understood the idea more simply than Hutcheon, may public utterance be subverted by the irony of its own silent meaning. The Critic reports Hutcheon's danger signal: the myriad "possible occasions for [verbal irony's] . . . misfiring in the context of democracy North-American style" because of the inherently communal, corrective and referential nature of its wit. (One concedes that verity, expressed some years ago in a short article by Paul Wohlfarth, "*War Conrad ein Englischer Dichter?*, a delicious musing on the reception by Anglosaxons of the Polish-born Conrad's ironies–his humour *vermisst*–expressing life as more or less paradoxical.) Puzzlingly, Hutcheon questions the existence of "an age of irony," so the Critic reports, even as he sets the obvious question: must a writer withhold verbally ironic (and, by contemporary reputation, purportedly elitist) saying because of its potential for being missed by an earnestly unknowing collection of groups of non-communicants from isolated quarters? A product from a Full Professor, Romantic ironist and supervisor of many a doctoral dissertation, Hutcheon's book so unfavourable to verbal irony, so the Critic remarks at the outset of his commentary (with apparently amused regret), "is well designed to convey some of [its author's] astonishment and uneasiness" in the face of public questions regarding "competency" among educators at "high" levels. And, quite fittingly, La Bossière's sifting of the ever-prudent Hutcheon's *The Theory and Politics of Irony* ends with a warning delivered with a self-denying moderacy: "But prudence in and of itself is not necessarily or entirely virtuous." There is more than a little charity and forbearance in such understated utterance. The Critic's *meaning*, one thinks, is that there is more virtue, more reverence for life, in all the richly risk-taking shenanigans of Harlen Bigbear. (Harlen Bigbear? the reader asks. Yes. The patient traveller will encounter him at this Introduction's end, precisely at that point where the Critic's book begins.) Perhaps one is presumptuous in detecting in the Critic's inclusion of Hutcheon at just this juncture the Critic's own spiritual and intellectual unease, his own purgatory of doubt, the critical enterprise to which he has devoted much of his life being systematically deconstructed by legions of (post) modernists advancing across their shifting dunes.

Bearing in mind the possibilities of irony in structures and juxtapositions, it may be no coincidence that the Critic extends the reader's circular tour of doubt's Purgatory with his essay on tricky Montaigne as precursor to a Melvillean self-deceiving trickster, revealingly titled (after *Mardi*) "'The World Revolves upon an 'I'': Montaigne's Unknown God and Melville's Confidence-Man," which detects in their shared enterprise a confounding of the divine with the secular, ignorance with wit, God with Man, their solipsistic, Faustian attempts at an elision of the finite with the Infinite foundering on doubt and inconclusion, seducing the unwary into certain bafflement. The Critic's discernment, though, does provide some insight into an opposition: Montaigne and Melville's creatures represent the obverse and reverse of hope and despair. Detecting Montaigne's recourse to the rhetorical design of Renaissance disputation by the "high art of debating by paradox," the Critic states as his aim a disclosing of Montaigne's "sustantially unparadoxical construction" that advances "a religion of the unknowing self founded on doubt." Here, the Critic's ironic sense has full play to attempt a matching of the game of faith founded on doubt played by Montaigne, who *said* that he "never sought to dimish the gap between his own folly and divine wisdom." Such is the appointed role of a devil's advocate, for whom failure is triumph. In light of Montaigne's savingly humble pride, the Critic's treatment of Huxley in Chapter X, "Of Huxley and Davies," simply signs a short "of course" apostrophizing Huxley's acedia, which procceeds from his "quest for the absolute," an endeavour, so the merrily melancholic Davies would have it, that occludes the "'infinitely complex mingling of contrarieties' essential for the generating of 'a newer and stronger spirit in man'."

By this point, the Critic, perhaps sensing his danger of losing the relevance of a theme that by now he has made clear, and clear, and clear, brings all this playing at "chase the kitten" back to his own sources in his purgatorial "Past and Present: The Neobaroque Novel in French Canada," which with a certain, polite irony engages Gérard Tougas' *Destin littéraire du Québec*, approximately a revolutionary manifesto that portends the liberation of a Québec literature increasingly seeking to free itself from a medieval, and therefore purportedly dark past. Standing in opposition to Glassco's notion of memory, Tougas's *Destin* rather contradictorily asserts the vitality of an old Québec culture by rejecting it for an independent literary culture dependent on a model shaped in accordance with the American Renaissance of the nineteenth century as (re)invented by critics in the twentieth. Here, as pronounced by historian and critic Tougas, is a self-proclaimed autochthonous self, purporting to reject a tradition in order to proclaim the birthing of a new culture–something of a hopeful Teufelsröckh, a literary Nietzschean transvaluator. So much, then, revolves on Tougas' "I" (which like Emerson's essaying) posits itself as "a mirror for self-reflection. . . . Autonomy calls unto autonomy, invention unto invention."

With a smiling *secousse de tête*, the Critic turns Tougas's New-England authority back on itself, by invoking the (*soi-disant*) "American" appetite for "reviving Renaissance and Baroque texts." The essence of the Baroque, as the Critic claims (by now somewhat obviously), that "the roundabout dreamworld of contradiction appropriated by [nineteenth-century Romantic] idealism," has made many border- and time-crossings. Indeed, the Critic rather punctures the vauntings of deconstructionist post-moderns with his observation that their method and its literature "go back more than four centuries." Hence the unflattering inclusion of "Neobaroque" in the the title of the Critic's essay, which locates historian/critic Tougas's recollection in a tale long on enthusiasm and ideology and short on both logic and memory.

Unsaid, but surely implicit, is the Critic's sense of the arrogance of ignorance. His observation of amnesia and logical inconsequence brings to mind an old saw that Tougas might have found reason to heed: A youth thinks he is breaking trail, until one day he looks down and sees that he is walking in another's footprints. That is not to say, though, that the new literature of Québec does not have its own vitality and merits. Indeed, the Critic is respectful of the way(s) in which it abandons "realism" for older "encoiled" schema. The Critic takes the reader on a daunting, winding tour in a world of Québébois novels, "in circles of self-reflexiveness." But the "liberty conferred by Promethan self-reliance comes at a cost," he reminds the reader in commenting on the lot of Bérénice in Réjean Ducharme's *L'Avalée des avalés* (a title suggestive of the Critic's own critique of Tougas' manifesto for *la littérature du Québec).* Contradicting Tougas, the Critic ends his whirlwind tour with a *pronunciamento* of his own, one inspired by Antonine Maillet and her rewriting of the medieval *homo ludens* in *Crache à Pic*: "Working in the spirit of Albert the Great's *Liber de alchima,* she shares in the power to translate passed on from narrator to narrator, generation to generation." As the Critic goes on to observe, "The spirit blows where it lists, and Maillet follows its life-giving inspiration, an eau-de-vie, wherever it takes her, just as she sees her people to have done from their very beginning." "Chacun se sentait bien dans la peau de l'autre, et n'aspirait pas à l'autonomie"–so the Critic cites from Maillet to evoke "a condition alien to the restless solitaries at sea in the neobaroque novel of French Canada." "The past," certainly, has "gifts for the future; which promises to be a lively one made possible by the renewal of an ancient and unifying faith." So ends "Past and Present." La Bossière could well have quizzically observed or added, in sympathy with Martin Levin's *Globe and Mail* article, "CanLit on the Map" (24 August 2002), "Whither CanLit is itself a very Canadian sort of topic, the very of thing we joke about." And for the earnestly circling Gérard Tougas, one gathers, that's no joke.

9

Source of Parnassus in Paradise

'Who are you? were my words,
My voice filled with love it left unsaid.
Dante, *Paradiso*, Canto VIII

After the abnegations plaguing the questing reader with purgatorial doubt, Chapter XII, "Of Montaigne, Dostoevsky and Gide: A *Sotie*," offers a release into genuine farce evident enough to be shared *sans pudeur*. The Critic's playfulness heretore, one has reason to sense, has been exercised with "clenched teeth" (as it were), the serpent's grip on its hindmost self. I shall go on to hazard that the Critic writes himself into his Gide, so that the chapter comes as close as wit may allow to his own manifesto of criticism as art. Could the Critic writing of Gide be *révélateur-de-soi*? "The silence tantalizes," he writes. "Perhaps Gide is playing on his own reputation as professional *inquiéteur*, sounding a false alarm of the kind that signals self-parody." "Celebrated wily gadfly" Gide once again shows himself "in good form," his coupling of Dostoevsky with Browning "an act of rhetorical, ironic misdirection well designed to draw attention away [does the Critic mean equally, "to draw attention to?" one is bound to wonder] from the really subversive business at hand." Pointing to "the adept counterfeiter" Gide's "professed horror of contradiction" in himself, La Bossière thereby (and likewise) "makes plain enough that he and Montaigne share more than just one turn of thought." What's good for the goose: *à bon rat, à bon chat*, so to speak.

Indeed, the Critic is more or less at one with Gide's Montaigne, which latter offered a unity of (un)believing in his essay *De l'honneur*: "We believe what we do not believe, and we do not believe what we believe." On the other hand, the Critic appears for a moment to sabotage his sympathy with the Gide who yokes cool Montaigne with the flamboyant Dostoevsky: "Not for Dostoevsky, certainly, the middling way. . . ." The "spectacle" of them "in concert" has contradiction in it "enough to induce bafflement or provoke laughter." But therein lies the Critic's basic thesis: their "extraordinarily rich antagonisms . . .

constitute the essential grammar of existence . . . ; their synthetic vision faithfully renders the coincidence of opposites in a world of radical interminacy." The Critic's pronouncement on Gide may as well be self-reflexive: "[Gide] sees in the mirror of his Montaigne and Dostoevsky the lineaments of his own activity as artist," itself a testament to the Critic's own Catoptrism.

In Chapter XII, "Of MacLennan and Conrad," the Critic's text spirals a bit further upward towards adumbrating his self-ideal, by thrusting Hugh MacLennan, Canadian *littérateur* and teacher, into the company of Conrad, La Bossière's early literary inspiration for wonder at the coincident foldings of "things." Starting with the Swiftian paradox of the "satirist satiri[zing] himself" for his soporific talent as moral guide, La Bossière finds in MacLennan "a similarly driven self-reflexiveness," which he relates to a riven, all-to-ambiguous Canadian conscience suspended or mired in the Middle Way. MacLennan, so the Critic says, finds some amusement in his "own double function as aesthete for sedation and earnest life guide." How does one deal with "ethical indeterminacy," the Hobson's choise of "the artist's way or the moralist's"? La Bossière jars his reader awake with his answer that avoids the pain of choice entirely: sedation, in a Buddha-like silence akin to that of Conrad's contemplative Marlow, a narrator "elegant in his indolence." Having written at all denies his own assertion, of course. The Critic notes that Conrad chose "the artist's way." Rather obvious, one should think, in that Conrad wrote of Being as an enigmatic spectacle having no ethical import. The reader may recall that Conrad was always on the edge of a choice which Dostoevsky's Underground Man elevates depressingly to a philosophy: "[I]t is best to do no-thing! The best thing is conscious inertia!" (Conrad, we also recall, has suicidally sought unconsciousness as a first choice, ending his art before it had begun.)

MacLennan, on the other hand, "chooses both"–the way of the artist and the moralist (which is to say, he makes, in a sense, no choice at all). The "Canadian sage" committed to the negative way of the Golden Mean , "to the task [like Huxley's] of disseminating the divine principle of neoclassical equipoise," appears here as representative Canadian teacher and man of letters, an aesthete and a moralist with a mission, whom the Critic would emulate in his own life of the mind, advancing the wisdom of indolence through his own need to *do*, a paradox uniting two solitudes. As with MacLennan the *Montréalais*, so with his character Huntley McQueen, a mellowed Presbyterian financier eventually self-stymied by a do-nothing prudence embracing the Golden Mean as bullion and political gospel: he sits silently in his boardroom "located at the exact centre of the country's [corporate] heart." Silence is indeed golden. Now, *that* is a figure for the balancing or reconciling of opposite or discordant elements that has long been understood as representatively Canadian.

10

Sources of Love in Laughter

A Paradise of the Parnassian self-ideal realized is to plunge to purgatorial gloom, a drear scaling of Mont Blanc.

Not for the Critic the "melancholic" Mac Lennan (nor even the sadness-soaked merriment of Davies "Tristram-gistus"). A reconciliation or balancing of conflicting or disparate elements (French and English, artist and moralist, for instance) must needs be accomplished with an *éclat de rire*, a wit that awakens, bursting with the *joie de vivre* that celebrates difference. A matter of temperament, one may say, of a nation, a people, or anyone, whether contradictions are the stuff of Conradian torment or celebration, or of both: a marriage of heaven and hell, so to speak. They (contradictions, opposites, disparities, that is, not to speak of metaphysical conjunctions) are met in the Critic with joy; and he adjusts the imbalance of *angst* that the agonizing choices in Conrad and MacLennan imply, with a couple of essays given over to mirth. In Chapter XIV, "Pop Conrad and Child's Play," the Critic exults with Chesterton at "the sheer wonder of things," which in Conrad's *The Rover* collocates the child-nonsense of Edward Lear's *Jumblies*-unreason and the grown-up-realism-in-fantasy of Conrad's late novels with Cusan, Christian mysticism.

Harking back downwards to the hell just left, the Critic focuses a beam reflected from such improbably companioned texts as *The Jumblies* and Lowry's *Under the Volcano*, the latter "a model for a properly bifocal reading" of Conrad. The congruence of their azimuths marks the place of Conrad's oeuvre on a meridian where realism and fantasy, sense and nonsense, enchantment and disenchantment elide. With "child" as "father" at one pole, and "the man" at the other, the point of separation of modes of play, "the line" (as the Critic calls it) between them "can be devilishly hard to draw." "*La vida es sueño*" (Life is a Dream), so La Bossière is disposed often to recall, especially from texts by Calderón, Schopenhauer and Conrad, and thereby signalling a conflation of fantasy and the real.

Chapter XIV, "Of Bells, Words, Nurseries, Nonsense, and Trees," is a joyfully "quizzical, risky *jeu d'esprit en macaronique*" (as the Critic himself dubs it), the sense of which so approaches the nonsense of *The Jumblies* that the Critic begs his audience's indulgence (it was written for reading aloud), in imitation of his central theme of the mystery of forgiveness in Conrad's *The Rover.* "*De rien*" locutes a sense beyond mere *politesse* or *bienséance.* He shows the novel to be rich in a word-playing dependent for its humour on a due attentiveness to Conrad's bilingual wit. It is to be hoped that one doesn't usurp the Critic's voice: those who may read this chapter, in company with the Critic himself (and, indeed, all of us), need forgiveneness by our gods and by ourselves (if there is an invincible disjunction between the two). And the voice of forgiveness is laughter.

All this while, it appears, that La Bossière has been on a quest of sorts towards (among other things) his philosophical, artistic and pedagogical ideal. Seeking durable wisdom through an analytical yet aesthetic medium, the Critic/teacher as essayist has led the reader through doubt, through temptations to slothful despair of art and life, and finally to an accommodation with a paradox in a "marriage of earth and sky," as Ford explains his physically vital Valentine Wannop in *A Man Could Stand Up. . . .* There is no more exact exemplar of such a conjoining (or, so it would seem from the Critic's bifocal perspective on Imponderables) than Charles Pierre Péguy of Saint-Aignan, poet playwright, editor, publisher, Dreyfusard and socialist philosopher committed to living in accordance with genuinely Christian wisdom. Ostensible contraries were met in him, much as they were in Dostoevsky, in his dual role as "dogmatist," "publicist" or "philosopher," on the one hand, and disinterested aesthete or "indifferent artist," on the other (to cite from the Critic's parsing of the irony basic to wily gadly André Gide's portraiture of the author of *Crime and Punishment* with Browning and Montaigne).

The Critic's biography of Péguy (the essay was initially offered as an encyclopaedia entry) logs, as it were, something of a homecoming for Camille La Bossière, the life bearing remarkable parallels to his own. He writes of Péguy's spiritual and intellectual maturation: "[He] came to concern himself . . . with writing a life of the mystic-in-action Joan of Arc and . . . with immediately practical matters." The Critic recalls Péguy's concern in *Véronique* with "'the ligature of the eternal and the temporal'" enabled by an authentic Christianity; and in the down-to-earth poetry of his *Eve*, with its "reconciliation" of the "carnal" with the "spiritual." Conrad's secular term "practical idealism" describes the Métis Critic's own ideal, which surely invites comparison with the chiaroscuro woven into the palpable text of Péguy's quotidian spirituality and intellectual life.

11

Back to Sources

Look for God in men and nature before you start looking in the synagogue - or the church. It never works theother way round. George Gabori, *When Evils Were Most Free* (1981)

At this point, the reader, in company with the author of this Introduction, has run out of book, and has nowhere left to go but to the beginning, Chapter I, on an art more redolent of the Critic's own beginnings than anything that has followed. This last recourse for the reader is the Critic's treatment of writings from Canadian author Thomas King, whose characters have their home in (this, only for the sake of keeping our metaphor consistent) hell's second and third circles. There is Lust and Gula galore in King's tales, but not as vices updated from the medieval tradition; rather, they serve as representations of an appetite for life. The Critic has troubled to note in treating of Lear and Conrad, that in *Under the Volcano* Geoffrey Firmin accomplishes his much longer descent to "the bottom of a hell-pit with a dead dog for a compañero." It takes not much transliterative imagination to perceive that author/persona Lowry's God has died with his last mortal hopes. His Hirsch-like oscillations have diminished, then ceased, reducing him to the death-in-life of a reflexive witness, his disinterest occluding love. So much for Firmin-Lowry. Nothing could be more opposite than King's sprightly novels of hopeful appetite, which minister a devilishly strong lenitive for the torment of placidly despairing acedia figured in *Under the Volcano*.

The very fact of the Cherokee and Greek parentage of Thomas King, creator of the CBC radio show *Dead Dog Café* and the *Coyote* children's books, may account in part for the opening chapter's punning title, "Coyote Agape: Thomas King's Wording for Love." The Critic comes to a home of the spirit, writing about *Medicine River* and *Green Grass, Running Water*, and of the springs of passion that feed their cast of characters in a *comédie humaine*: of the do-nothingness of Eli Stands Alone; the exasparation of engineer for draining modernization Clifford Sifton; the impulse to Good-Samaritanship in Harlen Bigbear; the melancholy of Will, the Bartelby-like photographer who prefers not to dine on food or life but only to look on from the sidelines; and of delectation, in the persona of Jonnie Prettywoman, an ideal that Harlen Bigbear leaves alone with painful restraint. The risk-taking Bigbear has a lust for life of a measure celebrated in Amerindian lore with legends of tricky Coyote, rabbit-chaser often figured with shoulder-slung member. And why not, in the phenomenal realm of generation? In King's novels, *agape* couples with a rough *caritas*, which appetites come together for a lovely feeding of human hunger in a heavenly enough hell for this life.

Here, none of the privatives and privation of the kind that drain *Settlers of the Marsh*, no true indignity; poverty and literal ignorance, perhaps, but no hunger of spirit or flesh that need to be denied except wilfully. From King's wording of appetite for life the Critic assembles a catalogue of gustatory delights of a length and bizarre diversity that has the power of reducing the reader to tears of belly-shaking mirth. Not for King Msgr Savard's frozen moon and earth, but food for the belly; and good grub for the soul in the practical "charity" that drives Harlen. Not humankind-in-general, but people: gatherings of "two [Harlen one of them] or more Indians" anywhere, any time. The Critic shares author King's laughter with a sympathy for the tales, not only because of his own roots, but because of the warmth and humour radiating from this community of loving and lovable eccentrics. In the Critic's superficially objective word-responses there is an undertow, a silently subjective stream in which flows his own love of human beings back up from hell's inmost circle and down to earth, where his and their feet are planted firmly, their souls rooted in the soil of here-and-now.

12

Sources in Flesh, and Blood, and Bone

We live with not one soul but two, our father and mother - at the least! - the night and the day, if you will; . . . two souls I possessed that were equal to two matched horses - badly matched! - if one said yes, the other said no, and the poor driver was nothing but my own person who cast the deciding vote.
Tim, in Norman Mailer's *Tough Guys Don't Dance* (1984).

Whereas unthinking Harlen Bigbear has a sometimes fumbling appetite for Everything, the all-too-thoughful Nietzsche (than whom no one could be more opposite than Harlen, "harler" of rabbits) fed fastidiously, thoroughly, all-consumingly on Nothing. The author recollected in *The Will to Power* (1900) was temperamentally incapable of recognizing anything like meaning or value in nature's diversity, or of acknowledging an actuality beyond the Self. Implicit in the Critic's recollection that Nietzsche came to regard his *The Birth of Tragedy* as "too Hegelian" is the Overman's contempt for his early work extended to the integration of disparate elements which this collection of essays explores and, for the most part, celebrates. The Critic mentions that one of the comings-together that Nietzsche contemned was "the mixing of races and values," a position that would have dreadful consequences in the century just past. Still infatuated with Darwinism half-digested, the all-too-earthbound categorical logic of *un*knowing ignorance and *ersatz* science bereft of wisdom, children of Chaos imposed their destructively self-negating notions of "racial purity," supposedly violated by "miscegenation."

It is not surprising, then, that the Critic has given pride of place to King's novels, as cardinal among the works he has chosen for this collection, to show through his consideration of their art the substantial verity of selfhood multifold yet all of a piece, a cause for exultation in the riches of multiple heritage, the diversity of circumstance and event making up the necessity of human nature shaping and colouring the Divine Comedy, the heavenly hell of every life. The Critic's stock, like that of all "mixed" heritage, is not, as once was commonly held, "deracinated" and intractably dual or multiple. The Métis, like every separate soul, are a little world, a distinct people, their nationhood supposedly bestowed (but only a human reality recognized) in 2002, after almost two centuries of denial, by act of a Canadian Parliament self-congratulatory for its benignity.

Down the generations of his "forebears" understood

as extended family, the Critic numbers a great-grandmother of Huronia stock blended with Swampy and High-Plains Cree, a grandmother and mother born in the area of Nantes, an aunt from Austria, and other relations, cousins and friends from many places: Alsace, Italy, Normandy, Scotland, Switzerland, Ireland, the USA, Belgium and Québec; and a Manitoba Métis father and a maternal grand-father from the Val de Loire (to both of whom this book is dedicated by the Critic in gratitude, respect, and humility). These disparate elements were yoked not altogether without violence, as was the collective experience of the clash of native and European Canadians. Menfolk, made strangers in a strange land and deprived of liberty, stared out incomprehending from jails at mores not their own, their bafflement echoing the babble of silent incomprehension as European settlers gazed on Canada's vastnesses. Deprived of almost everything in a West Coast storm as figurative as it was actual, cousins of the Critic had not Why to ask, only a mute dignity and love for each other as bulwark against the enigmatic injustice of privative fortune. All this and more has shaped the subjective element of the critical voice in *Back to Sources*, a happy coming-together of parts that makes rare art of literary criticism.

13

The Critic as Source

I just paint. I leave the clever talk to the sods who can't.
Lawrence Olivier as Henry, in *The Ebony Tower* (1986) [from the novel by John Fowles].

Literary criticism has come in for some bad press, since not all that many folk read "literary" art these days; and "intellectual" reading has become largely the preserve of universities. "There are always intellectuals around," Anthony Burgess wrote, "who praise the incompetent as the profound." Predictably, perhaps, recent *exempla* of "The Emperor's Clothes" remain easy to find. In a *Time Magazine* essay of 9 June 1997, Roger Rosenblatt observes that "some precious few critics have an artist in them, but most are a desperate shrivelled lot who have found a way to touch art without making it." That rule, only too commonly true, is demonstrated by the incompetent lauding of the incompetent with extravangances of arcane argot, evidently because neither critic nor artist has an artist within. The indignation of a largely uncomprehending and bemused public is mollified only when folk see critic, artist and art, whether good or bad, adjudged fraudulent by some Jacobin of the critical (or pseudo-critical) milieu. The story is often very much the same for all-too-precious visual art critics, antiques aficionados, and expert *connaisseurs* discriminating among vintages. Perhaps committees of Public Safety for the Arts wouldn't be altogether a bad thing.

Intellectual flummery touching the hem of art leaves a nasty stain in the public eye. Ordinary folk may not be artists or critics, but if they're interested enough to look, they know what's what. If critical analysis is not to be the dessicating and fraudulent discipline it is so often accused of being, then indeed the critic must be an artist, whose medium is itself an art form; not *an* art, which is simply a craft used to an end, like tracking deer, but art itself. Life and literature both are implicit in the intellectual, scholarly, and imaginative work that is bona fide criticism. Inspired literature illuminates life, and inspired criticism illuminates literature. That kind of illumination is what Professor La Bossière offers refreshingly: not merely the art of criticism, but criticism as art, expressed with a cogency, simplicity and grace that surpasses the bounds of wizened commentary and sees into the life of its subject, its purpose (as Conrad said of his own writerly aim) "to make you see."

14

And this is the man that in his study sits.
Christopher Marlowe

At the end of a formal pedagogical life garlanded with merit, the Critic has edited this collection of his essays under one cover. It is about sources, beginnings–and not least, his own. From its epigraphs and dedications, through to its final recondite essay on Charles Péguy, this book is a loving celebration of his sources: the forebears, history, traditions, life, mentors and friends that formed him, the writers–the teachers and storytellers–who inspired him. The book, like this Introduction, and like Professor Camille La Bossière's life of letters, ends where it began, back at its sources.

G.W.S.B.
Sidney, British Columbia
October 2002

I

COYOTE AGAPE: THOMAS KING'S WORDING FOR LOVE

[*The River Review / La Revue rivière* 1(1990)]

(*in memoriam* Adeline et Malvina Orphilia Grenon)

I am the grub-man. Such gentlemen as have friends here [in the Tombs] hire me to provide them with something good to eat. Herman Melville, "Bartelby, the Scrivener"

At the roadside I buy a melon . . . suck the sweet juices, and taste my grandmother's MacIntosh, my mother's strawberries, my father's plums. Maurice Kenny, "Rain"

What fits, suits. Mia Anderson, "Have I Told You How Lovely," in *Appetite*

Exasperated by the rumpish stoicism of do-nothing Eli Stands Alone, who resists eviction from his ancestral log house that stands in the path of progress, Clifford Sifton, engineer for modernization in all things and overseer of the useless dam in *Green Grass, Running Water*, is brought to the pass of goading the seated-down Blackfoot with an exemplum from an anthology of old. "You know," Sifton is brought to recollect, his pose suggestive of a Hollywoody

Indian sage's as he prepares to bring a session of anything but idle palavering to a close, "when I was in high school, I read this story about a guy just like you who just didn't want to do anything to improve his life. He just sat on a stool in some dark room and said, 'I would prefer not to'." The most bookish of the characters in Thomas King's second novel, a professor emeritus of the University of Toronto with monographs on Shakespeare and Bacon and two Teacher of the Year awards to his credit, Eli is quick to interrupt his would-be mentor's lesson by flipping up a sign of clearer recollection: "'Bartelby the Scrivener.' One of Herman Melville's short stories." But Sifton's critique flows on unchecked by the professor's reminder, as if by nothing more than a stick of learnèd lumber and consequently a thing of no practical or contemporary value, dead: "I guess. The point is that this guy has lost touch with reality. And you know what happens to him at the end of the story?" Seasoned scholar and teacher that he is (and one apparently au fait with Robert Scholes' *The Fabulators*) Eli has savvy enough to recognize railroading when he sees it coming, and to jolt with paradox (even tautology) when real thinking has stopped: "It's fiction, Cliff," the man of letters once again throws up a hard fact to the man of facts who argues from letters.

For all of that retort's invincible canniness, though, it does bespeak something of a bluntness in Eli, a kindred want of finesse in making distinctions. And Sifton, as though swept forward by the force of poetic justice, barrels past the old Liar Paradox reset by his antagonist to drive his point home. Rather like an emeritus authority pronouncing with arms folded, Sifton answers even himself with an undeniable verity, the fact of Bartelby's end: "He dies." That would seem to settle that. But venerable academicians, often like many other white-haired sages, do like to have the hushing last word, even in fiction. Whether glib or poignant, wise or inane, the professor's observation that marks the end of this *tête-à-tête* over the question of life's connection with letters makes as tight a point on earthly existence as there is: "We all die, Cliff" (119-20).

The discussion so ended, though, is hardly so final as the fact of human mortality: dead-ending is not King's brief. On this occasion, and as so often happens in *Green Grass, Running Water*, one fact secretes another in a process of revelation by witty understatement. Of the pertinent matters passed over in silence in the matching of conspicuous Melvillean facts between Eli and Sifton, the most obviously salient is the cause of Bartleby's demise: from a daily diet of a few ginger-nuts and a morsel of cheese taken without ale or tea or coffee, he graduates to eating and drinking nothing at all. Nor does the text of "Bartelby, the Scrivener," even as it tantalizes with its wily discretions, make a secret of the motive occlusions behind that death by starvation: the copyist for a Wall Street lawyer labours in service to a charity at once severed from theological virtue and uprooted from that "natural love" which has long been understood, in the language of a wisdom at least as old as Aristotle's, as "an inclination inherent in every being which causes the natural appetite to seek a good fitting for its nature" (Cunningham 92).

Set to the "very dull, wearisome, and lethargic" task of doing nothing more than copying texts, their every jot or tittle, of getting them straight, so to speak, in a world of neoclassical values (a bust of Cicero, looking down with "a certain calm disdain," dominates the lawyer's office) where "charity" has accordingly been made over into a balancing, negative "prudence" conducive to paralyzing indecision, indifference, melancholy, Bartelby has good cause to lose all appetite, not to want to (Melville 40, 29, 20, 43, 52). A recessional for humanity prompted in a prudential man of law as he casts his mind back to his scrivener's funeral wraps up this Melvillean instancing of the dead(ening) burying the dead; and the working-out of Bartleby's nothing-doing, an effect of stasis answering unto stasis, inanition unto inanition, tropes the much-storied saying that the letter kills but the spirit, cognate with love, gives life.

It is, I would propose, on the point of this principle that the 'spirituality' of King's fiction and Melville's in "Bartleby, the Scrivener" show substantial agreement. Potentially at least, the glossing over of the literal cause of Bartleby's death in the Eli/Sifton stand-off serves up a gentle reminder of the biggest point made by Melville's story, even as it discreetly encourages and sustains a reading of King's fiction as a wording for the appetite that is love and the absence of which necessarily kills.

Certainly, *Green Grass, Running Water*, like his first novel, *Medicine River*, is so heaped with references to food and feasting, their natural efficacy and ritual occasions, that it would be difficult not to notice them: the pages of both books run over with words of Sun-Dancing and weddings, of snacks before, during and after sex, of kitchens and supermarkets and restaurants, of breakfasts and lunches and dinners, of pizzas and beer galore, of noodles, cupcakes, fry-bread, minestrone, family pinics and birthdays, bananas, raisins, soup of mushroom or tomato, Cheerios, octopus, Tortino sans Carciofi with Ribollita, hot chocolate, soda crackers, macaroni, asssorted cookies and pop, Hawaiian Curdle Surprise with Moose, apples, hot dogs, ratatouille, corn, extra-crispy fried chicken, apple pie, chow mein, sundaes, cheese, fish, chips, melons, whale meat, Belgian waffles, milkshakes, eggs fried or scrambled, marshmallow whip, sausages, tarts, meatloaf, cinnamon toast, ice cream, peas, ketchup, oranges, omelettes, candies and cakes, hash browns, grapefruit, mashed potatoes, artichokes, fries, sardines, elk stew, croissants–all the good things that the cafés Casey's, Casper, and Dead Dog have to offer; and to cap things off, pots of tea or coffee with lots of cream and sugar.

What such a cataloguing is not intended to say, though, is that every object of appetite in his novels is presented as a good genuinely beneficial to consume. The product of an anatomical wit that remains sensible, patently hip to the times, King's ordering of feasts is not quite gargantuan: there are limits and distinctions to be respected. Cheer is one thing, alcoholism another; and to enjoy a good smoke is to participate in something of an oxymoron. The conspicuous consumption practised, for instance, in the bar of Medicine River's American Hotel, "a great dark hole filled with blue smoke and dead people," indicates a malnutrition of sorts, of the kind that results from an appetite grown too big, gone awry (*Medicine River* 145).

*   *   *   *

“I looked at the menu, but I wasn’t hungry,” the narrator of *Medicine River* remembers from his time in a greasy spoon not far from the Custer Monument, Wyoming (107). Nor did the sight of the mess of meatloaf and white sauce gorged by his driver and travel companion on that occasion, the ever-cheerful Harlen Bigbear, do anything to help quicken the appetite of a Will still fresh from the high life and haute-cuisine of Toronto. But more than a question of good taste is at issue in the narrator’s recollection of his experience at the Casper Café. Time and again in Will’s story of his life, the loss or absence of appetite signs the “depression” or “melancholy” that attends the baffling of natural inclination, a turning away from love (84, 102). A highlighting of that sign invites a recognition of *Medicine River* as a book of confession, an act of spiritual discernment that reaches down into the origins and registers the effects of the most unmarrowing of the besetting deficiencies a human can (and in Will’s case, does) suffer.

A photographer by trade and profession, Will would prefer to do nothing but contemplate existence from the sidelines. His response to Harlen Bigbear’s invitation to join in a “pot-luck-eating, cash-and-other-valuables hand game” puts his ruling disposition in a nutshell: “I just want to watch” (60, 64). The game is too risky, too rich in possibilities for the pain of losing, of getting into a mess, to be entered into willingly by one whose disappointments in love have led him to prize indisturbance and safety above all. For the uprooted Will fully orphaned in his middle years,[1] life has lapsed into a prudential huddling, a stoic-like taking of refuge from feeling and pain (thus his apathy and indolence). Given that inward state, neither his season of preference nor the negative character of its appeal is surprising: summer he finds too hot, winter too cold, autumn almost just right; and spring, or autumn topsy-turvied, is the cruellest since the most spirited of times, when the wind blows where it lists, to the raising of dust, the loosening of gravel, the cracking of windshields and the renewal of life. Altogether in character, Will's response to "wind the powerful mover," lifter of eagles and buzzards and storks, giver of being with all its mysteries and hazards, and "bringer of tears," is to turn his back to it (146, 15, 164, 52-53, 92-93).

The little hunger there is for Will to experience in his condition of spectator sportsman and huddler from love represents a parody of real appetite. What food there is for him to eat is nothing much more substantial than celluloid:

> [At ten on Sunday mornings] . . . I'd eat [some cereal] and watch Coyote chase Road Runner or Elmer Fudd chase Bugs Bunny or Sylvester chase Tweety. Around eleven . . . I'd watch the Blue Jays chase the Yankees or the Vikings chase the Rams or the Bucks chase the Rockets.

As the narrator of *Medicine River* himself has the probity immediately to go on to confess (though still not altogether repentantly), "It was a waste of a Sunday. I knew that. But it was relaxing, and to be honest, I enjoyed it" (236). The Will as would-be sabbaticant from existence savours the liberty to kill time watching the world go by and nursing his melancholy in the shelter of his solitude. Like many another tale of delight in retreat and bedevilment by apathy told by neoclassical-style spectators, idlers, observers and drones before him,[2] Will's story of his life rehearses the long-understood effects of love resisted, of the self's drawing back behind a shield to ward off a good fitting for its nature.

If Will's is a story of love resisted, though, it is not a story of love denied. In the absence of any force to resist, all resistance is futile, of course. A name for that motive force behind events in *Medicine River* is "charity," the virtue of which works its effects mainly through the providential meddling of an all-too-human harler of rabbits from the family of Bigbear.[3] Naturally annoying friend to the unhungry and stoically disengaged Will that he is, Harlen is remembered as "one of the most charitable people [he has] . . . ever known" (151). And, like the features of love resisted, the signs of its embracement are so raised in *Medicine River* as to make for plain viewing.

For better or for worse, Harlen follows the active way to the point of troubling himself with almost too many things. He is a player, coach and coordinator of community sports of many kinds (from basketball to gambling games of sleight-of-hand, from dancing to doing parody); a risk-taker willing time and again to try *terra incognita* and chance making a fool of himself; a weaver of webs of relation, a peace- and match-maker who remains undaunted by breaks or setbacks or foul-ups; and, above all, a promoter of feasting whose appetite for life understandably drives his abstemious, demurring friend Will to take refuge behind wit: "Helping was Harlen's specialty. He was like a spider on a web" (31); "Harlen chewed on a lot of people" (136); "Knowledge accumulated in Harlen's brain like brown grocery bags in a closet" (201).

But Will's tributes to the man of charity are not always so half-begrudging, nor so hedged with funny irony: the fact that Harlen "took on a lot of weight" indicates nothing of avoirdupoids (2). Nor is there an inkling of Harlen-as-nuissance in Will's recollection from the year of the Catholic wedding of Jonnie Prettywoman with Cecil Broadman, when "the wheat had been good": "Any time there was a gathering of two or more Indians in a hundred-mile radius of Medicine River, chances were one of them was Harlen" (89). As the narrator of *Medicine River* is brought to acknowledge *malgré lui*, there is something in his friend of a humanity for all seasons. Even the various mistakes Harlen has made (and they are plentiful: too much beer and a bungled hoop-dance and his persistent misrepresentation of things as they are, for example, not to mention his turning away from the wind on one occasion in mid-life, in fellowship with Will) are redeemed by the naturally spiritual intention that they serve, by the fact that they are mistakes born of a charity embraced in a suitably natural way–which is to say, imperfectly.

It is thanks in large measure to Harlen's words and actions, his example and counsel, that Will is brought to make his way back a long way towards the land of the living. The story of that gradual change-of-heart begins with Will's rescue on the evening of his mother's funeral as he sits by himself waiting to return to Toronto and self-exile: "I was slipping from melancholy to depression when Harlen walked through the double glass doors of the terminal" (94). Prompted by the hovering, circling man of charity, Will's decision to remove his habitation from Toronto back to Medicine River opens the door to the series of successful rescues that follow, each in the form of a suggestion made to entice him away from pining and withering away in privacy into a life among communicants. “Good food’ll cheer you up”: such are Harlen’s words of encouragement to his companion in the Casper Café, who (initially, at least) cannot bring himself to eat or to phone his more-or-less-beloved Louise Heavyman and her child South Wing back home (107); but they are words which gradually take hold in Will’s mind and bear fruit.

The last facts of Will’s story evoke a Christmas day (*muk osh kesh i kaw*), when, after an eve alone, he is reconciled with his brother, plays with, then packages, a spinning top for South Wing, makes lunch (“the most important meal of the day,” according to Harlen [32]), and goes out for a long walk in the snow. No television that day. Thanks in no small way to the meddling of Harlen Bigbear, Will comes to regain something of his natural appetite, to find himself restored in/to a community, and from thence to begin weaving his own story of all his relations. He is now ready to turn to the inspiriting and consequently perilous life of creation, to face the wind, so to speak, the animating principle that in *Green Grass, Running Water* will move in concert with an element no less old than the hills: the primordial waters.

* * * *

“There are no facts, only interpretations,” in the words of Nietzsche’s *Will to Power* (par. 482), just as “there are no truths . . . only stories,” in the words from the “I” of *Green Grass, Running Water* to a greedy, wily Coyote who swears to "the truth" of the heroic deeds of his own imagining (326). These are daunting absolutes, their forcefulness directly proportioned to the hunger to see everything, be in control, that drives imaginations vasty on the scale of Ralph Waldo Emerson's ("What is needed is a good gizzard that can digest religions, railroads, & make poetry of them all" [Emerson 12.46]); or, to come down a few rungs on the scale of Transcendental ambitioning, Buffalo Bill Bursum's: the television marketer with Machievelli's *The Prince* for his bible in *Green Grass, Running Water* would capture the whole of Canada and the United States in the lines of his vision projected as "The Map" (109, 108).

But to readers in a different way, unplatonic, who with eyes no bigger than their stomachs look to take in what nourishment texts may have to provide, these commanding cautions from Nietzsche and King need not be altogether forbidding. There remains the possibility that some stories, like some verbs, are made to have objects. As full of sound and fury and as rich in causes for "depression" as the world must come to seem to Dr. Joseph Hovaugh, the second mapmaker in *Green Grass, Running Water*, who strives to graph the every movement and meaning of his four Indian patients on a "chart . . . literal, allegorical, tropological, anagogic" that comes strangely to resemble a ring of endlessly expanding circles (62, 324), the tale in which he lives does signify something. Like the earthquake that it features, and like mystic circles, even those writ on water, *Green Grass, Running Water* has an epicentre, out from which ripple the movements and meanings that it inscribes, naturally, in roundabout ways.

While not quite as certain as the fact that Nietzsche's works have been interpreted, it is true that King's second novel respins that old moral fable of appetite baffled by a resentful police: the Dog-in-the-Manger. The renewing of that fable by *Green Grass, Running Water* begins with its first two pages, which tell a story of genesis, of the birth by a "Coyote Dream" of a being who "gets everything backward" and so imagines himself "GOD." In the three-hundred and fifty-eight pages that follow, readers are set on the spoor of this doggy promethean, whose tracks through time, enigmatic and devious though their patterning is, are so clearly imprinted as to make an identification of the kind of creature that makes them a matter of course.

The DOG of *Green Grass, Running Water* is the perverse GOD of the scribes, lawyers and politicians who make a virtue of stagnation, inanition, not-doing. Set against the spirit that animates, this dead(ening) divinity of the deaden(ing) letter would claim as his own and deny to others the good stuff he himself will not eat:

> Pardon me, says the Tree [in the garden made by First Woman], maybe you would like something to eat. That would be nice, says First Woman, and all sorts of good things to eat fall out of that tree. [. . .] And First Woman and Ahdamn eat those apples and that pizza and fry bread. Old Coyote eats those hot dogs and the melon and the corn. That GOD fellow doesn't eat anything. He stands in the garden with his hands on his hips, so everybody can see he is angry. Anyboby who eats my stuff is going to be very sorry, says that GOD. There are rules, you

know. (33, 57)

This jealous GOD fellow as risibly pretentious DOG means (and is meant) to be taken seriously, since no sun sets on the effects of his resentment. First Woman and Ahdamn are sent for a ride with the Cheyenne, Kiowa, Comanche and Arapaho railroaded by goverment policy in the 1870s to spiritual starvation in a vacationland swamp (82). And such dog-in-the-mangerish work continues a century later in the historical present of *Green Grass, Running Water*, in the raising of a dam that, like the "leaden-headed obstruction" maintained by the resolutely indecisive High Court of Chancery in *Bleak House*, serves only to clog (136; Dickens 1.3). The "gray" construction overseen by Clifford Sifton kills a river, suppresses the annual floods that feed the cottonwoods, "the Sun Dance Tree" around which food is shared. Thanks to a paralyzing jurisprudence, the sole positive effect of that construction is to produce the stagnant pool of "Parliament Lake" around which "the semi-idle, semi-middle class" that it profits gather privately to contemplate (312, 116, 99, 238). The middling man of law of "Bartelby, the Scrivener" would suffer little in the way of *dépaysement* by translation there.

In a manner foreign to Melville's, though, King's tale of the letter that kills comes expressly to affirm the principle of love that it invokes. The tie-ups of a law against the spirit in *Green Grass, Running Water* are brought to an end that leaves neither Sifton's dam nor Eli and his old log house standing. The dead waters of Parliament Lake are set dancing, then loosed, by the energy of an earthquake in cahoots with the creative imagination. And after the flood, a family of women, the weight of whose spirit has given headaches to the DOG jealous of the fruits they are empowered to produce, take up the work of building their ancestral home anew. They are led, with poetic justice, by the resourceful Latisha Red Dog, owner of a robust appetite and presiding genius of the Dead Dog Café: "Come on. . . . We'll catch lunch at the Dead Dog, get changed, and get to work" (354). The homecooking Latisha (or *Letitia*, "gladness" or "joy") is of a mind with Harlen Bigbear, at least when it comes to the virtues of eating and doing, communal good cheer. Much as in the story of re-energizing and regeneration told by *Medicine River*, a spirited natural love in the end does conquer all in the world according to *Green Grass, Running Water.*

ENDNOTES

1. Fully orphaned, that is, in a non-Native sense that accords with Will's as 'Torontonian.' Arnold E. Davidson observes: "By Native definitions, a big family is everyone, every cousin's cousin, ever brother-in-law's ex-wife's new stepchild. The distinctions don't matter" (195).

2. The narrator of prospect-painter James Thomson's *The Castle of Indolence* (1748) and the poet of William Shenstone's "Ode to Indolence" (1750), for instance, along

with the melancholic lawyer of "Bartleby, the Scrivener," provide cases in point. For an account of "the wise disease" of melancholy and indolence among the Augustans see Moore; for an account of Melville's response to that disease, La Bossière.

3. See "harl" in the *OED*: "To tangle twist, or knot together."

WORKS CITED

Anderson, Mia. *Appetite*. Ilderton, ON: Brick Books, 1988.

Cunningham, Francis L.B. *The Christian Life*. Dubuque: Priory Press, 1959.

Davidson, Arnold E. *Coyote Country: Fictions of the Canadian West.* Durham: Duke UP, 1994.

Dickens, Charles. *Bleak House*. 1853. With an introduction by Vladimir Nabokov. Toronto and New York: Bantam, 1983.

Emerson, Ralph Waldo. *The Journals and Miscellaneous Notebooks of Ralph Waldo Emerson.* Eds. W.H. Gilman *et al.* Cambridge: Belknap P of Harvard U, 1960-82. Vol 12.

Kenny, Maurice. "Rain." In *All my Relations: An Anthology of Contemporary Canadian Native Fiction*. Ed. Thomas King. Norman: U of Oklahoma P, 1992. 136-45.

King, Thomas. *Green Grass, Running Water*. Toronto: Harper-Collins, 1993.

----------. *Medicine River*. 1989. Toronto: Penguin, 1991.

La Bossière, Camille. "The Cosmopolitan, the Philosopher, and the Old Gentleman." In *Transactions of the*

NorthWest Society for Eighteenth-Century Studies. Ed. John Stephen Martin. U of Calgary, 1991.

Melville, Herman. "Bartleby, the Scrivener." 1853. In *The Piazza Tales*. New York: Russell & Russell, 1963.

Moore, Cecil A. *Backgrounds of English Literature, 1700-1760.* Minneapolis: U of Minnesota P, 1953.

Nietzsche, Friedrich. *Basic Writings of Nietzsche*. Ed. W. Kaufmann. New York: Modern Library, 1966.

II

OF WORDS AND UNDERSTANDING IN GROVE'S *SETTLERS OF THE MARSH*

(*in memoriam* Damien Thomas-Azarie La Bossière)

[*University of Toronto Quarterly*, 54 (1984/5)]

Les mots . . . l'infinie matière de mes doutes.
Félix-Antoine. Savard, *Journal et souvenirs II*

Ah, Jarl! so true and simple, that the secret operations of thy soul were more inscrutable than the subtle workings of Spinoza's. Herman Melville, *Mardi*

A philistine is only a man who is in the right without knowing why. G.K. Chesterton, "The Song of the Flying Fish," in *The Secret of Father Brown*

Michel de Montaigne, ironic assayer of perception and judgment, once observed that what may seem hot to one individual or group is not unlikely to seem cold to another. There is much in the criticism of the first of Frederick Philip Grove's prairie novels, *Settlers of the Marsh* (1925), to suggest that the sceptic's ancient wisdom has worn well with time and much use. On the one hand, there is commentary such as Desmond Pacey's in the *Literary History of Canada* (1965): while admitting to "some improbabilities" in the relations of the three main characters in that fiction, he finds in favour of Grove's "acute and profound" analysis of "the motives" of the protagonist Niels Lindstedt and praises the "brilliant fidelity" with which the author describes the northern Manitoba bush country and the homesteader's life there (681). In 1969, Ronald Sutherland also finds great virtue in the "psychological depth" of the novel, judging *Settlers of the Marsh* Grove's "finest achievement" (47, 51). More recently, a reader's guide restates the value of "the psychological realism of Grove's characterizations and the naturalistic description of the farms laid precariously upon the northern Manitoba landscape" (Moss 108).

On the other hand, some commentators have found Grove's work deficient in realism or truth to life and have assessed its artistic value accordingly. Edward McCourt, for one, in the 1970 revised edition of his *The Canadian West in Fiction* (1949), seems equally certain that "Grove's knowledge of human nature was not, unfortunately, as broad or as deep as his knowledge of physical environment," and that, consequently, he was "not equal to the task which he sets himself in *Settlers of the Marsh*," that of "making the central character . . . believable" (59, 65). Margaret Stobie's *Frederick Philip Grove* (1973) develops a parallel thesis, criticizing the author for his "reluctance to admit his limitations" and for his "pretensions to experience or knowledge that he clearly did not have." Grove's deficiencies are manifested in the "often wooden and ludicrous" characters in *Settlers of the Marsh*, where, according to Stobie, the chastity of Niels Lindstedt borders on "sheer stupidity" (189, 93).

It would seem that something of a critical tradition

has raised itself up in the more than half-century of commentary on that novel. Warning of the collision of realities or understandings sketched above may be detected as early as November 1925, in some of the first reviews to greet *Settlers of the Marsh*: G.V. Ferguson, in the *Manitoba Free Press*, for instance, writes of Niels' "simplicity" that it "passes all reasonable understanding," while Austin Bothwell, in the *Saskatoon Phoenix*, distinguishes the central character's innocence, his "denseness to certain implications," from mere "stupidity," to conclude that "he is drawn with skill, is consistent, is real" (cited from Pacey, ed., *Frederick Philip Grove* 108, 109).

But there is a consonance, too, discernible in the record of discordant voices. All seem agreed on the grounds for literary judgment in this case: Grove's (in)fidelity to the reality of people and/or places and things. And it is perhaps the harmony rather than the disagreement which proves the more instructive at bottom, for the commentary, taken as a whole in its broad lines, may be seen obliquely to mirror the 'problematic' of misunderstanding, understanding and language acted out by the *dramatis personae* of *Settlers of the Marsh* and incorporated by the novel itself as linguistic artefact and investigative device. As commentators have implied, *Settlers of the Marsh* is 'about' knowledge and its articulation. Their responses help define, by extension, the basic issues at play in the fiction: the (in)vincibility of human ignorance and the (in)ability of words to grasp and convey whole truth. Each group of conflicting responses hits the mark, then, by focusing attention on the novel's intellectual and artistic centre, the nature of which the reader is encouraged to draw out and clarify. An inquiry into the agency of ignorance and words in *Settlers of the Marsh*, making explicit the grounds which the work offers for its own interpretation, would seem the next logical step in the critical conversation it continues to invite. The following words attempt an advance in that direction, by a search through the text to discern a way of reading the novel appropriate to itself.

The search begins in *terra incognita*–this is where the author immediately locates his central character Niels. It is early November, and, in the gathering dusk, the twenty-four-year-old native of Blekinge, on the southeast coast of Sweden, is headed north from the Canadian praire town of Minor. But he has no precise sense of where he is. Only three months away from home, he navigates by the faith he has in his companion's savvy: Lars Nelson, three years in the New World, "knew the road." The "engulfing dark" (16) and a blinding snowstorm, however, deprive guide Nelson of his bearings. "Danged if I know where we are," he comes to admit aloud in English (17), presumably to the added mystification of Niels, who knows little or no English. Only a stroke of luck and the laconic directions provided by an ornery old Icelander, partly in broken English, in response to questions in Swedish, permit Nelson, after an hour's groping, to find the way ("Now I know" 19) to the Amundsen farm, where a job of well-digging awaits the two Swedes. What Niels makes of the Icelander's words is unsaid. At this point, the narration is less than five pages along, and, already, in at least two languages, each rendered as English, the author has framed the condition of a stranger in a strange land.

The remaining thirty or so pages of the first chapter

specify the lines of that stranger's entanglement in unknowing so compactly figured at the outset. "The word of the Lord," the hard facts of farm life and the meaning of the world may seem "perfectly clear" (23) in the eyes of the self-righteous, prosperous, self-deceived Amundsen, now seven years in the country. For this casuist, only the literal sense of the "spoken word" is "binding" (20). Matters stand otherwise with the uncorrupted newcomer Niels: unfamiliar as they are to him, the signs in his field of vision appear truly enigmatic. Finding himself "somehow" attracted to Amundsen's only child Ellen, in her late teens, Niels cannot read "any meaning" in the look she gives him (21, 22). What her general "attitude spoke of" was "a somewhat defiant aloofness," as the narrator vaguely recalls of her effect on people (21). Nor can Niels follow another kind of language, the German and English spoken by visitors at the Amundsen farm the first Sunday after his arrival there. That same day, at the Lund place, his sense of estrangement is all the more heightened when he is introduced to another group of visitors, including the vivacious and exotic widow, Clara Vogel: names "go past his ear in bewilderment" and the English sounds he hears are "quite beyond his understanding" (29, 30). With reason does he feel "outside of things" (25).

But there is an important difference between these two kinds of language. One is verbal, the other not. When, three years later, Niels encounters Mrs Vogel a second time –the occasion is Olga Lund's marriage to Nelson, in English at a German church–the widow recalls with a nicely suggestive choice of word: "When I first met you, you were dumb." "I did not know any English," Niels ingenuously replies (51). As Mrs Vogel suspects, there yet remains a language foreign to him, of a kind untaught by the male teacher at the night-school in Minor. Now, as at their first meeting, when the nature of Mrs Vogel's "impression" on him "did not become clear to Niels in articulate thought," he feels "awkward, dumb" before the "something in him" which this mysterious woman stirs up, a "dumb, passionate longing," "a hardly articulate impulse" (30, 46, 51). "What did it all mean?" (55) summarizes Niels' incomprehension before the innuendo in the widow's sly words of parting. While study over three years has given him some competence in one language, it has not enabled him to translate what "words" leave unsaid or to give expression in "words" to "the mysterious powers" at work in his "innermost being" (45, 46). The heart having its own reasons, the effect of his inability is to sharpen his desire for someone "who could understand the turmoil in his heart without an explanation in so many words" (54). His hope is to make himself known to others wordlessly. It is the only way he has.

The source of Niels' dumbness, however, goes deeper than a mere want of experience, for, even when he does understand something, he is unable to put his insight into words. Mrs Lund's pathetic dream of the future, for example, confessed to him in Swedish during his first visit to her decaying home, sets off resonances in Niels' mind, prompting him to a recollection of his own life with his poor mother and a review of his own dream of prosperity as a man. Not only had he "understood" Mrs Lund, so the narrator recounts, but he had been an acute interpreter, reading a tale of despair beneath the hope of her words: "suddenly he understood far more than mere words" (33). Fully sensing as he does the unspoken truth of the Lund story, he does not need to explain it. And when, in his mother tongue, Nelson gives voice to his special feeling for land that he himself has cleared (not for him the buying of a ready-made farm with wage-money) Niels grasps what his companion's distinction really means, though he himself cannot express what that meaning is: "Niels understood. That was his own thought exactly, his own unexpressed, inexpressible thought. . . " (36). The suggestion here is that the privation Niels suffers is beyond remedy. He cannot articulate what he really is and feels and believes, even when he recognizes what that is, because its truth is quite literally "inexpressible." What clarity is available to Niels comes in a motion as wordless and as sudden as that of a half-blind man's forked branch divining a hidden stream below (34). And so, as the last page of the first chapter transcribes, it becomes "very clear" that the vague emotion he feels for Mrs Vogel originates in that darkest and strangest of regions, where words cannot fully penetrate, "his innermost self" (56). Dumb as he remains at age twenty-seven, he has come clearly to see that what he does not understand is himself.

There is hardly a page in the second and third chapters in the history of Niels' progress along the way to enlightenment which does not directly advance the governing theme: the obscurity of the innermost life and the powerlessness of words to grasp and comunicate the truth of that life. As in chapter 1, Niels' "powers of vision" are weak; "his tongue is tied" (60, 79). "Searching for something," he gazes into his beloved Ellen's "inscrutable eyes," puzzling over the code of her "inscrutable look" (57, 58, 64). But no certain answer comes. Visiting Ellen shortly after her father's death by mishap, Niels looks at her, "dully, incomprehendingly" (64). On another occasion, he goes to her in "a dull and incomprehensible excitement," completely at a loss for what to say (68). There are no words between them to make public what each privately feels: "Always their intercourse had been full of silences" (93). And when he hears the dying Sigurdsen's delirious utterances, "trailing off into Icelandic," raising up "strange disquieting things" from a wild past at sea, Niels understands "only half" of what the sounds say. Such speech is "incomprehensible" (84). What the garbled words from the lips of the former sailor echo is the voice of the "hardly articulate impulse" in the man attracted to Clara Vogel (51).

Vaguely articulated as well is Niels' sense of the "things beyond the remedy of words" which separate him from Ellen and his dream of domestic bliss (80). Chapter 3 reveals what those things are. After a chance meeting with Clara, during which her eyes seem "to deprive him of his speech" (88), Niels runs to Ellen, hoping to get from her an unequivocal expression of her feelings for him. None is given. "Imponderable things, incomprehensible waves of feeling passed to and fro between them: things too delicate for words" (94). Ellen cannot "understand" (99) why she cannot help but not marry Niels, offering him no explanation; and he responds to her incomprehension and his own with silence. "He does not know what to do, what to say"; he does not "understand" (100). After the death of Sigurdsen, Niels returns again, this time desperate for enlightenment: "I have got to know. I have got to get this clear" (103). The thirty-year-old suitor stands "in helpless incomprehension" before Ellen, who now struggles to compose her "story," not knowing whether she can "tell" it, not knowing whether he will "understand" it or not (105). "If you are to understand, I must strip my soul of its secret," she warns him . . . she will have to speak of those things which are "skipped in silence" (105). The story of the appalling cruelties inflicted by Amundsen on his wife, however, clarifies only the facts. Unveiling one secret, it is testimony to another, more profound: the inscrutable syntax of life, "a dumb shifting of forces" (101). Niels cannot understand that inarticulate shifting. He withdraws in silence, speechless before the testament of Ellen's life.

The figure implied, of Niels as dumb and baffled reader before the enigmatic text of existence, is made explicit in chapters 4 and 5. On at least two occasions, he is perplexed by the "abstruse phraseology" of "a volume on National Economy" and discovers nothing in his troubled search for "something that might enlighten him" in *Madame Bovary* (147, 136). When he does find the "truths" of his own experience in another text, the Book of Ecclesiastes, what he reads, ironically, is that life is an enigma beyond human ability to solve (172). In the mirror of Solomon's words, he sees the language of his own ignorance. And while he is able to "read in a glance and a nod" the truth of the Dahlbeck couple, he has "no means of reading the mind" of Clara, whom has taken to wife susequent to a passive and wordless obedience to "strange, incomprehensible impulses . . . dimly felt, not distinctly told of in thought" (161, 164, 121). Niels cannot translate the hidden sense of Clara's "words" that he not leave her for an instant, since these only hint at "dark, incomprehensible things," "things unimaginable, horrors unspeakable," as he comes to dread (125, 128, 149). Beneath surfaces and words are "unsounded depths" he cannot "fathom" (166, 145).

When he is eventually enlightened by the last word of the Dahlbeck woman's brutal taunt–"You married the district whore"–the words of Clara's repeated warnings and the language of her mystifying actions over the several years of their marriage are illuminated in "a flash of real lightning" (177). But if the fact is not plain enough to Niels (to other characters in *Settlers of the Marsh* and readers less innocent it has been evident for some time before), it is another of those facts "inaccessible to any reason" which make up the "tangled labyrinth of his life" (168, 159). Again Niels is struck dumb. "With unseeing eyes, unthinking brain," in a speechless, somnambulistic trance, he staggers home (182-83). In a world of almost "utter darkness," where what vision there can be is by a light "very dim, almost divined" (185), he obeys another impulse. A single shot from his hunting rifle ends the life of Clara. "And he that increaseth knowledge increaseth sorrow," Niels recalls the "certain words" (189) from Ecclesiastes (1:18). He has come to experience the truth of that wisdom in a tragedy of unknowing confirming the words of his earlier meditation on the invincibility of ignorance in this world: "A dumb shifting of forces. Grass grew and was trodden; and it knew not why" (101). He still does not know the underlying why of things; he continues in his role as a perplexed reader of an inscrutable text. "However much man toils in searching" after a complete understanding of himself and the world, writes Solomon, "he does not find it out" (8:17).

It has been argued that the sixth and final chapter of *Settlers of the Marsh* is a *non sequitur* of sorts. The reunion of Ellen and a forty-year-old Niels, sending them off in search of possible happiness, detracts from the novel as an artistic and intellectual "entity," states Thomas Saunders: *Settlers of the Marsh* "should have ended with the tragedy," an end more consistent with the novel's internal design and more in keeping with Grove's view of life (xiii). Read in the context of a drama of ignorance and understanding, however, "Ellen Again" is a logical continuation of what has come before. From its opening page, the final chapter returns the reader to the question of "words," their agency and limitation, and the vagueness of human knowledge. At his trial, Niels does not utter "a word which might throw light on the crime or his motives" (192). What he does record before society is a written plea, "guilty to the charge of murder," set down in "plain, unequivocal terms" (192). Ironically, and perhaps even amusingly to the disinterested spectator, the very fact of the prisoner's impatient insistence on the certainty and veracity of his confession to a capital crime raises doubts as to its complete truthfulness; and Niels is found guilty of "manslaughter with attenuating circumstances" (193).

While in federal prison, Niels is introduced to yet other ways by which mankind strives to unravel mystery. After four years, he begins to attend classes, learning "something of French and Latin, of Algebra, Geometry, Science," and acquiring "a vocabulary which would enable him to read real books" (195). He progresses in erudition, but his final lesson is in detachment: "Finally he was amused. He learned to laugh at man's folly in puzzling out such curiosities of the mind" (195). Having passed his examinations, he concludes with the Solomon-like query: "What had it all to do with the real problems of life" (195). Niels, it would appear, has grown to a condition akin to the "negative capability" described by Keats, "when man is capable of being in uncertainties, Mysteries, doubts, without any irritable reaching after fact and reason, content with half knowledge" (cited from Woodring 525). Content now with truth "understood only half" (*SM* 84), and convinced of how little of life even his new knowledge and vocabulary can illuminate, he is in a position dispassionately to contemplate his ambiguous reality as a man who has both sinned and been sinned against. The less anxious Niels is now able to develop a more comprehensive sense his entanglements in the moral life, of his guilt and innocence.

Nor are words said to speak more eloquently of the heart of the matter when the man who "does not understand in articulate terms" (215) rejoins Ellen after serving less than seven of the ten years of his sentence: "Words were not needed" (213). In a "state of dusk," Niels and Ellen converse in "mutual wordless comprehension" (213). "Both know; and each knows what the other knows" (214). And what each knows is that each is partly responsible for what has happened, that "life has involved them in guilt," and that "never again must they part" (216). Here the author repeats almost verbatim the sentence from chapter 3: "imponderable things, incomprehensible waves of feeling pass to and fro between them: things to delicate for words" (214-15). Earlier, those "things" had been "somehow full of pain" (94); now, they are "somehow full of joy" (215). If words are powerless to make up the deficiency which is ignorance, they are also powerless to express the plenitude which is knowledge. So comprehensive is the range of silence, in fact, that it can speak of joy and sorrow at once: "They stand and look, their feelings half joy, half sorrow. . . . No need for words" (216). As the fiction nears its end, Ellen tells Niels of her belief that they can "live down" the past, that the distance still between them can be bridged. But she is not certain: "And whether we can or not we must try. . ." (217). They have a chance, it is clear, and perhaps blind fortune will favour them. In a dumb universe, beyond the ken of reason and words, they may by hap and by effort come to fulfil the promise of bliss. The reader last sees Niels and Ellen as they set off for home, hand in hand like Adam and Eve in the final lines of *Paradise Lost*, though without "Providence" for "their guide" (12.647). Where the remainder of their lives will take Niels and Ellen, whether to tragedy or felicity, is left to silence. They disappear from sight, bound for *terra incognita*.

There remains at least one extension of eloquent speechlessness which the reader of *Settlers of the Marsh* is left to puzzle over once the story of the characters' lives is done. It is the conundrum set by the story-teller's persistent reflection on words, so often repeated as to encourage the reader to focus on the 'written' nature of the tale: unlike his characters, Grove as author cannot limit himself to silence if he is to express what he understands of the 'inexpressible.' He is bound to find in words the least imprecise way of saying what he has to say. And what that language is has as much to tell of Grove's art and vision in *Settlers of the Marsh* as the story of Niels' life has to tell of the character's failure to see and articulate. Perhaps what is most significant in the language of *Settlers of the Marsh* is the absence of knowledge it implies in its author, the partiality of his vision. The privatives repeated in the novel are a defining feature of Grove's expression, which draws heavily on the vocabulary traditional to negative speculation. "Unseeing," "imponderable," "inarticulate," "unspeakable," "speechless," "inscrutable" and "incomprehensible" are examples already cited. Also, there are the limitative words to suggest a deficiency of comprehension. Of these, "almost" is the principal, repeated no fewer than seventy-eight times in the two hundred or so pages of the novel, more than fifty times in the last hundred. "Almost visible" (50), "almost transparent" (50, 88), "almost dark" (55, 198), "almost knew" (84), "almost palpable" (91), "imperceptible almost" (94, 215), "almost forgotten" (120, 176, 177), "almost complete" (141), "almost furtive" (170) and "almost happiness" (199), for example, signal an ongoing search for the precise expression of what is known only in part, "almost divined" (185) but not quite. Only slightly less prominent by frequency is "something," with the ignorance such anonymous naming implies. As well, the wide deployment of subjunctive "as if" constructions (these number more than fifty) shows a mind grappling with riddles, attempting to translate by supposition and hypothesis, rather than an eye certain of actualities. If Grove's semantics of privation may be heard to voice anything positive and certain, it is the author's understanding that his vision is unclear, his conviction that life is an unanswerable riddle.

Attention to the negative and limitative language of *Settlers of the Marsh* opens a way to a larger comprehension of this elusive writer. Since, as Pacey had occasion to write in 1965, Grove's novels show "a thoroughly worked out and consistent philosophy and a technique . . . fully adapted to his intentions" (*Literary* 685), the case of *Settlers of the Marsh* is not unlikely to be atypical of its author. Just how fundamental the semantics of privation is to the articulation of Grove's thought and art is suggested by the following passage from *In Search of Myself*, published more than two decades after *Settlers of the Marsh*. Grove here records the powerful feeling evoked in him by the imagined song of fictional Kirghiz herdsmen:

> But when he had left them a quarter of a mile behind, suddenly, unexpectedly, almost startlingly, the whole column broke into a droning song, with the effect of a ghostly unreality. It was a vast, melancholy utterance, cadenced within a few octaves of the bass register, as if the landscape as such had assumed a voice: full of an almost inarticulate realization of man's forlorn position in the face of a hostile barrenness of nature; and yet full, also, of a stubborn, if perhaps only inchoate assertion of man's dignity below his gods. (153)

It goes without saying that this passage, read by Pacey in 1965 (*Literary* 682) and Sutherland in 1969 (*Frederick* 9) as a summary of Grove's "philosophy," is sonorous with the language of limitation, negation and uncertainty. "Unexpectedly, almost startlingly," "a ghostly unreality," "an almost inarticulate realization," "yet," "if perhaps only inchoate": such is the linguistic correlative of Grove's "thoroughly worked out and consistent philosophy." Understandably, the identity of that philosophy has never been easy to define in positive, unambiguous terms. "What Was Frederick Philip Grove?" asks the title of Sutherland's contribution to *The Grove Symposium* (1974), in search of the "highly complex and profound thinker" (10). The riddling words of *Settlers of the Marsh* may serve as oblique reply:

> Are there in us unsounded depths of which we do not know ourselves? Can things outside us sway us in such a way as to change our very nature? Are we we? Or are we mere products of circumstance? (166)

Thomas Saunders offers this considered response to the interrogatives set by *Settlers of the Marsh*: "But there is no ready answer." The reader's response echoes the author's; "the novelist, through his characters," Saunders goes on to say, "arrives at no final answer" (xi). The negative surely confesses to a degree of bafflement. But is there is another answer, less ready, to the identity of Grove's intellectual creed? John Moss, in 1981, proposes a formulation consistent with the language of unknowing in *Settlers of the Marsh*: "quasi-determinism" (110). Man is almost free to choose, almost not; almost unfree, almost not. (*Quelle articulation!?* one might say.) It might reasonably be argued that, in the Grove universe, there can be no knowledge other than this nor any syntax more articulate for an understanding of responsible man's lot below his grimly playful gods.

The Kirghiz-song passage also characterizes Grove's art, according to Pacey's affirmation in the *Literary History of Canada*: "This is an apt description of Grove's own prairie novels" (682). Each, then, is a "song" with an effect of "ghostly unreality," a voicing of "an almost inarticulate realization," to repeat the words from *In Search of Myself.* But there is a difficulty when literary historian of ideas Pacey goes on in the same paragraph to set the artist Grove squarely in the "school of naturalists." "Like the novels of Zola and Dreiser and Hamsun, Grove's have strength and solidity, present masses of accurate sociological detail, and embody in plain prose a deterministic view of human character" (683). Grove's "apt description" of his own work, however, is hardly plain prose naming solid stuff, though it is very much like the prose of *Settlers of the Marsh.* Nor does it seem very much in tune with the language of *Sister Carrie* (1900), for example, Dreiser's literary imitation of what, in its own words, "has been shown experimentally" (362). Some three times the length of *Settlers of the Marsh*, Dreiser's novel compels its author to "almost" about half as many times; nor does it resound with the privatives of Grove's work. Clearly, there is a dissonance in the comparison.

In 1970, Pacey himself comes to suggest a corrective to the disjunction just below the surface of his earlier acccount. Introducing his collection of pieces from the history of Grove criticism, he remarks that commentators have not grasped "the nature of Grove's symbolic art," the fundamentals of which are not to be learned simply in the school of "Naturalism" (7). "Symbolic" is a valuable hint to the reader who would consider Grove's continuity with a tradition of writing more in harmony with the negative semantics of *Settlers of the Marsh.* The qualifier brings to mind a corpus of doctrine affirming the power of the imagination, a faculty beyond reason, for the perception of essential, inscrutable truth, and emphasizing the role of silence and symbol as means of expressing that truth. Sceptical of positive science, it is a body of doctrine having *Sartor Resartus* (1833-34), not Zola's *Le Roman expérimental* (1880), as a cardinal text in the history of its development. As Carlyle reflects in "The Life and Opinions of Herr Teufelsdröckh," "not our Logical, Mensurative faculty, but our Imaginative one" can see into the underlying reality of this "Universe of Nescience," the nature of which is literally "unspeakable" since hidden from our knowledge (148, 152, 146). Silence, so the argument follows, is the appropriate and complete expression of man's unknowing.

The impasse of silence responding to nescience, however, is not entirely insuperable: it may be solved, though only in part, so *Sartor Resartus* proposes, by the action of symbolic utterance. The word-symbol, taking its vocabulary from the language of finite things, not only speaks of the world man can know but also expresses, by what it leaves unsaid, that which is beyond knowing and saying. By that "doubled significance," of "Speech and Silence acting together," writes Carlyle, the symbol allows for a positive articulation even as it simulates "the inarticulate mystic speech of Music" (100). The analogy earlier suggested by Pacey, between Grove's prairie novels and his verbal account of an imagined song of Kirghiz herdsmen, "an utterance . . . full of an almost inarticulate realization," seems all the more apt when read in the light of the fundamentals of "symbolic" art conceived in this way.

If almost dumb, then, as Carlyle's account speculates and Grove's self-description reflects, the music-like symbol almost articulates as well. Symbol's agency, in this regard, is not wholly incompatible with a realism of the kind aimed for in the *La Fortune des Rougon* (1870), "a simple exposé of facts" by a "scientist," according to Zola's manuscript "Plans" (cited from Wimsatt and Brooks 456). There is, in principle, no "dédain de la nature" enjoined by the symbolic artist's "néo-mysticisme," in the words of an 1892 letter from the musician and poet Camille Saint-Saëns to the autobiographer, novelist and mariner Pierre Loti (cited from Millward 326).

And practice has confirmed principle. Certainly, there is no disregard for surface reality or its language celebrated in the work of Joseph Conrad, for example, a reader of *Sartor Resartus* and one of Grove's favourite authors, who strove to render as much of "the mystic nature of material things" as his art would permit (Conrad, *Personal* 130). As Conrad illustrates in *Typhoon* (1903), a tale exploring "the mysterious side" of a taciturn literalist's "stupidity," words may serve to describe facts with "perfect accuracy"; but, like facts, they also serve as mute witnesses to the unspeakable underlying truth of man and the universe. "Facts can speak for themselves with overwhelming precision" (*Typhoon* 4, 3, 15, 9).

A similar "doubled significance" manifests itself in *Settlers of the Marsh*. It may be found, for instance, in Grove's much-celebrated description of a sudden prairie storm, remarkable as much for its precise reflection of appearances as for its symbolic evocation of the unseen. Parts of the description follow, its added ellipses here enhancing the effect of silence natural to the book's unspeaking:

> The air is breathless: even the slight, wafting flow from the east has ceased. . . . The wall of cloud has differentiated: there are two, three waves of almost black; in front, a circling festoon of loose, while flocculent manes, seething, whirling. . . . A winking of light runs through the first wave of black. A distant rumbling heralds the storm. . . . The bush . . . stands motionless, breathless, blackening as the sun is obscured. Birds flit to and fro, seeking shelter, silent. . . . Then a huge suction soughs through the stems. But already the lash of the wind comes down: like the sea in a storm tree tops rise and fall, the stems bending over and down and whipping back again, tossed by enormous pressures. They dance and roll, tumble and rear, and mutely cry out as in pain. . . . A misty veil rushes over the landscape, illumined by a bluish flash which is followed by nearer and nearer growlings and barkings. The first rain drops fall, large, but few. . . . Down comes the rain in a cloudburst, forming a wall. . . . Flashes of lightning break on the slough like bombshells; rattling thunder dances and springs. (98-99)

The semantics of privation featured in *Settlers of the Marsh* figure only slightly in this passage. There is continued absence, though, in the form of what is unsaid, in the negation which is silence. The facts of nature, their power figuratively to converse with humanity confirmed by the presence of simile and metaphor here, "mutely cry out," by symbolic suggestion, what is unspoken and invisible in the turbulent, silent conversation of Niels and Ellen as they sit and observe in profound incomprehension of themselves before the storm. "Niels and Ellen still are silent" (99), a condition partially shared by their author, who articulates from the appearances of nature images for the mute expression of his characters' interior lives. Even as they inscribe such knowledge as an outward eye can give, Grove's words strive, it seems, to translate what is beyond the power of words expressly to say. As Dick Harrison remarks, Grove's sentences often have an "opaque qualilty" (115). Confronted by "the enigmatical spectacle" of "the visible universe," in the words of Conrad's Preface to *The Nigger of the NARCISSUS* (vii), Grove finds what expression he can for his vision of that universe in the speech and silence of symbol, or in a language of partial or complete privation.

What, then, is to be learned from the words of this teacher and student of languages and self-professed quester after "psychologic truth?" (*It Needs* 70). Large claims have been made. The concluding sentence of a paper read at the Grove Symposium (University of Ottawa, May 1973), Louis Dudek's "The Literary Significance of Grove's Search," for example, avers that we may learn much: "Through them you may learn to know yourself, and to know the universe and the gods" (99). *Settlers of the Marsh* provides a clue to some of the particulars we may come to know, though the patterning of these hardly seems so positive. Specifically, there is tuition to be found in the story of silence and ignorance that the novel tells, in the negative, limitative semantics of its author, a language fully adapted to the expression of what is known only in part if at all. It is instruction in a tongue somewhat foreign to the ear unattuned to silence, in a knowledge partly hidden from the eye unadjusted to obscurity. "His mind was a lonely hunter through the intricate mazes of the words of seven languages, through the secret places of the heart," Kay Rowe eloquently commemorates Grove in the Spring 1949 number of the *Manitoba Arts Review* (cited from Pacey, *Frederick* 199).

That Grove searched for the innermost truth through a labyrinth of words can be verified from *Settlers of the Marsh*. That he actually found that truth, though, is something less certain. A secret, after all, is a secret. Faced with the question of Grove's (in)fidelity to the reality of people and things in a fiction tracking the inscrutable ways of man in an inscrutable universe, the reader may understandably come to answer with the motto of another seeker after psychologic truth, Montaigne. *Que sais-je*? is no unfit response to the truth of a fiction riddling in words of absence and uncertainty, signs of a fundamental privation also discernible in the mute speech of symbol. Here, perhaps, in a confession of reasoned doubt, not a certain profession of whole ignorance or knowledge, the reader is on solid ground. At bottom, the lesson of *Settlers of the Marsh* seems a lesson in limitation.

WORKS CITED

Carlyle, Thomas. *Sartor Resartus.* 1833-34. London: Routledge, 1888.

Conrad, Joseph. *The Nigger of the* Narcissus. 1897. Preface 1914. Ed. Robert Kimbrough. New York: W.W. Norton, 1979.

----------. *A Personal Record.* 1912. London: Dent Collected Edition, 1946-51.

----------. *Typhoon, and Other Stories.* 1903. London: Dent Collected Edition.

Dreiser, Theodore. *Sister Carrie.* 1900. New York: Modern Library, 1932.

Dudek, Louis. "The Literary Significance of Grove's Search." In *The Grove Symposium.* Ed. John Nause. Ottawa: U of Ottawa P, 1974.

Grove, Frederick Philip. *In Search of Myself.* Toronto: Macmillan, 1946.

----------. *Settlers of the Marsh.* 1925. Ed and with an introduction by Thomas Saunders. Toronto: M&S, 1966.

Harrison, Dick. *Unnamed Country: The Struggle for a Canadian Prairie Fiction.* Edmonton: U of Alberta

P, 1977.

McCourt, Edward. *The Canadian West in Fiction.* 1949. Toronto: Ryerson, 1970.

Millward, Keith C. *Pierre Loti et l'esprit 'fin de siècle'.* Paris: Nizet, 1955.

Moss, John. *A Reader's Guide to the Canadian Novel.* Toronto: M&S, 1981.

Pacey, Desmond. "Fiction: 1920-40." In *Literary History of Canada*, gen. ed. Carl F. Klinck. Toronto: U of Toronto P, 1965.

------------, ed. *Frederick Philip Grove.* Toronto: Ryerson, 1970.

Stobie, Margaret. *Frederick Philip Grove*. New York: Twayne, 1973.

Sutherland, Ronald. *Frederick Philip Grove*. Toronto: M&S, 1969.

------------. "What Was Frederick Philip Grove?" In *The Grove Symposium*, ed. John Nause. Ottawa: U of Ottawa P, 1974.

Wimsatt, William K., Jr., and Cleanth Brooks. *Literary Criticism: A Short History.* New York: Vintage, 1967.

III

LE SILENCE CHEZ FÉLIX-ANTOINE SAVARD

[*Cultures du Canada français* 1 (1984)]

Je tourne toujours autour des mêmes idées. F-A. Savard, *Journal et Souvenirs II*

"Nul n'aura de peine à situer ce que nous n'annonçons pas de ce livre, soit dans l'axe vertical ou les extrêmes se touchent, le corps retrouvant selon son destin le niveau de l'âme et l'harmonie des cieux; soit sur la ligne horizontale ou rampent les excès parasitaires et inassumables de l'esprit égaré." Bruno de Jésus-Marie, "Liminaire," *Magie des extrêmes*

Les libres chemins du papier. . . .
F-A. Savard, *Journal et Souvenirs II*

Dans le présent article, j'aimerais aborder la question du paradoxe *horizontal/vertical* chez Monseigneur Félix-Antoine Savard, dans une perspective qui nous permettra d'avoir sous les yeux à la fois non seulement le désaccord, mais encore l'harmonie dans sa pensée. D'une part, "une sorte de dualisme régit tout le jeu de notre nature," avoue Savard lors d'une conférence prononcée en 1939. Par conséquent, "une instabilité" et "une inquiétude tragique" auxquelles nous ne pouvons échapper "règnent dans le théâtre de nos éléments." D'autre part, l'intention optimiste de synthèse, d'ordre, et de paix est nettement marquée dans son oeuvre. Si, d'après la déclaration que Savard nous fait dans le premier volume de son journal, "la révélation de la vérité" se fait par "l'accord des extrêmes," comment cette révélation arrive-t-elle à se faire et à s'exprimer chez cet auteur consacré à la recherche de la vérité et plié à la règle d'un jeu dualiste et forcément tragique? Sa vie durant, sa réponse est toujours la même: par la poésie. C'est le poète qui chante "le bonheur de l'ordre et l'hymne de la réconciliation" (*Carnet du soir intérieur I*).

Et par quel processus la poésie tente-t-elle d'effectuer cet accord où se situe cette vérité? Ecoutons la réponse que nous fournissent les grands précepteurs de Savard en ce qui concerne la poétique, Paul Claudel et l'abbé Henri Brémond, tous les deux de l'école de Thomas Carlyle.

Le conflit des contraires se résout par l'opération de l'imagination poétique, selon le credo claudélien dans l'*Art poétique*: la pensée moderne de l'imaginaire se fonde sur "une nouvelle logique. . . . L'ancienne avait le syllogisme pour organe, celle-ci a la métaphore . . . l'opération qui résulte de la seule existence conjointe et simultanée de deux choses différentes." Carlyle, suivant en cela S.T. Coleridge, avait devancé Claudel quand il tenta de réaliser la vérité de l'intégration par la voie du symbole, de l'imagination–"the faculty by which opposite or discordant qualities are balanced or reconciled," Coleridge avait médité sur la question dans *Biographia Literaria.* Chez ceux-ci, comme chez Claudel, le processus symbolique effectue la réconciliation du FINI et de l'INFINI. "Natural Supernaturalism" et "The Gospel of Silence," les chapitres de *Sartor Resartus* tellement utiles à l'Abbé Henri Brémond dans *La Poésie pure*, mettent ce thème en valeur.

Carlyle lui aussi, qui s'est inspiré de la littérature allemande et de la philosophie de l'Est, propose ici que le silence soit l'expression négative de l'inexprimable ("the unspeakable"), de la vérité qui dépasse la logique du FINI; et que seul le symbole est capable d'exprimer cet inexprimable d'une façon positive et concrète:

> It is by Symbols that opposites are harmonized . . . In a Symbol there is concealment and yet revelation; here, therefore, by Silence and by Speech acting together comes a doubled significance. . . . By Symbol, the inarticulate speech of music, the Infinite is made to blend itself with the Finite. Like and Unlike are united. (*Sartor Resartus)*

"La poésie pure est silence . . . pensée musicale," souligne l'Abbé Brémond. Et Savard est d'accord: "c'est du "symbole" que sort "la plus authentique poésie," l'expression des "inexprimables silences de l'enffable," lieu de "l'amour" et de "la souffrance du poète" (*Carnet du soir intérieur I).*

La pratique de Savard est conforme à sa poétique. Les silences de *La Folle*, par exemple, chantent "une sorte de musique" qui exprime ce que l'écrivain se sent "impuissant à dire." "Se sentant incapable d'exprimer par mots" la vérité des sentiments qu'il éprouve dans *Menaud*, l'auteur, comme le Lucon, reprend "sa musique." "Je cherche la vérité dans l'équilibre de l'étale," explique Savard dans son journal. Il cherche l'unité dans la poésie, dans un équilibre analogue à celui auquel Claudel et maintes artistes amoureux du symbole et du silence on aspiré.

"Si ce que tu à dire / n'est plus beau que le silence / tais-toi." Le sens de ce proverbe chinois, mis en exergue du recueil de haï-kaï composés par Savard (*Aux Marges du silence*), pourrait se traduire comme suit: "l'expression écrite doit prendre part à l'accomplissement de la beauté par le silence." L'expression écrite ainsi que la beauté participent *du* silence et *au* silence. Convenablement, les haï-kaï, "poèmes qui se contentent de contempler avec douceur la sérénité, l'ordre et la beauté" du monde," sont diserts dans leur silence. "Le papier dit plus que le texte," dit Savard dans l'édition de luxe de son recueil de petits poèmes. La blancheur silencieuse du papier dit plus que les mots noirs.

Le silence à l'intérieur du discours poétique nous fournit un moyen de retrouver la parole face à l'INFINI. D'après Savard, "c'est le souverain privilège de la poésie de survoler l'histoire et de réunir . . . l'immense et le transcontinental" (*Journals et souvenirs I*). Et de survoler le temps et l'espace. La lune, la terre, la truite, l'arbre, l'eau, le caillou, la neige, la corneille, la tourterelle, l'étoile– tous communiquent sans paroles avec le vieux poéte aux marges du silence qui entend en tous lieux le discours symbolique, la musique analogique qui lie deux mondes. Ce discours silencieux est pour quelque chose dans l'oeuvre d'un prêtre et d'un poète qui se réjouit, selon la parole de Karl Rahner, "des conversations avec le Dieu du silence."

Bien sûr, ces "échanges sans paroles" (*Journal et souvenirs II*) ne peuvent s'accomplir sans mots, sans images tirées de ce bas monde, le seul monde qu'on connaît, le monde de chez nous. Monseigneur Félix-Antoine Savard *vixit*. Nul idéalisme sans réalisme chez lui; nulle poésie/ parole sans silence. Pas moyen d'échapper à cette condition d'intégrité paradoxale. "Équilibre, ai-je dit. Après avoir divisé, pesé, analysé, c'est à ce mot qu'il faut toujours revenir," explique Savard aux forestiers du Québec en 1950. La forêt est "un merveilleux poème debout entre ciel et terre et tout foissonant de rhythmes, d'analogies, de symboles, de correspondances." Au sein de la forêt se chante le *sacrum silentium.*

Trois envois:

"Toute musique enfin!" (Savard, *Symphonie du Misereor*).

"Le silence . . . la mystérieuse syntaxe de l'amour" (Savard, *Le Barachois).*

"François d'Assise le chante: '*Laudate si, mi Signore, cum tutte le tue creature / Spezialmente messer lo fratre Sole'*." (Savard, *Journals et souvenirs II).*

IV

COMPASS OF THE CATOPTRIC PAST: JOHN GLASSCO, TRANSLATOR

[*Canadian Poetry* 13 (1983)]

"Oh, heart! Oh, blood that freezes, blood that burns!" Robert Browning, *Love among the Ruins*

"*El original es infiel a la traducción.*" Jorge Luis Borges, *Sobre el* Vathek *de William Beckford*

"All of John Glassco's works have been eccentric achievements, more attached to the values and fashions of the past than to those of post-war Canada."[1] So summarizes Frank Davey in *From There to Here* (1974), as though to confirm, *à rebours*, the theme of one-way transferral which the title of his guide implies and encapsulates. But such a division of here from there, past from present, seems far from *à propos* in the case of John Glassco. The precocious youth who steamed to the Old World as supercargo on the CANADIAN TRAVELLER, in flight from "lingering Victorianism,"[2] was to join the society Steven Marcus has named "the other Victorians." The author of *The English Governess*, burlesqued in a "mock-Victorian psychosexual romance,"[3] Glassco came to body fully the aphrodisiac fragment left at Beardsley's death in 1898.[4] "May I ask: are you yourself already a Canadian avatar of someone else, and if so of whom?," a British novelist in Paris responded mischievously to Glassco's claim for the existence of several Canadian throwbacks to Old-World writers.[5] For Glascco, who conversed with Catullus, Samuel Daniel, Bishop Berkeley, Thomas Love Peacock and Baudelaire, to name only a few of his acquaintances, the past is not a complete stranger. For Glassco, home is where the mind has been. And his had been to many places. He presently recalls in *A Point of Sky* (1964):

> From here the only way is turning back
> To join the links of casual circles leading
>   back
> Home, or somewhere else I have been before.[6]

Like other travellers before him, he goes forward *à reculons*. He takes home with him wherever he goes.[7]

In all of his writing, Glassco travels with his gaze in "the rear-vision mirror," as he reflects near the end of the historical poem *Montreal* (1973).[8] It is his cardinal habit of mind. Recounting Montreal from the conception of its island in "a boiling sea / Full of devil-fish" (ll. 21-22), through the golden age of the "Happy Savage" (l. 53) and the advent of Christianity, to the city of the poet's childhood and, now, of his advanced age, Glassco blurs the line between then and now by partly remaking the past in his own image. He writes of the natives of Hochelaga before the arrival of Cartier, for example:

> All the exquisite enjoyment

Of the torturing of prisoners
And consumption of their livers–
All these lovely pranks and pleasures
Soon shall disappear forever! (ll. 63-67)

Pranks and pleasures of the kind, of course, have not disappeared at all. The Chevalier Tannhäuser,[9] the sexologist Eulenberg,[10] Harriet Marwood[11] and John Glassco have kept them alive. The augury, "Soon shall disappear forever," is ironic in fact: for a moment, Glassco here has transported Hochelaga to late-Victorian England. The pre-Christian Amerindians and the poet of Foster, Québec, join to celebrate "the *agape*" of "fornication" (ll. 70-73). Thus the facetious lauding of "the many blessings / Of a European culture" (ll. 93-94) appears unwittingly ambiguous. Glassco himself places the Amerindians, by parallel, in *fin-de-siècle* Europe. As he confesses, his poem is made of "quaint analogies" stimulated by "nostalgia" (l. 213). The history of Montreal is, as it must be in part, a pretext for the expression of Glassco's private legend. "All is not lost," he muses in the poem "Second Sunday after Trinity."[12] His memorial imagination permits him to salvage something personal from time.

But, as with all salvage operations, there is loss. Montreal is not what it once was:

City, city of my childhood
I know you only by the names of streets
Gone from me now like old mistresses. . . .
(ll. 604-6)

Memory provides reflections only, not warm bodies. The past still lives, though now by similitude only, as names and images in the mind. "Translate thy vision," Glassco addresses himself in *The Deficit Made Flesh* (1958); it is all the poet can do.[13] His work is to harrow up "a new-made ghost," a moving image of the dead life.[14] Past and present, image and object, expression and thought are but analogies of each other. Between them, there is silence, a great distance, since similitude is not identity:

> And as what they are for me, here and now,
> As the translated pegs and props, characters
> In the fable of being–infinitely
> Remote: I mean, daffodils in a vase,
> Sail on the water, sunlight on the grass.
>
> "Hail and Farewell"[15]

Such is the tension, "the darkness and distance,"[16] which all translators must experience: between speech and silence, signifier and signified. It is on this intermediary ground that Glassco's translation of his own vision and that of other poets come together. As a maker of elegiac word-analogies "caught / Between silence and the failure of any words" ("The Crows"), Glassco was ideally suited to the invaluable, futile and costly craft of literary translation. The following words, as justly as they can, will suggest that he practised that craft with courage and skill, with a success proportionate to the silence and distance he came to evoke and diminish.

"At worst," according to Glassco in the Introduction

to his *The Poetry of French Canada in Translation* (Toronto: Oxford UP 1970), the translator provides "a bridge of sorts" between folk of different languages (xxii). In this respect, the translator does nothing much more than provide a social service, though it is one which Glassco manifestly judges valuable. He tells us in the same Introduction that his purpose here as anthologist and translator is to give "the English reader his first extended view of the beauties, development and direction of the poetry itself" (xvii). With close to two hundred works, three-quarters of which had not been published before 1970, *The Poetry of French Canada in Translation* continues to stand as an impressive bridge. In fact, the collection approximates Guy Sylvestre's *Anthologie de la poésie canadienne-française* (fifth ed. 1966) in both scale and matter: one quarter of the poems included by Glassco are to be found in Sylvestre; and all but a few of the more than forty authors collected there are also represented in Glassco's anthology.

It goes without saying, though, that the poetry itself is the material cause of Glassco's anthology. At best, so he observes in the volume's Introduction, the translator is "transported" to a vision by the poem he proposes to communicate in another language. He returns, to speak another poem, "a poetic creation in itself" (xxii). In the words of Clément Moisan, *The Poetry of French Canada* is at once "une très bonne anthologie de la poésie québécoise des XIXième et XXième siècles" and a quite separate work "d'excéllentes traductions, souvent faites par des poètes."[17] Fred Cogswell, John Robert Colombo, George Johnston, A.J.M. Smith, Jay Macpherson, Ralph Gustafson and F.R.

Scott are among the twenty-two authors to have their translations recorded in the anthology. But more than of any other poet, it is Glassco's work. More than one-third of the translations log his own travels across the field of poetry from French Canada that he has surveyed.

Glassco's translations in the 1970 anthology precisely reflect the nature and difficulties of the work he describes in the Introduction to that volume. He is, in this sense, his own best reader/critic. While agreeing with John Denham, seventeenth-century translator of six books of the *Aeneid,* that "'the subtile Spirit of poesie evaporates entirely . . . unless a new, or an original spirit is infused by the Translator himself,'" Glassco emphasizes that the process of re-creation must be ruled by the "architecture" of the original (xx). The translator's vision, of course, cannot be merely emotive or passive. He must look. And what his eyes seek out is the poem's "intimate structure" (xx). Such scrutiny may be so searching in some cases that it "may leave [the poem] . . . nothing but its intellectual content or 'meaning,' its images and inner pulsation" (xx). Consequently, "the scales of translation are . . . weighted in favour of a poetry marked by clarity of thought and expression, spare and striking imagery, and a simple internal movement"; like the "analytical critic," the translator of poetry finds matter most sympathetic to his eye in a work of distinct and simple lines (xx).

Glassco's rendering of "Grotesque," from René Chopin's *Le Coeur en exil* (1913), for example, shows how clearly and imaginatively he can read a poem's design. The work of a writer noted for "sa recherche de belles formes, son culte de l'art,"[18] "Grotesque" readily lends itself to the translator's architectural interpretation. The poem is cited in full:

> C'est Pierrot avecques encore
> Sa souquenille, un teint blafard,
> Sa face mince qui décore
> Une lèvre qu'ensanglante le fard.
>
> Sous le balcon de Colombine,
> Il grelotte et rêve aux appas
> La neige qui tombe, blanche farine.
> Qu'on lui refuse et ne sent pas
>
> Grimacier que le vent flagelle,
> De ses doigts bleuis et trembleurs
> Sur sa joue il essuie un pleur
> Puis pince le bout de son nez qui gèle. . . .[19]

Glassco translates:

> See, t'is Pierrot, affecting still
> The domino, the wry grimace,
> The lantern jaw whose painted mouth
> Incarnadines a powdered face.
>
> Shivering beneath her balcony
> Lost in a dream of Columbine,
> (Who has refused him) he ignores
> The snow descending, floury-fine.
>
> A grinning clown lashed by the wind,

With fingers pinched and blue he goes
To wipe a tear away–then rubs
The end of his frostbitten nose.

The first stanza of the translation immediately sets out the sense that is clarified only in the final stanza of the original. "Affecting still" (1) responds to "Grimacier" (9), as "wry grimace" (2) makes plain. Glassco sets out with Chopin's entire poem in mind, and proceeds, from the beginning, to articulate as simply and directly as possible what he takes to be its fundamental intention. The translation has a meaning all its own as well: it goes beyond Chopin in emphasizing Pierrot's affectation and the harmonious discord of posturing and doing which follows from it. While Chopin has Pierrot react to both unrequited love and frostbite, Glassco appears to imagine not quite so sentimental a lover who bypasses a gesture of love to react sensibly. Whereas feeling and emotion incongruously come together in Chopin (Pierrot, who in the second stanza is said not to "feel" the whiteness and coldness of snow and, by extension, of Colombine as "appas," comes to feel the effects of both in the end), Glassco simplifies the associations in the middle stanza, finally to paint a ludicrous contrast of gesture and harsh reality.

Glassco's reading of François Hertel's "Soir automnal," from *Strophes et catastrophes* (1943), shows a similar process. Beginning with the poem's final simile, "comme un navire" / "like a vessel,"[20] he renders "une rose" in the first stanza as "compass-card." This rose is ambiguous in Hertel's Petrarchan sonnet. The subject is love. It is only in the end that its significance as a "rose des vents" comes clearly into view for the reader:

> Je suis comme un navire arrimé sur la grève
> Qui part à la conquête de l'Amour.

In this instance, though, "une rose" ("Je n'ai plus un ami, je n'ai plus une rose"; l. 2) and its ambiguity might have been preserved in translation, since "a rose" also is a compass-card. As in "Grotesque," Glassco chooses for a greater simplicity. On other occasions– his translation of Jean-Guy Pilon's "Et Brûleront les navires" (*L'Homme et le Jour*, 1957) exemplifies the variation–Glassco will graft rather than prune to achieve this same purpose. "The Dry Season" extends Pilon's poem:

> And when, some day, the tree
> Protestant of her purity
> Displays her naked limbs,
> We shall know shame if any shame is left.

The poem's meaning as a whole is drawn out by the adding of a witty and transparent equivocation: shame should be in those who do not act from love, not in the shame of nakedness.

His translation of "Janvier," by Louis-Honoré Fréchette (according to Sylvestre "le plus grand poète canadien" of the nineteenth century),[21] may further suggest the clarity of Glassco's reconstruction of a poem's intimate design. Here is the sonnet, from *Les Fleurs boréales* (1879):

La tempête a cessé. L'éther vif et limpide
A jeté sur le fleuve un tapis d'argent clair,
Où l'ardent patineur, au jarret intrépide,
Glisse, un reflet de flame à son soulier de fer.

La promeneuse, loin de son boudoir tépide,
Bravant, sous les peaux d'ours, les morsures de l'air,
Au son des grelots d'or de son cheval rapide,
A nos yeux éblouis passe comme un éclair.

Et puis, pendant les nuits froidement idéales,
Quand, au ciel, des milliers d'aurores boréales
Battent de l'aile ainsi qu'étrangent oiseaux,

Dans les salons ambrés, nouveaux temples d'idoles,
Aux accords de l'orchestre, au feu des girandoles,
Le quadrille joyeux déroule ses réseaux.[22]

The translation, later to be incorporated into Glassco's *Montreal* (ll. 506-19), reads:

The storm has ceased. The keen and limpid air
Has spread a silver carpet on the stream,
Where, on intrepid leg, the skater glides
With shimmering flame upon his iron shoe.

From her warm boudoir, a lady braves
Beneath her bearskin robes the biting air;
With a sound of golden bells her rapid sleigh
Flashes like lightning past our dazzled eyes.

And later, through the nights' ideal cold
While thousands of auroras in the sky
Flutter their plumage like fantastic birds,

In ambered salons–deity's new shrines–
T'orchestral strains, 'neath sparkling chandeliers,
The gay quadrille unreels its sinuous web!

The scales of translation are weighted in favour of poetry of this kind. With its simple internal movement, imaging sharply defined parallels of motion and light, "Janvier" advances at a sprightly pace from dance to dance. Glassco follows the "sinuous web" of Fréchette's "quadrille joyeux" with a skill which makes his imitation of the dance seem almost effortless.

But such harmony by faithful representation is not always so attractive or congenial. When the translator sees his author beckoning him downward, however slightly, the fidelity counselled by Wentworth Dillon in his *Essay on Translated Verse* (1684) becomes trying: "'Your author always will the best advise; / Fall when he falls, and when he rises rise'" (Introduction xxi). Every good translator experiences "the temptation to beautify and 'improve,' and thus perhaps carry the process of betrayal a bit further," so Glassco reflects on the wry old equation of *traddutore, traditore* (xxi). Beautification for art's sake tacitly reveals what the translator finds blemishing. Glassco does not have to add that the better and more creative poet the translator the greater the enticement. His remaking of Propertius' *Elegiarum*, from the Second Book, recalls that he himself succumbed elegantly and discreetly on occasion:

> Aut cum Dulichias Pallas spatiatur ad aras,
> Gorgonis anguiferae pectus operta comis–
> (ll. 7-8)[23]

the literal sense of which might be rendered "Or like Pallas when she passes before the altars of Dulichium with her breast covered with the snaky head of the Gorgon," Glassco embellishes in this way–

> Or *Pallas* pacing to the Altar-rite,
> Her breast with curl'd Medusa locks o'er-woven.[24]

A few of the pieces of *The Poetry of French Canada* testify that there were occasions when the temptation to improve proved to be even more enticing.

"The Dead" is perhaps the most striking case in the anthology of the translator as critic whose interpretation confesses his author's sinning against art. It represents an improvement on Octave Crémazie's "Les Morts."[25] Glassco follows Crémazie closely through the first seven stanzas, then omits the following ten, to add two concluding stanzas of his own. The compression in "The Dead" (the title should read "From 'The Dead'") better serves art. While the poet of "Les Morts," a commemorative poem inspired by All Souls' Day, turns directly to address a moral lesson to his living public as of stanza 8, Glassco continues to address the dead:

> Our selfish hearts, given up to present things,
> See in you but the pages of a book
> We have already read. . . .

Glassco's page artfully recalls the reader's attention to what he is doing, to his own moral condition, while it continues in conversation with the dead of Crémazie's pages. Glassco's own poem shows a greater control of voice; his is an artistic aim that fixes its gaze intently on a tighter and simpler structure.

"The Dead" also raises the issue of another kind of betrayal translators are sometimes inclined to commit: the (*soi-disant*) improvement of moral sense. It is "not only the ideas and progression of the poem that are exposed by translation: the temper and complexion of the poet himself are . . . mercilessly revealed," as Glassco in his probity is bound to observe (Introduction xxi). Since he too is a poet, what may also be exposed is the translator's own temper, his own moral values. Again, Glassco is a telling critic in his own case. In the instance of "Les Morts," the stanzas that Glassco omits speak of life after death, of the remission of temporal punishment for sins, of the theological virtues of faith, hope and charity. Crémazie's poem (as anthologized in Sylvestre) ends:

> Et les mourrantes fleurs du sombre cimetière,
> Se ranimant soudain au vent de la prière,
> Versent tous leur parfums sur les morts endormis.[26]

The Resurrection of the Dead is to come. Glassco's poem, on the other hand, progresses to a grim and quizzical incomprehension:

> To us, what does the world of suffering mean
> Which groans beyond this vast and dreary wall

That death has reared?

The difference suggests that the translator is substituting his own creed for Crémazie's. Dante, pilgrim from Inferno through Purgatorio to Paradiso, is absent from "The Dead," though not from "Les Morts" (st. 9).

Like "Les Morts," Simone Routier's "Psaume,"[27] pubished in the decade of her membership in the Dominican Institute of Philosophy (1940-50), is improved by Glassco's translation. Though, again, the improvement by compression, the tightening of structure, is gained, to some extent, at the expense of the French poem's theology. Glassco omits stanzas 5-9 (here the poet sees herself in the dress "de luxe et de péché" and is moved to hope by God's love and mercy made tangible in the "Sacrements"), to continue from stanza 10, which returns to the soul's loneliness, pain and malady. "Delivering happiness from the breast of pain" (st 5) / "Délivrant le bonheur au sein de la souffrance" (st. 10) calls Glassco back to Routier. Such feeling, it would seem, is congenial to the translator; the analogy may sound nostalgic to the reader of Glassco's own registering of pleasurable pains in *The English Governess* and *Montreal.* Stanzas 17-20 also are omitted. They are bright with hope and joy:

> Car le Soleil est là comme un vivant symbole
> Du drame répété sur l'archaïque autel. (st. 18)

And when, in stanzas 27-28, Routier praises the beauty and splendour of God reflected in Nature, Glassco again leaves off. By omission, he seems to give despair and loneliness a stronger voice than does his author. As Glassco himself was well aware, the translator exposes the poet's temperament. Omission or silence, while it may serve art, also serves to define the differences between two analogous visions.

Striving to translate Glassco's vision, the above reflections may bring to mind that all of his oeuvre turns about a central theme: between the author remembering and the author remembered, there is speech and silence. In the prefatory note to *Memoirs of Montparnasse* (1970), a fifty-nine-year-old Glassco recalls of the youth he once was and still is in the guise of a "new-made ghost": "in my memory he is less like someone I have been than a character in a novel I have read."[28] Similarly, we too are caught up in an ironic remembering and unknowing as we read Glassco's words, here and elsewhere. It is by speech that he can name the middle ground shared by analogous texts, of others and of himself; by silence or omission that he expresses the differences which separate them. Consequently, as the above words, taking their direction from Glassco's own poetry and criticism, have suggested, his medium cannot avoid but be "unequal and opaque" (Introduction xix) at bottom, even as it is clear and measured in its architectural interpretation of things.

On infrequent occasion, though, there is injustice in the translation more than is unavoidable, when its opacity relative to the original is pronounced more than the craft makes inevitable. At such times, Glassco's "compass of the catoptric past"[29] may be seen to image his own temper more clearly than it does the faith of those who have spoken before him. Then the silence between the author remembered and the author remembering grows. It is a measure of

Glassco's success, his fidelity to the intimate structure of poems not his own, that he is only rarely so provincial.

ENDNOTES

1. Frank Davey, *From There to Here: A Guide to English-Canadian Literature since 1960* (Erin, ON: Porcepic, 1974), 122.

2. Leon Edel, Introduction to Glassco's *Memoirs of Montparnasse* (Toronto: Oxford UP, 1970), vii.

3. From Glassco's June 1975 Preface to his *Harriet Marwood, Governess* (rev ed 1976), initially published with that title, anonymously, by Grove Press in 1967. First published as *The English Governess* (1960), in Paris, under the pseudonym Miles Underwood.

4. *Under the Hill . . . by Aubrey Beardsley, now Completed by John Glassco* (New York: Grove, 1959).

5. *Memoirs of Montparnasse* 32.

6. John Glassco, "Luce's notch," in *A Point of Sky* (Toronto: Oxford UP, 1964).

7.Cf. André Berthiaume, *La Découverte ambiguë: essais sur les récits de voyage de Jacques Cartier et leur fortune littéraire* (Ottawa: Le Cercle du Livre de France, 1976), chap 4 in particular. See also, Camille R. La Bossière's review of Berthiaume in *Le Voyage et la découverte du monde:Cahiers roumains d'études littéraires* 4 (1980). The traveller in foreign lands, like the translator, can express what he sees only in its analogical relationship to what he already knows. In that sense, he remembers as he sees. The lexicons appended to Cartier's *Le Bref Récit* figure large in Berthiaume's argument. At home everywhere, the traveller is at home nowhere. Glassco writes in "One Last Word": "No port for those tasselled sails!" (*Selected Poems* [Toronto: Oxford UP, 1974]).

8. John Glassco, *Montreal* (Montreal: DC Books, 1973).

9. *Under the Hill* resurrects the medieval legend of Tannhäuser's participation in the revels of Venus.

10. Eulenberg is the author of *Sadismus and Masochismus* (1898), apparently the stimulation for Glassco's writing of *The English Governess*.

11. The deliciously cruel disciplinarian who gives her proper name to *The English Governess* in its 1967 version.

12. John Glassco, *The Deficit Made Flesh* (Toronto: M&S, 1959). Indian File Books 9.

13. "A Devotion," in *The Deficit Made Flesh.*

14. "Deserted Buildings under Shefford Mountain," in *The Deficit Made Flesh.*

15. "Hail and Farewell," in *The Deficit Made Flesh.*

16. "Villanelle," in *The Deficit Made Flesh.*

17. Clément Moisan, *Poésie des frontières: étude comparée des poésie canadienne et québécoise* (Cité de La Salle: HMH, 1979) 20.

18. Réginald Hamel, John Hare and Paul Wyczynski, "René Chopin," in *Dictionnaire pratique des auteurs québécois* (Montreal: Fides, 1976) 142.

19. *Anthologie de la poésie canadienne française*, edited and with an introduction by Guy Sylvestre (Montreal: Beauchemin, 1966). Fifth ed.

20. Sylvestre 201.

21. Sylvestre 19.

22. Sylvestre 25.

23. Propertius, *Élégies*, ed. D. Paganelli (Paris: Les Belles Lettres, 1964) 38.

24. Glassco, in *A Point of Sky* 50.

25. Sylvestre, ed., 9-12. In his other translation of Crémazie

in *The Poetry of French Canada,* "From 'The Old Canadian Soldier'," Glassco slightly heightens the militancy of his author's fustian.

26. Sylvestre 12.

27. Sylvestre 161-67.

28. Glassco, "Prefatory Note" to *Memoirs of Montparnasse* xiii.

29. Glassco, from the title poem of *A Point of Sky*.

V

DU PAIN, DU PAPIER, ET DES CANNIBALES: M. CARLYLE ET SA RÉVOLUTION

[*Carrefour* 12 (1990)]

> "Il y a des humeurs fantastiques et sans discours qui ont poussé non des hommes particuliers, seulement, mais des peuples à se deffaire." Montaigne, "Coustume de l'Isle de Cea"

> "*La Révolution* . . . is verily devouring its own children." Carlyle, *The French Revolution*

> "The prevalence of suicide is the test of height in civilization." Havelock Ellis, *The Dance of Life*

Au printemps de 1835, la femme de ménage de John Stuart Mill, croyant n'avoir sous les yeux que de la paperasse, jette au feu l'unique manuscrit complet du premier volume sur la Révolution française que Thomas Carlyle est en train de rédiger. Carlyle fait mine de calme ("shows a smooth front to it"), comme si de rien n'était, lorsque Mill, confus, lui annonce la triste nouvelle.[1] Devant ce nouveau malheur qui le frappe (encore une fois il venait de prodiguer ses efforts en vain), Carlyle fait preuve d'un stoïcisme qui est tout à son honneur. "I began at the beginning," confie-t-il à Ralph Waldo Emerson dans une lettre du 13 mai 1835, "to such a wretched paralyzing torpedo of a task as my hand never found to do; at which I have worn myself . . . to the hue of saffron, to the humour of incipient desperation" (*CEC* 131). "A Kind Friend but a careless one," Mill avait emprunté le manuscrit avec les meilleurs intentions du monde: il voulait faire profiter Carlyle de ses annotations dans les marges (*CEC* 130).

En mai 1837, peu de temps après la parution de *The French Revolution*, Carlyle subit les foudres de Lady Sydney Morgan. Soucieuse du décorum, cette commentatrice traite l'écrivain de blagueur, l'accusant de traiter de façon cavalière l'histoire véritable, et qualifie son oeuvre d'assemblage incohérent. Selon elle, *The French Revolution* n'est tout compte fait qu'un chiffon de papier, "three long volumes of misplaced persiflage and flippant pseudo-philosophy." Ces trois volumes, prédit Lady Morgan, tomberont vite dans l'oubli, et c'est le sort qu'ils méritent.[2] Très attentif au bien de Carlyle cette fois-ci, Mill se lance à la rescousse du texte. Sa réplique au démolissage par Lady Morgan est retentissante: "No work of greater genius . . . has been produced in this country for many years," proclame-t-il dans *The London and Westminster Review*.[3] Emerson est du même avis. Grâce en partie à cet article élogieux et perspicace de Mill, l'auteur de *The French Revolution* peut s'attendre à un accueil chaleureux du public, ce qui ne tarde pas à le rassurer. Et en effet, ses lecteurs seront très nombreux.[4]

Carlyle et son public vont bénéficier de l'appui de Mill, qui porte *The French Revolution* aux nues et cherche à faire valoir le sens profond de l'oeuvre et la genèse de sa production. L'idée maîtresse de cet ouvrage, selon Mill, est l'intégralité, dans toute la force du terme. Il remarque tout d'abord que *The French Revolution* possède la cohérence et la véracité des grands récits comme ceux d'Homère ou de Milton et des pièces de Shakespeare: "It is the work of a great poet . . . [of] a creative imagination, which, from a chaos of scattered hints and confused testimonies, can summon up the Thing to appear before it as a completed whole." Les principaux personnages carlyliens sont conçus eux aussi de façon unitive. Ils jouissent d'une vie tout entière and véritablement humaine, grâce au talent du poète doué d'une vision large et englobante. A l'instar de Shakespeare, Carlyle donne vie à ses personnages en chair et en os ("beings of his own flesh and blood, not mere shadows and dim abstractions"). Ce sont des êtres humains qu'il nous donne à découvrir. Carlyle réussit là où David Hume, par exemple, échoue:

> Hampden, and Stratford, and Vane, and Cromwell;–do these in Hume's pages [in *The History of England*], appear to us like beings who actually trod this earth, and stretched out human hands in fellowship with other human beings; or like the figures in a phantasmagoria, colourless, impalpable, gigantic, and in all varieties of attitude, but all resembling each other in being shadows?

Pour Mill, il n'y a qu'une seule réponse valable. De même que la Révolution française, selon Carlyle, signale "the end of the Dominion of IMPOSTURE . . . of only Phantasms of Reality," "Shams,"[5] de même *The French Revolution*, aux yeux de Mill, met en relief l'incohérence, l'inhumanité et l'irréalisme caractéristiques des récits comme ceux de David Hume. Dans son compte rendu, Mill fait preuve qu'il n'y a aucun doute dans son esprit: qualifiée "the truest of histories," cette oeuvre poétique est empreinte d'une unité exemplaire. On ne saurait mieux décrire l'entreprise de Carlyle.

Il est donc ironique que cette tentative d'appui de la part de Mill ait contrarié son ami une fois de plus, car les propos de Mill ne concordent pas tout à fait avec le point de vue exprimé par Carlyle sur son propre travail. Contrairement à Mill, celui-ci est assailli de doutes au sujet de la véracité de son histoire et, par conséquent, de sa valeur intrinsèque. Il s'en confie à Emerson en 1837: "The unutterable *French Revolution* . . . a beggarly Distortion of which I know not whether the fire were not after all the due place!" (*CEC* 158-59). Comme d'habitude, Carlyle donne l'exemple à ses adversaires en faisant son autocritique, se disputant avec lui-même.[6] Lorsque Lady Morgan affirme que *The French Revolution* fausse les faits historiques et bouleverse la pensée bien ordonnée, que chez Carlyle "the grossest absurdity in speculation does not prevent his perceiving and adopting truths in the closest relation of opposition to it," elle ne fait que reprendre les propos tenus par l'auteur lui-même. Quand Carlyle qualifie son oeuvre de "my poor Book . . . a miserable scrap of paper," qu'il la considère comme un blague, une histoire de fou farcie de contradictions ("infinite contradictions") et chargée de scories ("great quantities of dross"), un essai qui n'aboutit à rien ("the Inane"), il se châtie lui-même devant Emerson (*CEC* 130, 172, 159). En se précipitant ainsi sur sa propre création, Carlyle prend le contre-pied de Mill, fait cause commune avec Lady Morgan et, part surcroît, applique le principe qu'il énonce à Emerson: "Revolt . . . is mean internecine work" (*CEC* 144). Il s'y connaît bien en la matière. Comme le laisse entendre Lady Morgan, il y a matière à rire aux larmes dans les écrits des penseurs qui se contredisent.

Le plus drôle de cette tragi-comédie d'opinions contradictoires, c'est que, tout en le desservant, le jugement que porte Carlyle sur *The French Revolution* concorde parfaitement avec l'élément d'audestruction présent dans l'oeuvre elle-même. C'est à Carlyle, critique impregné de scepticisme et d'humour noir, et non à Mill, qui adhère entièrement à l'oeuvre, que le lecteur à la recherche d'éclaircissements sur *The French Revolution* doit se fier, car le récit ne cesse de se démentir. A cet égard, l'histoire de Carlyle rappelle les essais de Montaigne et l'emblème traditionnel de leur autolecture, le serpent qui se mord la queue. Comme chez Montaigne, où les contraires se rejoignent et s'annulent, *The French Revolution* met en valeur la sinuosité artiste de sa composition, "the art of producing zero" (*FR* 1.6.1). "A self-combustion" (1.3.4), "an internecine duel" (1.3.4), "a suicide" (2.2.2), le texte carlylyien est proprement révolutionnaire, "consuming itself" (1.7.4; 3.2.1; 3.6.1), "fighting with itself" (3.7.5), "at war with itself" (1.5.7). Si la critique de Mill passe sous silence tout ce qui touche au suicide, Carlyle laisse entendre que l'essentiel de son récit réside dans l'autodestruction. Le principe d'intégralité présent dans *The French Revolution* se résume ainsi: tout ce qui est complet est double et se (re) plie sur soi-même.

"*Du pain; pas tant de longs discours!*" s'écrie le pauvre peuple dans le premier des trois longs volumes qui constituent *The French Revolution* (1.7.8). Ces vingt-cinq millions d'habitants réclament de quoi manger et une saine gestion du pays: "a Reality, not an Artificiality, not a Sham" (1.4.4). On leur répond: *qu'ils mangent du papier!* Carlyle consigne dans son récit:

> It is *Encyclopédies*, *Philosophie*, and . . . what innumerable multitude of ready Writers, profane singers, Romancers, Players, Disputators, and Pamphleteers, that now form the spiritual and Practical Guidance of the world. (1.1.2)

L'historien sympathise avec le peuple qui meurt de faim; on ne peut attendre rien de substantiel d'un roi qui se comporte en esthète et en comédien ("leader of a Troop of Players"; 1.1.2) dans un salon littéraire ("the Sceptre of the Sword has become the Sceptre of the Pen"; 1.3.5). Rien non plus des Assemblés nationales où les participants babillards rendent hommage "to the the gospel according to Jean-Jacques" (1.2.7) en rédigeant des constitutions de toute beauté mais sans substance ("only Phantasms, Paper models"; 3.7.8). "Paper is made from the *rags* of things that did once exist; there are endless excellences in Paper" (1.2.2), ironise Carlyle, qui se moque de "this Paper Age" (1.2.5), "a jargon of Babel" (1.3.7). "What has been written in books," note-t-il à maintes reprises, "is ineffectual for the empty National Stomach" (3.2.2; 3.3.1): "Philosophism has yet baked no bread" (1.4.3). Et comme cela était prévisible, Carlyle s'associe à l'événement décisif qui fait tout basculer: le 27 avril 1798, à Paris, une foule affamé ("with a deep fixed Determination to have done with Shams"; 1.4.4) se rue sur une fabrique de papier et réussit à y mettre le feu (1.4.3). *The French Revolution* et son discours de mille pages dénonçant le bavardage sont bel et bien entamés.

A la différence de Mill, Emerson saisit bien, lui, l'esprit de contradiction de l'auteur de *The French Revolution*: "Carlyle is a covenanter-philosophe . . . & sans-culotte-aristocrat."[7] Et contradiction et humour font bon ménage: "It is droll to hear this talker talking against talkers, and this writer writing against writing."[8] En effet, *The French Revolution* est une plaisanterie macabre, et son auteur un adepte du suicide spirituel. Comment garder son sérieux, par exemple, en lisant l'épisode concernant M. Dusaulx:

> As for the poor Legislative, the sceptre had departed from it. The Legislative did send Deputation to the Prisons, to the Street-Courts; and poor M. Dusaulx did harangue there. . . . He was wont to announce himself . . . as the *Translator of Juvenal*. "Good Citizens, you see before you a man who loves his country, is the Translator of Juvenal," said he once. "Juvenal?" interrupts Sanculottism: "Who the devil is Juvenal? One your *sacrés Aristocrates?* To the *Lanterne*!" (3.1.6)

Un peut inconséquent, mais pas fou, le député tient à sauver sa peau et s'empresse de quitter les lieux. Mais M. Carlyle, en bon ami du peuple et *Translator of Goethe* (une citation de cet auteur est reproduite en lettres gothiques au début de chaque volume de *The French Revolution*), harangue ses lecteurs, et en faisant ainsi, se pend lui-même. Toujours animé du même esprit de contradiction, le pendu accumule les diableries, "one boundless inarticulate Haha" (1.7.11).

Carlyle se délecte de l'inconséquence révolutionnaire à laquelle il participe et dont il se moque: "*Tout va bien ici, le pain manque*" (2.5.8). Même quand il traite de la Terreur, il ne cesse d'ironiser et de se trahir lui-même:

> There is no period to be met with, in which the general Twenty-five Millions of France suffered *less* than in this period which they name Reign of Terror. It was not the Dumb Millions that suffered here; it was the Speaking Thousands . . . who shrieked and published. (3.7.6).

A ses yeux, il ne fait aucun doute que ces derniers ont bien mérité leur sort: le diable emporte les bavards et les marchands de papier! Et comme le rire carlylien–"a kind of horrid diabolic horse-laughter . . . proclaiming *Vanity of vanities, all is Vanity*!" (1.1.3)–le laisse entendre, qu'il emporte *The French Revolution*! Le jeu de démenti va bien ici, le pain manque.

Comment expliquer que Mill ne fasse pas état dans son compte rendu de l'évidente propension de Carlyle pour le suicide? Sa critique serait-elle purement fantaisiste? La réponse qui s'impose est simple: ce qu'écrit Mill ne vaut pas pour l'ouvrage qu'il a sous les yeux, mais pour celui que Carlyle aurait *voulu* écrire. Lorsqu'il compare les personnages historiques de Hume ("like the figures in a phantasmagoria, colourless, impalpable, gigantic, and in all varieties of attitudes, but all resembling one another in being shadows") et ceux de *The French Revolution* ("like beings who actually trod this earth and stretched out human hands in fellowship with other human beings"), Mill s'appuie sur des points de vue que Carlyle exprime à certains endroits de son récit. Marat, par exemple, "is no phantasm of the brain, or a merely lying impress of Printer's Types; but a thing material," selon Carlyle, quelqu'un qui a les deux pieds sur la terre (3.2.1). Il en va de même pour Danton: "A Reality and not a Formula he. . . . It is on Earth and on Realities that he rests" (3.1.4). Ces révolutionnaires sont des nôtres.

Mais l'historien qui comptait décrire la réalité du quotidien n'en fait rien. Certes, il n'est pas facile "to find some firm footing . . . among Paper-vortexes" (1.6.2). Le Danton de Carlyle–"thou brawny Titan," "Titan of the Forlorn Hope" qui ne cesse de prêcher l'audace toute la nuit (3.1.4; 3.1.6)–et son Marat, un esprit héroïque de provenance infernale, "a living fraction of Chaos and Old Night" (3.2.1), ressemblent, en réalité, au Satan que Blake a cru voir dans les pages de *Paradise Lost*. La nuit, tous les anges et tous les hommes sont gris. Fantômes tirés d'un enfer littéraire, le Marat et le de Danton de *The French Revolution*, "this dim Phantasmagoria of the Pit" (3.1.6), font penser étrangement aux esprits 'titaniques' que Mill perçoit chez Hume. L'enfer de Blake/Milton inspire davantage Carlyle, homme de haute culture, qui s'identifie à Marat et à Danton, lorsqu'il fait sien le parti pris du Maître Fausseur, esprit généralement reconnu pour sa malveillance à l'égard de la race d'Adam: "Are not both Heaven and Hell made out of man, made by him?" (3.1.4; cf. *Paradise Lost* 1.254-56). Pour les lecteurs sensibles aux forces autodestructives de *The French Revolution*, la réponse qui s'impose n'est ni celle du Carlyle épris de diablerie romantique, ni celle ce son duc d'Orléans: "evil is his good" (1.4.3). En s'appuyant sur les aveux de Carlyle qui se voudrait des nôtres, Mill prend *The French Revolution* à contre-pied et ignore le nihilisme de l'oeuvre qu'il a entre les mains.

Et pourtant, il ne faut pas trop insister sur les silences du compte rendu de Mill, ni sur la pénurie de nourriture substantielle dans les trois volumes de *The French Revolution.* Si le nihilisme carlylien semble dépasser Mill, il n'en demeure pas moins que la critique de ce dernier touche indirectement à un aspect positif dont Carlyle, autocritique suicidaire, ne s'occupe guère. L'histoire de Carlyle, au fond, présente certaines des qualités des grands récits poétiques, et comporte une part de vérité prophétique. Ce que *The French Revolution* annonce, Carlyle le résume prophétiquement en ces termes:

> Some two centuries of it still to fight! Two centuries; hardly less; before Democracy go through its due, most baleful, stages of *Quack*ocracy; and a pestilential World be burnt up, and have begun to grow green and young again. (1.4.3)

En écrivant ces lignes, Carlyle retrouve son sérieux. Si, de nos jours, à l'âge postmoderne, le bouleversement générale amorcé pas la Révolution se poursuit (auto-destruction, guerres intestines, campagnes d'extermination réciproque), il reste que Carlyle a vu juste en prévoyant que l'événement aurait des retombées considérables et durables. Comme en fait foi son histoire, lui aussi en a subi les effets meutriers. Carlyle prophète, participant au bouleversement historique qu'il décrit, ne (se) trompe pas.

ENDNOTES

1. *The Correspondence of Emerson and Carlyle*, éd. Joseph Slater (New York: Columbia UP, 1964) 130-31. (*CEC*)

2. "Review of *The French Revolution*," dans *Athenaeum* 20 mai 1837: 353-55.

3. "Review of *The French Revolution*," dans *The London and Westminster Review* 27 (juillet 1837): 17-53.

4. *CEC* 170. Voir A.L. Le Quesne, *Carlyle* (Oxford: Oxford UP, 1982). Grand succès à l'époque de sa parution, *The French Revolution* continue de nos jours à susciter l'admiration des critiques qui voient en Carlyle un esthète désinteressé.

5. Thomas Carlyle, *The French Revolution* (New York: Modern Library, 1966) 3.7.8; 1.4.4.

6. Voir Murray Baumgarten, *Carlyle: Books and Margins* (Santa Cruz CA: U Library of U of California, 1980); et Camille R. La Bossière, *The Victorian* Fol Sage: *Comparative Readings on Carlyle, Emerson, Melville and Conrad* (Lewisburg: Bucknell UP, 1989).

7. Ralph Waldo Emerson, *The Journals and Miscellaneous Notebooks*, éd. William Gilman *et al.* (Cambridge: Belknap P of Harvard U, 1960-) 10.550.

8. Emerson 10.232.

VI

NIETZSCHE

[*Encyclopedia of Contemporary Literary Theory*,
ed. Irena Rima Makaryk (U of Toronto P, 1993)]

" . . . le délire dantesque. . . ." Hubert Aquin, *Neige noire*

(b. Prussia, 1844; d. Weimar 1900) Philosopher, poet, philologist, composer, historiographer, theothanatologist. Born of a line of Lutheran ministers (his father and grandfathers) many of whose ancestors were butchers, Nietzsche was christened Friedrich Wilhelm after the reigning Prussian king whose birthday he shared. The loss of his father (to a brain disease) and his infant brother left the five-year-old Friedrich with his mother, sister, paternal grandmother and two spinster aunts. An able musician by age twelve, he composed, on the eve of his confirmation, a fantasia for four-hand piano under the motto "Pain is the Keynote of Nature." The "a priori of doubt" took hold early in Nietzsche, attended by an enthusiasm for Byron's *Manfred*: in his first attempt at philosophical writing, at age thirteen, he "made God the father of evil" (Preface, par. 3, *Genealogy of Morals*). As a student of Pforta (1858-64) he acquired a fine classical education and a predilection for the natural religion of Theognis, Hölderlin and Emerson. After courses in theology and classical philology at the University of Bonn (1864-65), Nietzsche dropped divinity and moved to Leipzig, where he majored in classical literature but devoted his mind to the reading of Kant, Schopenhauer, and F.A. Lange. He accepted the chair of classical philology at the University of Basel in 1869, Leipzig having graced him with doctor's name without examination or thesis. Promotion to full professor came in 1870.

What little charm the world of workaday classical learning held for Nietzsche vanished soon after his arrival at Basel. The tragic pessimism and prophetic power of Schopenhauer's philosophy of will, Burkhardt's history of culture and Wagner's operatic poetry proved headier; the prospect of heroic solitude, more enticing. Like Mathilde Trampedach's refusal of his offer of marriage, his accelerated estrangement from scholarism evidently came as a relief to Nietzsche. Something of his disaffection from the toming philology of the time shines through *The Birth of Tragedy* [*Die Geburt der Tragödie aus dem Geiste der Musik*], a brief yet grand speculation, free of footnotes or Greek quotations, on the sublime as the artistic conquest of the horrible. To Nietzsche's mind, tragedy was born of the synthesis of two tendencies in the spirit of Greece–"the Apollonian" (harmony, proportion, restraint) and "the Dionysian" (ecstatic self-abandon)–then died with the advent of rationalism and moralism, epitomized in Socrates/ Plato. Late in life, Nietzsche would repudiate his first book, finding its patterning "offensively Hegelian," or moribund with the *logos* of metaphysical idealism ("Why I Write Such Good Books," in *Ecce Homo*).

A series of "untimely meditations" (*Unzeitgemässe Betrachtungen*) succeeded *The Birth of Tragedy*: on David Strauss as enlightened Darwinian and non-Christian yet still a philistine (1873), on the kinds and uses of history (1874), on Schopenhauer as teacher of self-reliance (1874), and on the return to pre-ethical drama once promised in Wagner (1876). The larger question of the genesis of "good" and "evil" in the history of mentalities came increasingly to preoccupy Nietzsche in the late 1870s. With *Human, All Too Human* (*Menschliches, Allzumenschliches* 1878), dedicated to Voltaire, he introduced his psychocultural notion of "moral prejudices" and their bicameral origin in hale "aristocratic morality" and life-denying "slave morality," rival reponses to "the will to power." By decade's end Nietzsche had taken his distance from a Schopenhauer now found contaminated with the otherworldliness and pity of slave morality and had broken with Wagner on the grounds of the nationalism and anti-Semitism, the "pandering" to Christianity in *Parsifal*. The synthetic amoralism of Heraclitus, the existential contradictoriness of Montaigne and the worldly optimism of Goethe had become more attractive.

Never good, Nietzsche's health so worsened at Basel that he resigned his chair in 1879. A pension, though modest, allowed him to move from place to place in France and Italy over the next ten years, and to prepare (and pay for the publication of) those works that were to make him a power in modern Western ideology: *The Dawn: Reflections on Moral Prejudices* [*Morgenröth: Gedanken über die moralischen Voruteile* 1881], *The Gay Science* [*Die fröhliche Wissenschaft* 1882], *Thus Spoke Zarathustra* [*Also Sprach Zarathustra* parts 1-3, 1883-4; part 4, 1891], *Beyond Good and Evil* [*Jenseits von Gut und Böse* 1886], *On the Genealogy of Morals* [*Zur Genealogie der Moral* 1887] and *The Twilight of the Idols* [*Die Götzen-Dämmerung* 1889].

In1889, not long after the completion of *Der Antichrist* (1895), Nietzsche lapsed into a complete paralysis of mind and body and was taken to an asylum at Basel; he subsequently passed into the care of his mother at Naumburg, then of his sister at Weimar. The diagnosis of Nietzsche's insanity as tertiary syphilis was to pass into modern legend, thanks in part to the portrait of the artist in Thomas Mann's *Doktor Faustus*. A year after her brother's death in 1900, Elisabeth Nietzsche's selection from his notebooks for 1884-88 appeared as *Der Wille zur Macht* [*The Will to Power*]. His mocking self-portrait in *Ecce Homo* was made public in 1908.

The substantial negativity of Nietzsche's major undertaking, its devaluation and discrediting of intelligibility and truth as such (cf. *Beyond Good and Evil* par. 334; *Will to Power* par. 493), makes any attempt at a discursive account of his oeuvre more than a little uncertain: "We are not yet rid of God because we still have faith in grammar" (*Twilight of the Idols* par. 5). Founded on a rejection of traditional logic and referential language, the Nietzschean text at its labyrinthine best builds towards minimal disclosure (*dévoilement*) with maximal unclosure, "the zero degree of discourse, a philosophy which never takes place" (Nancy 57). As deconstructionist readings have asserted, interpretation can never accomplish itself in the Nietzschean dis-ordering of things since there is no-thing at bottom to interpret. Certainly, the brilliantly playful self-concealment and self-contradiction, the endless ironies, maskings and shiftings in the extravaganza of metaphoricity that is *Thus Spoke Zarathustra* are not made to encourage authoritative reading. Nor is a logically coherent apprehension of Nietzsche's musical yet deterministic doctrine of "the eternal recurrence" (the repetition of what is, has been and will be, times without end; cf. *Thus Spoke* part 3) very likely to come in the forseeable future. But the Nietzschean tabling of new and proper values is not altogether innocent, enjoining as it does a universal theory of the will that portends "the mastery of all being" (Gadamer 230). When Zarathustra speaks in the language of Luther's Bible he tacitly appropriates at least as much authority as he burlesques (cf. *André Gide: Journal 1889-1939* [Dijon: Gallimard, 1948] 990). And Nietzsche himself recognized the potential of his works for empowering new absolutisms: "I am terrified by the thought of the sort of people who may one day invoke my authority" (letter of June 1884, to his sister). Such is the ethical indeterminacy of Nietzsche's text, as Jacques Derrida has acknowledged in his "Otobiographies," that any use may be made of it: "There are no facts, only interpretations" (*Will to Power* par. 481).

It is a fact, though, that Nietzsche's texts have been interpreted, and perhaps no more tellingly than by Nietzsche himself in the least undiscursive of his aphoristic works, the polemical *Genealogy of Morals*, which reviews his progress in decoding the ethics of power ciphered in the history of mentalities. His readings of the origin of good and evil in "the long hieroglyphical text of the past of human morality have ripened" since *Human, All Too Human*, have grown "clearer, more solid" (Preface). Part 1 of the *Genealogy* affords a fairly consecutive account of Nietzsche's matured sense of Western history as the victory of slave over hale aristocratic morality–that is, of Judea's values over Rome's:

> It is the Jews who, with a terrifying logic, dared invert the equation of aristocratic values (good= noble=beautiful=happy=beloved of the gods) and who maintained this inversion with a bottomless hatred (the hatred of impotence) . . . asserting that only the miserable are the good.

The coming of "vulgar" Jesus with his "love born of hatred," "the instrument of Israel's revenge," heralded master morality's demise and the triumph of the common man, the effects of which were the mixing of races and values ("a poisoning of the blood") and the nihilism of heavenly idealism. Shaken though it was during the Reformation, when free spirits attempted a restoration of classical values, the slave morality institutionalized in "the ecumenical synagogue of New Rome" held firm, "thanks to the movement of fundamentally populist *ressentiment*" against a worldly church's domination. Judea's victory was more complete yet in the French Revolution, when European nobility bowed before a populace enslaved to resentment. The present hegemony of democratic socialism in Europe represents "a monstrous atavism."

Part 2 of the *Genealogy of Morals*, on good and bad conscience, characterizes the manly hero to come after two millennia of resentment towards the world and its aristocratic morality. He is the *Übermensch* (Overman) heralded in *Thus Spoke Zarathustra* ("Of the Bestowing of Virtue" par. 3) and *Beyond Good and Evil* (par. 260), "the autonomous and supra-moral man" who, true to the instinct to mastery, has given style to his character (cf. *Gay Science* par. 290), achieved sovereignty over himself. So self-empowered to say "yes" to himself, he shuns all nationalisms or parties and the "bad conscience" that arises from "the will to mistreat onself" (cf. *Antichrist* par. 55). He is perforce irreligious, since "all religions at the bottom of themselves are systems of cruelty" or self-denial, the gods having been invented for "the autocrucifixion and the autoprofanation of man." Likewise anathema to the fully realized man are the moral pose and subjacent idealism of the socialists, anarchists, and anti-Semites, who represent "the man of resentment returned," yet another triumph for Judea (cf. part 3, par. 26). The hope for the coming of the Overman is secured by the ironic principle that "every good thing on this earth ends by destroying itself," including the Judaeo-Christian morality of "mercy" born of the "auto-destruction of justice by resentment": "this antichrist and this anti-nihilist, this conqueror of God and of nothingness, *he must come some day. . . .*"

In Part 3, Nietzsche reviews his diagnosis of the exhausted idealism of the West and speculates on the prospects for humanity on its inevitable demise. Like the philosophers and scientists before them, the free thinkers of his time have not broken with the otherworldliness of the herd (Christianity is a Platonism for the people), "since they still believe in truth." In their hunger for transcendent verity they have not yet considered "the *value* of truth"; nor have they come to see that "there is no 'vision' *but* perspective, no 'knowledge' *but* perspective." But the end of their moribund idealism is in sight, since the very acuteness of their illness assures imminent cure. In accordance with the law of life ("All great things perish of themselves, by an act of self-destruction"), this "will to truth" in populist Christian metaphysics (a multiple redundancy for Nietzsche) "will end by drawing the ultimate conclusion, the conclusion against itself," that there is no God, that "God," never more than a semantic fiction, is now "empty of meaning" (cf. "Prologue" par. 2, *Thus Spoke*; *Gay Science* par. 125). At that moment, all morality must crumble: "if nothing is true," as Nietzsche transposes from Dostoevsky's Ivan Karamazov, "all things are permitted." Projection into the two centuries to follow the "unconditional atheism" born of the "will to truth" affords "a horrifying spectacle, fraught with the unknown, and perhaps also with the highest hopes. . . ." His own transvaluation of all received values, so the author of the *Genealogy* anticipates, will have its long day.

The range and force of Nietzsche's impact on high Western culture ("I am no man, I am dynamite"; *Ecce Homo* par. 326) are difficult to overestimate. Its markings are distinctly visible, for example, in the poetry of Rainer Maria Rilke, Gottfried Benn and William Butler Yeats; in the novels of Robert Musil, Hermann Hesse, André Gide, André Malraux, Susan Sontag, Jack London, Romain Rolland, Nikos Kazantzakis, Jack London and Ayn Rand; in the elegiac historiography of Oswald Spengler; and in the social theory of Max Horkheimer and Theodor Adorno. Comparisons of Nietzsche with Sigmund Freud and Jacques Lacan on dream-thinking, with Mircea Eliade on the history of religions, with José Ortega y Gasset on mass culture and with Ludwig Wittgenstein on language have become relatively common. But it is in the direct shaping of a variety of existentialisms and phenomenologies that his influence has been most masterful: the writings of Dietrich Bonhoeffer, Karl Jaspers, Paul Tillich, Martin Buber, Martin

Heidegger, Albert Camus and Jean-Paul Sartre voluminously comment on the death of transcendent reality announced by Nietzsche. The theothanatology of Thomas J. Altizer, William Hamilton and Paul van Buren, prominent members of the U.S.A. avant-garde of the 1960s, represents an extension of that gloss. Among even the leading Christian existentialists at mid-century, Gabriel Marcel is exceptional in his unambiguous characterization of Nietzschean unreason as suicidal, fatal for theology and philosophy alike.

The importance of Nietzsche for contemporary critical theory is commensurate with his eminence in philosophy. Deconstructive criticism, as in Derrida, Roland Barthes, Paul de Man, Jean-François Lyotard, Gilles Deleuze and J. Hillis Miller, has found his theothanatology especially virtuous for the propagation of autogeneal, autotelic, 'grammarless' reflection; and Michel Foucault has credited the *Genealogy of Morals* with founding a new, radically inventive approach to 'history.' Given Nietzsche's relentless twitting of "the flatheads of socialism" (*Beyond Good and Evil* par. 203), his treatment at the hands of leading Marxist critics has been reasonable: Georg Lukács, for example, has denounced Nietzsche as the founder of irrationalism in the imperialist period; and Jürgen Habermas has lamented the effect of his mere aestheticism on the writings of Adorno. Marxist ideology, though, has substantially profited from the Nietzschean rejection of otherworldliness in all its forms: "with Jehovah buried," in the words of e.e. cummings, "Eternity is now a Five Year Plan." While Nietzsche's inversion of the 'masculine' principle of reason has appealed to feminist criticism, his actual misogyny understandably has not.

SOURCES

Primary

Nietzsche, Friedrich. *Basic Writings of Nietzsche*. Ed. and trans. Walter Kaufmann. New York: Modern Library, 1966.

----------. *The Portable Nietzsche*. Ed. and trans. Walter Kaufmann. New York: Viking, 1954.

----------. *Sämliche Werkj Kritische Studienausgabe*. 15 vols. Ed. Giorgio Colli and Mazzino Montinari. Munich: Deutscher Taschenbuch Verlad; Berlin: Walter de Gruyter, 1980.

----------. *Selected Letters of Friedrich Nietzsche*. Ed. and trans. Christopher Middleton. Chicago: U of Chicago P, 1969.

Secondary

Buber, Martin. *Eclipse of God*. New York: Harper and Row, 1952.

Deleuze, Gilles. *Nietzsche et sa philosophie*. Paris: PUF, 1965.

Derrida, Jacques. "Otobiographies: The Teaching of Nietzsche and the Politics of the Proper Name." In *The Ear of the Other*. Ed. Christie V. McDonald. New York: Schoken, 1985.

Gadamer, Hans-Georg. "The Drama of Zarathustra." In *Nietzsche's New Seas: Explorations in Philosophy, Aesthetics, and Politics*. Ed. Michael A. Gillespie and Tracy B. Strong. Chicago: U of Chicago P, 1988.

Heidegger, Martin. *Nietzsche*. 2 vols. Pfullingen: Neske, 1961.

Irigaray, Luce. *Amante marine: De Friedrich Nietzsche*. Paris: Minuit, 1980.

Jaspers, Karl. *Nietzsche: An Introduction to the Understanding of His Philosophical Activity.* South Bend: Regenery/ Gateway, 1965.

Murchland, Bernard, ed. *The Meaning of the Death of God.* New York: Vintage, 1967.

Nancy, Jean-Luc. "Nietzsche's Thesis on Teleology." In *Looking after Nietzsche*, ed. Laurence A. Rickels. Albany: State U of New York P, 1990.

Reichert, H.W. *Friedrich Nietzsche's Impact on Modern German Literature*. Chapel Hill: U of North Carolina P, 1975.

Shapiro, Gary. *Nietzschean Narratives.* Bloomington: Indiana UP, 1989.

Thatcher, David S. *Nietzsche in England 1890-1914: The Growth of a Reputation.* Toronto: U of Toronto P, 1970.

VII

OF ACEDIA, ROMANTIC IMAGINATION AND IRONY REVISITED: A SUPPLEMENTARY CONTEXT FOR *UNDER THE VOLCANO*

"What is this wondre maladie?" Chaucer, *Troilus and Criseyde*

"He goes reeling . . . from a natural drunkenness . . . like the cold and hot of fevers." Montaigne, "Of Repentance"

"In Mozart the balance of the whole is perfect. So equilibrium is preserved, but action becomes impossible. . . . Equilibrium produces indecision . . . . The disease of irony." *Amiel's Journal*

"I feel neutral . . . the terrible impression of being turned into a block of ice enveloped in fire." Sartre, *Nausea*

"This may be misery, but it is blest." Conrad Aiken, "Psychomachia"

Early in the history of its reception, Stephen Spender remarked of *Under the Volcano* that its "central paradox is . . . that it is a novel about action, that is, about action negated" (xxvii). According to Spender, Malcolm Lowry's big book spun about that self-contradiction tells of a life of ensnarement in a "despair . . . that is really acedia, the spiritual apathy of the the religious who have become, as it were, hermetically sealed off from the source of their religion" (xxviii). A host of other commentators in the 1960s–Walter Allen, Anthony Burgess and Douglas Day among them–[1] would effectively rehearse Spender's sense of the spiritual condition characterized in *Under the Volcano*, and would do so in a language likewise recollective of a medieval Christian frame of reference and value, of "*acedia* [as] . . . the negation of *caritas*" (Wenzel 55) or "the complete paralysis of the will" by "suspension in ambiguity" (Kuhn 39-40).[2] Sherrill Grace, in her *The Voyage That Never Ends: Malcolm Lowry's Fiction* (1982), proceeds quite traditionally, then, in a way faithful to a history and practice of spiritual discernment at least as old as the Schoolmen, when she recognizes in *Under the Volcano* "a book about failure and *acedia*," "about the hell man inflicts upon himself through his emotional sterility and *acedia*";[3] "it is a story of hellfire, and hellfire, for Lowry, means paralysis of the will" (41, 58). It goes without saying that the contextualizing of *Under the Volcano* in such terms presumes the virtue of *caritas*, the abiding pertinence of which is tabled anew.

On the face of it at least, commentary thus suggestive of a work of para-medieval inwit or conscience seems entirely apt, since Lowry's novel timed on an All Souls' Day fairly bristles with signs of an intelligence steeped in traditional Christian readings of Hell. Even Milton's monumental *Paradise Lost* constitutes a very much secondary source in the cyclopaedic history of a doomsday that *Under the Volcano* recollects for meditation. Certainly,

Lowry's tale of an exile in spiralling pilgrimage downward concludes in a place and a language the metaphysical sense of which had been established long before the composing of *Paradise Lost*: drinking deeply while "at an agonized standstill" in a cantina made to stand for "El Infierno," Consul Geoffrey Firmin feels as if he "were being filled with boiling ice . . . or there were a bar of red-hot iron across . . . [his] chest, but cold in its effect" (346, 349, 351).[4] The allusion here, to Milton's oxymoron resuming Hell's grammar, whereby "cold performs th'effect of fire" (*Paradise Lost* 2.595),[5] resonates with the power and sense of an even older wisdom literature. As the whole of the Lowry oeuvre invites the recognition, Dante's rhymes of the unlove and unreason dead-ended at the centre of the innermost frozen circle of the *Inferno*,[6] Chaucer's tale of charity stymied by ambiguity in the sublunary world of "cold . . . hete" that *Troilus and Criseyde* revisits,[7] Marlowe's tragicomedy of a devil's pact sealed by a feverish, would-be gnostic's indwelling in relentless illogic that concludes in despair,[8] and, more latterly yet, priest Calderón de la Barca's *La Vida es sueño*, a *commedia* of unremitting subjectivity set in an ambience of "*fuego y hielo*"[fire and ice],[9] figure prominently in the long line of texts that underwrite Milton's sense of the unreason basic to Pandemonium, the ultimate site of "includence" as "encapsulation in self-contradiction" (Tellenbach 146).

That extensive line of affiliation being understood, commentators attending to *Under the Volcano* as a story about the freezing hellfire of *acedia* have understandably shadowed (as it were) a Lowry in at least partial recursion to the theology on which books in the enduring tradition of

Inferno 'found' their ethical sense. "Accidie is lyk hem that been in the peyne of helle," so Chaucer wrote in the last of his tales of a pilgrimage to Canterbury (250.686), in the form of a sermon for repentance and charity from a parson alert to the injunction of Revelation 3:15: "I would thou wert cold *or* hot. . . ."[10] Working as it does to situate *Under the Volcano* in the progress of an oeuvre for undyingly fruitful, conscientiously moral action, Grace's affective response in 1982 accordingly casts an author impelled by a loving, ethical intention: as she senses it, "the strong ethical thrust" of *Under the Volcano* issues from a will keen "to close the emotional and imaginative gap between world and book, reader and text," to break out from the infernal interior circling that voyaging in "the Good Ship Solipsism" naturally entails (122). Sue Vice responds appositively when she distinguishes the affectivity of Lowry's masterwork from the "environmentally amoral" tenor of writings from postmodern gamesters enjoying themselves in the privacy of their funhouses: "his art is not heartless . . . . *Under the Volcano* . . . is a collage with a conscience" (135).[11] The truth of late-medieval Friar Luis de León's dictum that "*No se puede vivir sin amar*" [one cannot live without loving], twice blazoned in *Under the Volcano* (11, 199),[12] would seem to have retained its substantial cogency.

But readings of *Under the Volcano* as something of an exemplum even metaphorically consistent with a traditional Christian sense of charity and conscience have become increasingly difficult to maintain. As to why so, a readership attentive to the (post)modernist play of reflexiveness, terminal ambiguity or ambivalence, even whimsicality, in Lowry's big book has not been all that slow in coming to recognize. In his 1978 essay "Tragedy as a Meditation on Itself: Reflexiveness in *Under the Volcano*," to cite a particularly acute rejoinder, Stephen Tift deems "fallacious" such interpretations as work to suggest that "the crux of the Consul's tragedy" resides in "the inability to love" (46). The manifest signs of "shifting definitions of 'loving'," of a shiftiness consistent with Lowry's "ironic handling of the Good Samaritan theme," so Tift goes on to argue, point to "an ambivalence that can hardly be ignored" (47). "Lowry's Christian echoes are decidedly ironic," as Richard Hauer Costa agrees ("The Way It Was" 42), and as findings by David Markson (16), Duncan Hadfield (96) and Ronald Binns (41, 64), for instance, additionally confirm.

And, again logically enough in view of the superbly modern character of the aesthetic achievement that "the masterpiece of the forties" has been recognized to represent, the main body of Lowry commentators has increasingly come to find for the virtue of the "romantic irony" basic to *Under the Volcano* and the still abiding modernist sense of "the grammar essential to the best poetry" (La Bossière, "Irony" 573): "Irony," according to I.A. Richards in 1924, is "the bringing in . . . of opposites" in such a way as to achieve "a balanced poise" (250). Since it issues from "the recognition that the world in its essence is paradoxical and that an ambivalent attitude alone can grasp its contradictory totality" (Wellek 14), irony in that mode naturally serves to "make us at home in indecision" (Burke, *Counter* 14). Home is where the romantic irony is, which siting has proved congenial to a readership in affective sympathy with Lowry at his ambivalent, ambiguous, ethically indeterminate best. The complex of "ambiguities and uncertainties" available to readers of *Under the Volcano*, so Frederick Asals' contribution to Grace's edition of *Swinging the Maelstrom: New Perspectives on Lowry* (1992) speculates, "was probably instrumental to drawing us to it in the first place" (109). Asals' use of the extensive "us" is not without some justification.

Not surprisingly, then, commentary on *Under the Volcano* so closely associating itself with the appeal of a mode of ironizing now not so new has seconded the creative efficacy of a doubtful, since radically subjective, turn of mind cognate with the fallen Lucifer's in *Paradise Lost*. Like readers of *The Marriage of Heaven and Hell*, *Prometheus Unbound* and *Thus Spake Zarathustra*, students of Lowry have surely had occasion to revisit the notion that "The Mind is its own place, and in itself / Can make a Heaven of Hell, a Hell of Heaven" (*Paradise Lost* 1.254-55).[13] Nicely coordinate with that hypothesis, the reckoning that with *Under the Volcano* Lowry achieved "self-mastery" through "self-creation" has now become a commonplace.[14] In the words of Grace's introduction to *Swinging the Maelstrom*, the artist of *Under the Volcano* "constitutes himself" by an act that renders the world "a home for the human imagination": for Lowry as for the Nietzschean philosopher and Blake aficionado Ortega y Gasset, "the best image of man" is that of "the novelist who makes up his life as he goes along" ("Putting Lowry in Perspective" 3, 15). Recognition of the "dynamism" of *Under the Volcano* as a testament to "the never-ending act of creation" akin to "the Nietzschean state of becoming that underlies romanticism and expressionism" (Grace, *Voyage* 2, xvi) has ostensibly laid to rest the image of an artist riddled or overcome with apathy or spiritual paralysis.[15] Like the Coleridge of *Biographia Literaria* and *Aids to Reflection*–so Grace, for one, further historicizes the romantic thinker of *Under the Volcano*–a Lowry intent on realizing "the considerable synthesizing powers of . . . imagination" viewed life "in terms of polarities that must be balanced. He felt that the activity of unifying or balancing opposites reflects the vitality of the universe and illustrates the creativity of the mind" (*Voyage* 3).

For all the support that it lends to a latter-day-romantic artist's creativity, though, the locating of *Under the Volcano* in a tradition of ironic and imaginative reflection founded on the synthesis or balance of opposites sits perhaps all too well with a history of that principle's affiliation with the working of hellfire. As Grace's wide-ranging reference to nineteenth-century literary sages might call to mind, the most heady of English romantic writers found in "cold performs th'effect of fire" a sentence to illustrate his cardinal axiom, that "Extremes meet,"[16] a "proverb to collect and explain all the instances of which would constitute and exhaust all philosophy" (Coleridge, *Works* 4.110). Coleridge's own striving to achieve just such a cyclopaedic comprehension by way of the logic of burning ice–a grammar that "assume[s] to our Understanding a *circular* motion, the snake with it's Tail in its Mouth"–[17] is duly registered in the summa of his life in the way of philosophico-literary theorizing: "imagination" (so he translates from Schelling) is the faculty which "reveals itself in the balance or reconciliation of opposite or discordant qualities" (*Biographia* 14.12). As Grace's supple, necessarily abbreviated genealogy for Lowry the Coleridge-style philosopher suggests,[18] many an exponent of the creative imagination in the nineteenth century–among them, fellow readers of Coleridge and students of German idealism Carlyle and Emerson–took up the promise of whole comprehension held out by that definition. What such a genealogizing for world- and self-creation might also call to mind, though, is the inducement to encapsulation in hellish self-contradiction repeatedly signed by leading imaginative thinkers in "the Reflective Age," "the age of the first person singular," or, again in the words of Emerson, "the Age of Suicide" (*Journals* 5.366, 12, 198; *Letters* 2.445).

Certainly, the reckoning that "on a fundamental level" Lowry "retains ties with the nineteenth-century moralists such as Coleridge and Carlyle" in an "almost religious vision of self and world . . . passionately, personally expressed" (Grace, *Voyage* 121) squares nicely with Carlyle's own intense apperception of the logic, intention and reach of the creative imagination as he seems to have understood it. "Imagination," according to "The Hero as Poet" (1840), "is the faculty which enables him to discern the inner harmony" at "the Centre of Being" (*On Heroes* 337, 325). Again, Dante's *Inferno* is made to provide representative testimony: the medieval poet's "mystic" song of "fiery snow" reflects a depth and an integrity of insight matched only by Shakespeare (329, 321, 325). Pole "rhymes" with pole at "the innermost heart" of all that exists, which "inward harmony of coherence" only the imagination's "*musical* thought" can encompass, and only the poet's vatic song, "a kind of inarticulate, unfathomable speech" can express (316).

Carlyle himself had achieved a degree of poetic integration comparable to his Dante's just a few years before *On Heroes*, with the production of *Sartor Resartus*. Spun from the wisdom of "the Serpent of Eternity," *Sartor* images the "fever-paroxysms," "delirious vertigo," "circumambulations" and "circulations" of a metaphysical wanderer brought to peer into the mirror of "the Infinite Brine" under the sun of an arctic June midnight (153, 87, 78, 130, 153). The "dizziquilibre" so imagined (Ducharme 94) would come to find a duly double-sided response, from Jerry A. Dibble's celebratory *The Pythia's Drunken Song*, for example, on *Sartor*'s resolution of "the style problem in German idealist philosophy"(56),[19] to Kenneth Burke's relating of Carlyle, writer of the "Zero Moment," with the "Light-Bearer" at the centre of Dante's *Inferno*, who "cancels himself, as the beating of his wings . . . sends forth draughts that freeze him all the more" (*Language* 120). As his good friends and antagonists John Sterling and Ralph Waldo Emerson found ample occasion for perplexed observation, often to funny effect, a suicidal logic of fiery snow subtends the whole of Carlyle's endeavour as moral guide.[20] "A Truth in art is that whose contradictory is also true," nice critic of *Sartor* and *The French Revolution* Oscar Wilde would come to observe (*The Artist as Critic* 432). A.L. Le Quesne's *Carlyle* (1982), then, strikes a still contemporary note when it affirms its subject not as a would-be prophet and teacher of ethics, but as an artist *malgré lui*, a seer gifted with "double vision" and a player adept "at keeping opposites in balance" (82, 93).

A devotee to the thought of Colerige and Blake and

the main disseminator of *Sartor* in America, Ralph Waldo Emerson saw and juggled in much the same way. Indications are that the Sage of Concord seconded the Sage of Chelsea's perception of the harmony underlying the superficial differences in their way of seeing things: "I see," so Carlyle wrote to Emerson in July 1850, in response to *Representative Men*, "where the rock-strata, miles deep, unite again; and the two . . . souls are at one" (*Correspondence of Emerson and Carlyle* 459). Unlike the more wary Carlyle, though,[21] Emerson could be altogether forthright, celebrative in announcing the substantially infernal character of his imaginative enterprise. "The Mind is its own place, and in itself / Can make a Heaven of Hell, a Hell of Heaven," he copied in his journal of 1823 (even as he prepared to become a Unitarian preacher), adding the comment: "There is no danger of any excess in the practice of this doctrine" (*Journals* 2.330). Supported in that conviction by Blakean-style readings of Dante and Milton,[22] Emerson more often than not is happy to identify the grammar of his own synthetic, balancing turn of mind with the logic of Hell: "Extremes meet: there is no straight line," as he untiringly repeats in concert with Coleridge's *Aids to Reflection* (*Works* 7.181, 9.14; *Journals* 4.383, 8.397, e.g.). "It is cold flame; what health, what affinity!" Emerson writes of the "truth" of the universe such as only the fully insightful poetic imagination can embrace (*Works* 3.171):[23]

> Line in nature is not found;
> Unit and universe are round;
> In vain produced, all rays return;
> Evil will bless, and ice will burn. ("Uriel")

Using "bitumen, fastest of cements," drawn from "the floor of the Pit," the poet makes "all things cohere" (*Works* 4.24, 17). Like Nietzsche the singer of "a divine hell" in "The Intoxicated Song" that wraps up *Thus Spake Zarathustra* (330), Emerson the poet of "Bacchus" celebrates the power of the synthetic poet to create "equilibrium" or "unity" from "spin": "He turns the woe of Night, / By its own craft, to a more rich delight" (*Works* 9.125).[24]

Now, the topsy-turvying of traditional Christian sense by the nineteenth-century literary thinkers and moralists with whom Lowry retains fundamental ties logically enough entailed a transvaluation of acedia. Shrewd historian of ideas Aldous Huxley, cited in Lowry's "Those Coal to Newcastle Blues" (*Collected Poetry* 44), makes precisely that point in his early essay "Accidie." Proceeding with due circumspection, Huxley retraces to the onset of "romanticism" the "triumph of the *daemon meridianus*," "the progress" of a medieval "deadly sin" to the status of "a literary virtue, a spiritual mode," "an essentially lyrical emotion fruitful in the inspiration of much of the most characteristic modern literature" (*On the Margin* 21, 22).[25] The cases of master of negative capability Keats' "Ode on Indolence," Baudelaire's Spleen Poems in *Les Fleurs du Mal*, Sue's *La Paresse*, Bysshe Vanolis Thomson's "Indolence: A Moral Essay," suspension-obsessed Genevan professor of aesthetics Henri-Frédéric Amiel's *Journal intime*, Symons' "The Dance of the Seven Deadly Sins," the chapter of Joyce's *Ulyssses* set deep in Lotusland, Evelyn Waugh's essay "Sloth" and, of course, Huxley's own wryly ambivalent compositions inspired by a witting acedia, as in

Crome Yellow,[26] to cite but a few of the host of available instances, eloquently attest to the cogency of his timely recollection. The fact of romantic lyrical sloth as a medieval vice transvaluated and prolonged in Huxley's own time seems obvious enough.

The intention of this essay in the form of background notes, then, is to suggest that the reading of *Under the Volcano* as a book of and for *caritas* and, consequently, against *acedia,* is substantially partial, perhaps even mistaken. The text of Lowry's novel 'about' hellfire itself makes that point, and eloquently, in Chapter 8, where the reponse of "frozen," "stone[d]" folk in a bus, finding it "impossible to make up their minds," doing "nothing" to help a dying Indian lying on the side of a road (248, 251), is cast in a language referring to an I.A. Richards invoking Coleridge on "'the balance or reconciliation of opposite or discordant qualities'."[27] Spender's dictum, that *Under the Volcano* is a book about "acedia, the spiritual apathy of the religious who have become, as it were, hermetically sealed off from the source of their religion," might consequently be revised to read, more aptly, as follows: all-too-humanly embracing the values of a prolonged romanticism, the Lowry of *Under the Volcano* was anything but sealed off from the source of his religion. Indwelling a region where "cold performs th'effect of fire," he suffered the travails of ethical paralysis attendant on fidelity to the central paradox of his art.

ENDNOTES

1. Though "clear-sighted in the imprisonment of his sloth," so Allen observes of the protagonist of "the masterpiece of the forties," he is "yet unable to make the necessary gestures . . . that would heal the breach between himself and the world" (419-20). In Consul Geoffrey Firmin, according to Burgess, Lowry creates "a giant character whose sloth or accidie . . . etches the desired opposite, whose inability to love defines what love is" (*Modern Novel* 60; cf. *The Novel Now* 69). For Day, in one of his several accounts of the writer of "the greatest religious novel of the twentieth century," like character, like author: "deadly sloth . . . accidia is his worst enemy" ("Preface" xx).

2. "The word [*acedia*] itself has become quite fashionable among the literati," Siegfried Wenzel had cause to remark in 1960, in the preface to his *The Sin of Sloth:* Acedia *in Medieval Literature and Thought* (vii). Evelyn Waugh says as much in "Sloth," his contribution to Ian Fleming's project of *The Seven Deadly Sins* (1962): "the man of sloth, in all his full theological implications, has become one of the stock figures of the stage and novel" (58). See also Robertson Davies' 1962 secular sermon "The Deadliest of the Sins." Perhaps even more appositely engaging for readers of Lowry, Reinhard Kuhn's study of the *daemon meridianus* in Western literature makes substantial reference to Conrad Aiken's poem "Psychomachia."

3. Grace's use of italics here indicates the Late Latin from which the Middle English "accidie" derives. "Acedia" has

its own entry in the 1953 College Edition of *Webster's New World Dictionary*.

4. Reference is to the Penguin Modern Classics edition (1963).

5. This allusion is unmentioned in Ackerley and Clipper's *A Companion to* Under the Volcano.

6. See La Bossière, "*Conrad e Dante*," for an account of the logic of agony imaged in the *Inferno*.

7. "For hete of cold, for cold of hete, I die," as Chaucer's Troilus at sea is brought to lament (395.420). F.N. Robinson specifies Boethius and Dante as the major sources for "the idea of fate" discussed in this tale (389). In his short story "Through the Panama," Lowry cites this Chaucerian text in the voice of a Troilus at sixes and sevens: "All stereless within a boot am I / Amid the sea, betweexen windes two / That in contraries stand evermo" (*Hear Us* 87). References to Blake and the legend of the doomed, endlessly voyaging Flying Dutchman also figure in "Through the Panama" (84, 91).

8. In his 1967 essay "Harlequin Faustus: Marlowe's Comedy of Hell," Gerald Morgan observes that "'the tragical history' of the doctor and devils may be seen to belie its title, except in that degree to which we involve Marlowe in our own 'hyperpathetic' assumption of subjectivity, which seldom allows other than hellish mirth" (27). Morgan's essay provides a close analysis of the illogic that Marlowe's over-reaching, funny gnostic actually short

science is logically made to practice. For an account of the artist as "solipsist or egotist" in *Under the Volcano*, see McCarthy (47).

9. See La Bossière, "*La Vida es sueño* and the *Coincidentia Oppositorum.*" Teresa Scot Soufas's *Melancholy and the Secular Mind in Spanish Golden Literature* might similarly be of use to readers interested in the history of acedia as an aid to interpretation of *Under the Volcano*. For another contextualizing of Lowry's response to "the aesthetics of somnambulism," see Ackerley.

10. See Robinson 769.

11. Grace likewise remarks: "The cool, ironic distance, the parody, the anti-realist foregrounding of language in Barth, Nabokov, or even Joyce are foreign to Lowry's work because the reader must respond with and to Lowry's writing emotionally" (*Voyage* 121). Richard K. Cross anticipates Grace and Vice in this regard when he disassociates *Under the Volcano* from the "narrower sort of avant-garde writing, the . . . game-playing manner of men like Nabokov, Borges, and Pynchon," on the grounds of Lowry's concern with establishing "relations between the self and the larger world" (ix). According to O'Kill, "the verbal and cultural texture of *Under the Volcano* is largely pre-modernist" (11). John Orr, on the contrary, affirms that *Under the Volcano* "belongs firmly in the modernist tradition we associate with Eliot, Joyce, Woolf, Proust and Kafka" (18). Mixed signals seem to be indicated, all round.

12. For a reading of "the precious and aesthetically elegant manner" in which that dictum is inscribed, see Hadfield (96). Terence Wright remarks the "static" character of Lowry's art in *Under the Volcano* (67).

13. See, e.g., Woodcock, "The Own Place of the Mind." In a reading of *Under the Volcano* that parallels Woodcock's, Michael Cripps is able to affirm that, like Blake, "Lowry the novelist was able to follow the path 'right through hell' that is closed to the Consul, because, unlike Geoffrey Firmin, he was able to see far beyond the self and see clearly" (99). But, ironically enough, the case that Cripps advances seems to rely on the representation of a second Blake likewise in agreement with the epistemology of Milton's Satan and yet who distances himself from "the absolutism of the self" which that figure promulgates (99).

14. Falk (53), New (575), and Costa (*Malcolm Lowry* 127) provide representative instances.

15. The efficacy of *Under the Volcano* for inducing sympathetic participation in this regard is amply demonstrable. According to Binns, for one, here is a novel that "puts the reader into the situation of sharing the uncertainties and doubts" of its "four leading characters" (39). Costa responds not all that differently when he remarks that what "interweaves" the four main characters of *Under the Volcano* resembles "that galvanic negative capability which caused Melville's Bartleby *to choose not to* and Camus's Meursault to remain impassive at his mother's funeral. Not since Hemingway brought Jake Barnes and his entourage to

good fishing and bullfights at Pamplona has a group of fictional characters so moved us by their inability to move" (*Malcolm* 72). As Stanford A. Lyman's response to Camus' tale of the "acedic French clerk Meursault" appositely indicates, "even [the representation of a character] indifferent even to his own indifference" can somehow be stimulating, though to ethically deadly effect (40). Like the arch-expressionist Kafka's art as well, Lowry's has the effect of "making us feel the absence of passion passionately," in the words of Geoffrey Clive's *The Romantic Enlightenment* (182).

16. "Extremes meet" heads the list of the aphorisms meditated in Coleridge's *Aids to Reflection.* The illustration of that proverb with "cold performs th'effect of fire" is recorded in *The Notebooks of Samuel Taylor Coleridge* (1: item 1725).

17. From the Coleridge letter to Joseph Cottle dated 7 March 1815 (*Collected Letters* 4.545-46). Coleridge's concern here is to make the point that "the common end of . . . *all* Poems is to convert a series into a *Whole*." The image of the Ouroboros has similarly been invoked in Lowry criticism (see Cross 60, e.g.), though not nearly so often as in writings about Melville, a close reader of Coleridgean-style idealism and a fellow mariner who helped inspire *Ultramarine* (see La Bossière, *Victorian* 66). Coincidentally, in Melville's *Mardi*, the Ouroboros represents "the god of suicides" (2.26-27). For additional historical background, see R. L. Colie's *Paradoxia Epidemica: The Renaissance Tradition of Paradox,* which highlights Donne's *Biathanatos*, a treatise on suicide; and H.B.C. De

Groot's 1969 essay "The Ouroboros and the Romantic Poets: A Renaissance Emblem in Blake, Coleridge, and Shelley," which, by contrast, celebrates the figure. For a reading of *Under the Volcano* as "a suicidal discourse," see Bromley (294). The Spanish common name for fireworks in the shape of "fiery serpents' tails" is "*borrachos* (drunks)" (Lambert 226).

18. "Philosopher" Lowry, since "he wrestled constantly with epistemological questions about the nature of perception and consciousness" (Grace, *Voyage* 1). I write "suggests," since Grace does not explicitly refer to the perhaps all too obviously analogous case of Emerson. For an indication of Lowry's substantial affinity with an Emerson likewise wrestling with such questions, see his letter of 1942 to John Stuart Bonner, in which he cites two entire paragraphs from Emerson to make the point that "'The possibility of interpretation lies in the *identity* of the observer and the observed'" (*Selected Letters* 44; emphasis added). For an account of the "solipsistic entrapment" idealized in the Emerson oeuvre, see Doherty.

19. According to Dibble, the Editor in *Sartor* comes to transcend his differences with his subject, to rise to "a higher state of consciousness which contains and cancels all opposition" (56).

20. See Sterling's diagnosis as documented in his *Tales & Essays*: Carlyle makes "all manner of random and amorphous assertions [which] . . . like bursting cannon and reverting Congreve-rockets, injure his own cause" (1.307). Proceeding with characteristically flamboyant, whimsical

panache, Emerson chides Carlyle for his logic of contradiction: "covenanter-philosophe & . . . sansculotte aristocrat" Carlyle "denies the books he reads . . . denies his own acts & purposes; By God I do not know them–and immediately the cock crows" (*Journals* 10.550, 343). For sustained accounts of Carlyle's entanglement in self-contradiction, see Ikeler, Baumgarten, and Harris. La Bossière remarks "l'élément d'autodestruction" fundamental to the author of *The French Revolution*'s "'art of producing zero'" ("Du pain" 82, 83).

21. "Poor . . . souls. . . . Poor devils!"–so Carlyle qualifies the condition he takes himself and Emerson to share in his letter of answer to *Representative Men* in 1850.

22. See Emerson's *Journals and Miscellaneous Notebooks* 16.90, for example; and Blake's notion that "Heaven is Hell, Hell Heaven," but only "When view'd from Hell's gate," in the words of his "Upside-Down" reading of the *Inferno* ("Notes on the Illustrations to Dante," in *The Portable Blake* 594).

23. "I think if I were professor of Rhetoric . . . I should use Dante for my text-book," Emerson wrote to himself in 1849, shortly after his return from Craigenputtock Farm with the page proofs of Dr. John Carlyle's translation of the *Inferno* in his luggage (*Journals* 11.133).

24. For all of his delight in the transformative power of the roundabout logic imaged in "cold fire" and "the snake with its tail in its mouth" (*Works* 9.140; *Journals* 8.246, e.g.), Emerson could also occasionally discern "the Lunatic Asy-

lum" at "the end of these fine streets [of bitumen]" (*Journals* 11.15).

25. Mark Williams' 1989 essay on Lowry as "muscular aesthete," though, works to make the point that the author of *Ultramarine* "has none of . . . the tiresome intelligence of Aldous Huxley" (79).

26. For a detailed account of Huxley's wrestling with acedia, see La Bossière (*Progress*, chap 5).

27. Cited from Ackerley and Clipper (321).

WORKS CITED

Ackerley, Chris. "Malcolm Lowry and Hermann Broch: The Aesthetics of Somnambulism in *Under the Volcano* and *The Sleepwalkers.*" *The Malcolm Lowry Review* 26 (1990): 10-15.

Ackerley, Chris and Clipper, Lawrence J. *A Companion to* Under the Volcano. Vancouver: U of British Columbia P, 1984.

Allen, Walter. "The Masterpiece of the Forties." In *On Contemporary Literature*. Ed. Richard Kostelanetz. New York: Avon Books, 1964. 419-21.

Amiel, Henri-Frédéric. *Amiel's Journal*. Transl. Mrs Humphry Ward (Mary Augusta Arnold). 2nd ed. New York: A.L. Burt, 1890.

Asals, Frederick. "Revision and Illusion in *Under the Volcano.*" In *Swinging the Maelstrom*. 93-111.

Baumgarten, Murray. *Carlyle: Books & Margins*. Santa Cruz: U Library of the U of California, 1980.

Binns, Ronald. *Malcolm Lowry.* London: Methuen, 1984.

Blake, William. *The Portable Blake*. Ed. Alfred Kazin. New York: Viking Press, 1968.

Bromley, Roger. "The Boundaries of Commitment: God, Lover, Comrade–Malcolm Lowry's *Under the Volcano* as a Reading of the 1930's." In *The Politics of Modernism*. Eds. Francis Barker *et al*. Essex: University of Essex, 1970. 273-96.

Burgess, Anthony. *The Modern Novel in Britain and the United States*. New York: Norton, 1964.

----------. *The Novel Now*. London: Faber & Faber, 1967.

Burke, Kenneth. *Language as Symbolic Action*. Berkeley: U of California P, 1968.

----------. *A Rhetoric of Motives*. Berkeley: U of California P, 1969.

Carlyle, Thomas. *Sartor Resartus* and *On Heroes*. London: Dent, 1908.

Chaucer, Geoffrey. *The Works of Geoffrey Chaucer*. Ed. F.N. Robinson. 2nd ed. Cambridge MA: Riverside Press, 1957.

Clive, Geoffrey. *The Romantic Enlightenment: Ambiguity and Paradox in the Western Mind (1750-1920)*. New York: Meridian Books, 1960.

Coleridge, Samuel Taylor. *Biographia Literaria*. Ed. John Shawcross. 2 vols. Oxford U P, 1907.

Coleridge, Samuel Taylor. *The Collected Letters of Samuel Taylor Coleridge*. Ed. E.L. Griggs. 6 vols. Oxford: Clarendon, 1956-71.

----------. *The Friend*. Ed. Barbara Rooke. Vol 4 in *The Collected Works of Samuel Taylor Coleridge*. London: Routledge & Kegan Paul, 1969.

----------. *The Notebooks of Samuel Taylor Coleridge*. Ed. Kathleen Coburn. Vol. 1. London: Routledge & Kegan Paul, 1957.

Colie, Rosalie L. Colie. *Paradoxia Epidemica: The Renaissance Tradition of Paradox*. Princeton: Princeton U P, 1966.

Costa, Richard Hauer. *Malcolm Lowry*. New York: Twayne, 1972.

----------. "*Under the Volcano*–The Way It Was: A Thirty-Year Perspective." In Smith. 29-45.

Cripps, Michael. "*Under the Volcano*: The Politics of the Imperial Self." *Canadian Literature* 95 (1982): 85-101.

Cross, Richard K. *Malcolm Lowry: A Preface to His Fiction*. Chicago: U of Chicago P, 1980.

Davies, Robertson. *One Half of Robertson Davies*. Toronto: Macmillan, 1977.

Day, Douglas. *Malcolm Lowry: A Biography.* New York: Oxford U P, 1973.

----------. "Preface" to Malcolm Lowry, *Dark as the Grave wherein My Friend Is Laid.* Eds. Douglas Day and Margerie Lowry. New York: New American Library, 1968. ix-xxiii.

de Groot, H.B. "The Ouroboros and the Romantic Poets: A Renaissance Emblem in Blake, Coleridge, and Shelley." *English Studies* (Amsterdam) 50 (1969): 553-64.

Dibble, Jerry A. *The Pythia's Drunken Song: Carlyle's* Sartor Resartus *and the Style Problem in German Idealist Philosophy.* The Hague: Martinus Nijhoff, 1978.

Doherty, Joseph F. "Emerson and the Loneliness of the Gods." *Texas Studies in Literature and Language* 16 (1974).

Ducharme, Réjean. *Les Enfantômes.* Paris: Gallimard, 1976.

Emerson, Ralph Waldo. *The Complete Works of Ralph Waldo Emerson.* Ed. Edward Waldo Emerson. 12 vols. Boston and New York: Houghton Mifflin, 1903-04.

----------. *The Journals and Miscellaneous Notebooks of Ralph Waldo Emerson.* Eds. William Gilman *et al.* Cambridge: Belknap Press of Harvard University, 1960- .

----------. *The Letters of Ralph Waldo Emerson.* Ed. Ralph L. Rusk. 6 vols. New York: Columbia U P, 1939.

Falk, David. "Lowry and the Aesthetics of Salvation." In *Swinging the Maelstrom.* 52-60.

Grace, Sherrill. "Putting Lowry in Perspective." In *Swinging the Maelstrom.* 3-18.

----------. *The Voyage That Never Ends: Malcolm Lowry's Fiction.* Vancouver: U of British Columbia P, 1982.

Hadfield, Duncan. "*Under the Volcano*s 'Central' Symbols: Trees, Towers and Their Variants." In *Apparently Incongruous Parts: The Worlds of Malcolm Lowry.* Eds. Paul Tiessen and Gordon Bowker. Metuchen: Scarecrow, 1990. 80-109.

Harris, Kenneth Marc. *Carlyle and Emerson: Their Long Debate.* Cambridge: Harvard U P, 1978.

Huxley, Aldous. *On the Margin.* London: Chatto & Windus, 1971.

Ikeler, A. Abbott. *Puritan Temper and Transcendental Faith: Carlyle's Literary Vision.* Columbus: Ohio State U P, 1972.

Kuhn, Reinhard. *The Demon of Noontide: Ennui in Western Literature.* Princeton: Princeton U P, 1976.

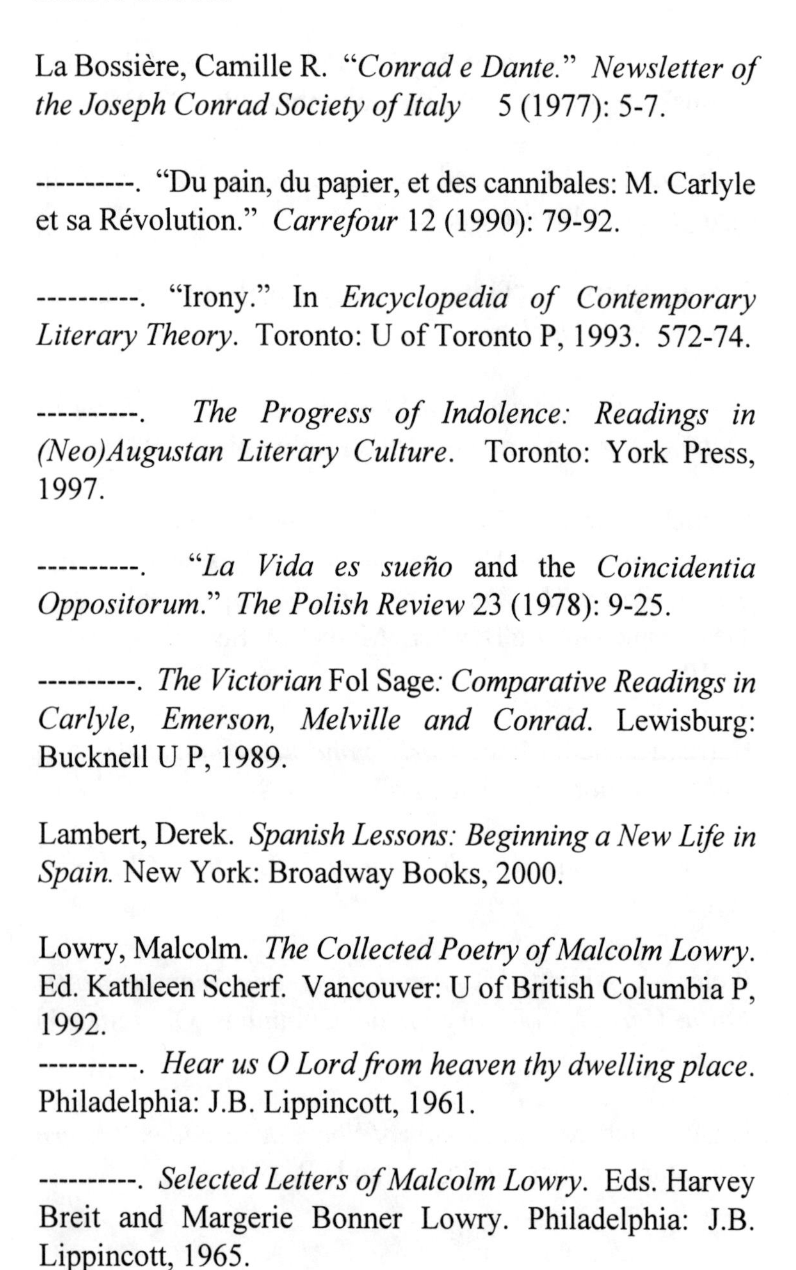

La Bossière, Camille R. "*Conrad e Dante.*" *Newsletter of the Joseph Conrad Society of Italy* 5 (1977): 5-7.

----------. "Du pain, du papier, et des cannibales: M. Carlyle et sa Révolution." *Carrefour* 12 (1990): 79-92.

----------. "Irony." In *Encyclopedia of Contemporary Literary Theory*. Toronto: U of Toronto P, 1993. 572-74.

----------. *The Progress of Indolence: Readings in (Neo)Augustan Literary Culture*. Toronto: York Press, 1997.

----------. "*La Vida es sueño* and the *Coincidentia Oppositorum*." *The Polish Review* 23 (1978): 9-25.

----------. *The Victorian* Fol Sage*: Comparative Readings in Carlyle, Emerson, Melville and Conrad.* Lewisburg: Bucknell U P, 1989.

Lambert, Derek. *Spanish Lessons: Beginning a New Life in Spain.* New York: Broadway Books, 2000.

Lowry, Malcolm. *The Collected Poetry of Malcolm Lowry*. Ed. Kathleen Scherf. Vancouver: U of British Columbia P, 1992.

----------. *Hear us O Lord from heaven thy dwelling place*. Philadelphia: J.B. Lippincott, 1961.

----------. *Selected Letters of Malcolm Lowry*. Eds. Harvey Breit and Margerie Bonner Lowry. Philadelphia: J.B. Lippincott, 1965.

Lowry, Malcolm. *Under the Volcano*. 1947. Harmondsworth: Penguin, 1962.

Lyman, Stanford M. *The Seven Deadly Sins*. Rev. ed. Dix Hills NY: General Hall, 1989.

Markson, David. *Malcolm Lowry's* Volcano*: Myth, Symbol, Meaning*. New York: Time Books, 1978.

McCarthy, Patrick A. "Wrider/Espider: The Consul as Artist in *Under the Volcano*." *Studies in Canadian Literature* 17 (1992): 30-51.

Melville, Herman. *Mardi*. 2 vols. New York: Russell & Russell, 1963.

Milton, John. *The Portable Milton*. Ed. Douglas Bush. New York: Viking Books, 1949.

Morgan, Gerald. "Harlequin Faustus: Marlowe's Comedy of Hell." *Humanities Association Bulletin* (Canada) 18 (1967): 22-34.

New, William H. "Fiction." In *Literary History of Canada: Canadian Literature in English*. 2nd edition. Gen. Ed. Carl F. Klinck. Toronto and Buffalo: University of Toronto Press, 1976. 3.233-83.

Nietzsche, Friedrich. *Thus Spoke Zarathustra*. Ed. Oscar Levy. New York: Russell & Russell, 1964.

O'Kill, Brian. "Why Does Nobody Write Like This Any More?" In *Malcolm Lowry Eighty Years On.* Ed. Sue Vice. New York: St. Martin's Press, 1989.

Orr, John. "Doubling and Modernism in *Under the Volcano.*" In *Malcolm Lowry Eighty Years On.* Ed. Vice. 18-34.

Richards, I.A. *Principles of Literary Criticism.* 1924. New York: Harcourt, Brace and Co., 1938.

Slater, John, ed. *The Correspondence of Emerson and Carlyle.* New York: Columbia UP, 1964.

Smith, Anne, ed. *The Art of Malcolm Lowry.* London: Vision Press, 1978.

Spender, Stephen. "Introduction" to *Under the Volcano.* 1947. Rpt. New York: New American Library, 1965. xi-xxx.

Sterling, John. *Tales & Essays.* Ed. Julius Charles Hare. 2 vols. London: W.H. Parker, 1848.

Swinging the Maelstrom: New Perspectives on Malcolm Lowry. Ed. Sherrill Grace. Montreal and Kingston: McGill-Queen's UP, 1992.

Tellenbach, Hubertus. *Melancholy.* Transl. Erling Eng. 2nd ed. Pittsburg: Duquesne UP, 1980.

Tift, Stephen. "Tragedy as a Meditation on Itself: Reflexiveness in *Under the Volcano*." In Smith. 46-71.

Vice, Sue. "The *Volcano* of a Postmodern Lowry." In *Swinging the Maelstrom*. 123-35.

Waugh, Evelyn. "Sloth." In *The Seven Deadly Sins*. Ed. Ian Fleming. 1962. Freeport NY: Books for Librairies Press, 1970. 55-64.

Wellek, René. *A History of Modern Criticism (1750-1950): The Romantic Age*. New Haven: Yale UP, 1955.

Wenzel, Siegfried. *The Sin of Sloth:* Acedia *in Medieval Literature and Thought*. Chapel Hill: U of North Carolina P, 1960.

Wilde, Oscar. *The Artist as Critic*. Ed. Richard Ellmann. 2nd ed. Chicago: U of Chicago P, 1982.

Williams, Mark. "Muscular Aesthete: Malcolm Lowry and 1930s English Literary Culture." *The Journal of Commonwealth Literature* 24 (1989): 65-87.

Woodcock, George. "The Own Place of the Mind: An Essay in Lowrian Topography." In Smith. 112-29.

Wright, Terence. "*Under the Volcano*: The Static Art of Malcolm Lowry." *Ariel* 1 (1970): 67-76.

VIII

OF POLITICS AND *IRONY'S EDGE*

[*English Studies in Canada* 22 (1996)]

Linda Hutcheon's *Irony's Edge: The Theory and Politics of Irony* (London and New York: Routledge, 1994) is well designed to convey some of the astonishment and uneasiness experienced by its author in her attempt "to figure out how and why people choose to express themselves" in the "bizarre way" of irony (1). Writing in the first-person singular, Professor Hutcheon certainly succeeds (for one reader, at least) in immediately inducing an edginess cognate with the feeling that informs the whole of her narrative of how irony has "happened" for her in the 1990s (12), by the very naming of *The Theory and Politics of Irony.* "As the title of the book hopes to suggest," so Hutcheon informs us, "the book is both a continuation and a revision" of one of her many influential monographs (3), *A Theory of Parody* (1985).

But between "a" and "the" there is all the difference in the world, a difference Hutcheon herself has been at pains to impress upon her readers for some time now. Does *The Theory and Politics of Irony*, then, as its title apparently indicates, announce less a resumption than a revisionist upending of an established attitude? Not so. For all the range of its scholarly reference (a bibliography of some thousand items stands behind it) and the depth of its aesthetic cultivation (see, for example, Hutcheon's elegant reflections in Chapter 5, on her experience of *Der Ring des Nibelungen* at Le Théâtre de la Monnaie, Brussels), this book is actually quite modest in what it intends and achieves. *The Theory and Politics of Irony*, in fact, surveys but one kind of irony from a particular and by now distinctly familiar point of view.

The irony of immediate interest to Hutcheon is neither "Socratic" nor "romantic," but "verbal" (3), of the kind long understood as "a figure of speech in which the intended meaning is opposite to that expressed by the words used" (*OED*). Hutcheon's concern, however complicated by "nervousness and self-consciousness" it may be, is "simply" with "the intentional transmission of information and evaluative attitude other than what is explicitly represented" (3, 11). Nor is Hutcheon any less forthright in directing attention to the position in theory from which she writes: "Risky Business," the heading of her first chapter, is borrowed from Stanley Fish's "Short people got no reason to live: reading irony" (1983). Reader-response criticism continues to hold its own: "After all, the final responsibility for deciding whether irony actually happens in an utterance or not (and what the ironic meaning is) rests, in the end, solely with the interpreter" (45); "nothing is an irony signal in and of itself" (159). One of the virtues of Hutcheon's reprise of Fish is that it both highlights and rehearses "the double bind of democratic discourse" (16) that has vexed and liberated reader-response critics. *The Theory and Politics of Irony* is nothing if not reader friendly, even as it registers a sensibility unfriendly to radically private enterprise on the part of some: "It is less that irony creates communities . . . than discursive communities make irony possible in the first place" (18). Given the inherently communal, corrective, referential nature of verbal irony, the possible occasions for its misfiring in the context of democracy North-American style are certainly plentiful and obviously problematic, as Fish has often indicated, and as Hutcheon continues to emphasize. For all the elegance of its performing, then, the theory that holds *The Theory and Politics of Irony* together is itself old hat.

Hutcheon as political pragmatist, by contrast, shows a capacity for considerable innovation; as, for example, in her response to the fact of public dissent from much of contemporary literary theorizing. Much to her credit, Hutcheon clearly intends by *The Theory and Politics of Irony* to help "restore public confidence" in a profession that continues to expose itself to "press attacks" (7). The profession of literary criticism has lost public confidence because its practitioners have tended to ironize, so she makes the point by way of introduction. Having taken to heart the spirit of "Regulation VII: '*No irony*'," from the "Regulations for Literary Criticism" promulgated in 1993 by the "Teachers for a Democratic Culture," Hutcheon is quick to assure readers of her intention to avoid "exclusion and embarrassment" (15), not to offend: "I hasten to add: this is a book *about* irony, and not an ironic book" (7). And she does strive to keep her word, proceeding gingerly, with a circumspection that culminates in Chapter 7, "The End(s) of Irony: The Politics of Appropriateness," in her balancing of various and therefore conflicting community responses to the exhibition "Into the Heart of Africa" presented by the Royal Ontario Museum (Toronto) in 1989-1990 (176-204). From beginning to end, prudent Hutcheon means to take no side ("on the one hand . . . on the other," she repeats time and time again). It would take a dogmatic and undemocratic journalist indeed to find fault with the position recapitulated in the last sentences of *The Theory and Politics of Irony*: "Whether it will become too dangerous, too risky [to attempt irony] is for the future to decide. Will there ever be another–safe–'age of irony'? Did one ever really exist?" Who knows? or could possibly know for certain? And who could be offended by such a profession of solidarity in 'unknowing'?

As the old saying goes, there is no virtue without prudence. But prudence in and of itself is not necessarily or entirely virtuous. The strategy Hutcheon adopts for quietening the press is surely wise, but it does pass over in silence a matter of much more broadly based popular concern than effronteries to democratic sensibility from ironic littérateurs. If there is one thing in contemporary literary theorizing that has affronted a North-American public increasingly concerned with (in)competency in education, it is the proposition (as broadly understood) that neither texts nor teachers should have authority in the classroom. Hutcheon sidesteps that political problem, and prudently so in view of her own disposition as theorist and educator: "What is usually called interpreter 'competence,' is a term which has, for me, uncomfortable connotations which bespeak the exclusion of those who cannot see through to the 'depths' . . . of intended meaning or to climb to the 'heights' of superior knowledge" (18). Now *that*, surely, is a statement of affective political value of a kind unlikely to increase or encourage public confidence in the literary academy as an institution of higher learning.

IX

"THE WORLD REVOLVES UPON AN 'I'": MONTAIGNE'S UNKNOWN GOD AND MELVILLE'S CONFIDENCE-MAN

(*in memoriam* John Spencer Hill)

[*The Dalhousie Review* 77 (1998)]

"Les mestis qui ont . . . le cul entre deux selles, desquels je suis. . . ." *Montaigne,* "Des vaines subtilitez"

"*Deus est anima brutorum.*" Oliver Goldsmith, "The Logicians Refuted"

YEA AND NAY–
EACH HATH HIS SAY:
BUT GOD HE KEEPS THE
MIDDLE WAY.
Herman Melville, "The Conflict of Convictions"

Late-modern scholarly accounts of Montaigne and his oeuvre attest to the still elusive, beguilingly ironic character of his humanism. On the one hand, the author of the *Essais* has invited recognition as "a critic of humanism, as part of a 'Counter-Renaissance'."[1] The wry upending of such vanity as Protagoras served to model for Montaigne –"Vrayment, Protagoras nous ont contoit des belles, faisant l'homme la mesure de toutes choses, qui ne sceut jamais la la siennne," according to the famous sentence from the "Apologie of Raimond Sebond"–[2] naturally comes to mind when he is thought of in this way (Burke 12). On the other hand, Montaigne has been no less justifiably recognized by a long line of twentieth-century commentators as a major contributor to the progress of an enduring philosophy[3] "qui fait de l'homme, selon la tradition antique, la valeur première et vise à son plein épanouissement" (Micha 1.19). The Athenian text in translation that lends its high lyrical dignity to the last page of "De l'expérience" (and of the *Essais* as a whole) signs the nature and lasting appeal of that valuation:

> *D'autant es tu Dieu, comme*
> *Tu te recognois homme.*

If on occasion he stands for nothing much more than a wretched little creature whose proud *bêtise* makes a dog seem all the wiser, Montaigne's "man" can also be remembered walking arm-in-arm with the paragon of Pico's *De hominis dignitate oratio* (Burke 11-12).

How, then, to account for such an apparent contradiction?

Modern scholarly answers to that question have been many and varied, but more or less of a piece. Broadly speaking, explanations of Montaigne's (anti)humanism have relied on a historicizing along one or both of the following lines: true to the protean, mutable being he aimed veritably to represent, Montaigne shifted his position with the passage of time logged in his writing's progress, which as he says and shows, runs round and round, all on wheels without entermission;[4] and like many a wit among his contemporaries, Erasmus and Pierre Boaystuau for instance, he practised the Renaissance high art of debating by paradox, in a way consistent with the old verity that "*Ogni medaglia ha il suo riverso*" (*E* 3.11.246; Burke 12). Reference to the existential fidelity of Montaigne's self-writing or to the fact of the rhetorical set-pieces for and against the dignity of man by other intellectuals of his age would seem to account adequately enough for the eccentric yet representative character of the individual mentality and the ironic humanism embodied in the *Essais*. In each or either case, the knot of contradiction is explained, if not cut, by descriptive reference to Montaigne's contemporary circumstance.

The aim of this essay, which issues from yet another mode of historicizing, of a transtemporal and consequently more 'philosophical' kind, is to work towards yet another apprehension of Montaigne's (anti)humanism, though in a context that would suggest its substantially unparadoxical construction. The preliminary outlining of that context proceeds from a recollection of the holying or theologizing of Montaigne and his enterprise during the nineteenth-century Renaissance that Walter Pater was prompted to resume under the sign of "*Que sçais-je*?"–[5]an age when Charles-Augustin Sainte-Beuve could imagine Pascal, Saint-Évremond, Hume, Keats, himself and perhaps all of his contemporaries as a line of followers in Montaigne *l'enchanteur*'s funeral cortege;[6] when pilgrim to Saint-Michel-de-Montaigne John Sterling found occasion to companion

Luther with Shakespeare's Hamlet and Montaigne's "Saint Socrates" in a religion of the unknowing self founded on doubt;[7] and when Harvard Divinity School graduate Ralph Waldo Emerson invoked "Saint Michel de Montaigne," "this prince of egotists," as guide, familiar and patron in his own apostolate for invincible whimsicality and self-reliance.[8] If such a secular theologizing sits somewhat awkwardly with the more or less strong disjunction between faith and reason, sacred wisdom and secular folly as subtly advanced in "Of Praiers and Orisons," for example, where Montaigne observes "That this fault is oftener seene, which is, that Divines write too humanely, than this other, that humanists write not theologically enough" (*FM* 175), it remains entirely consistent with his twitting, as in "Of Experience," of those wisdom-lovers who would divorce godly from human savvy: "Philosophie . . . brings forth a childe . . . when she betakes herselfe to her Quiddities and Ergoes, to perswade us, that is it a barbarous aliance, to marrie what is divine with that which is terrestriall . . . . It is not that, which *Socrates*, both [her] . . . and our Maister, saith" (*FM* 663). Montaigne the humanist and Montaigne the divine have aptly been wed–and not only by the extensive body of nineteenth-century sages whose sense of his wisdom-writing helped sustain, even inspire, the development of their own.[9] Celebrations of that marriage have endured well into the late-modern age. At bottom, there is arguably little to distinguish the divinely ludic humanism that impels André Gide's *Essai sur Montaigne* and Michel Butor's *Essais sur les Essais*, for example, from Emerson's spirituality in "Montaigne, or The Skeptic," the essay that centres his *Representative Men*.

But of all the instances of Montaigne's canonization that might be adduced from the now very long nineteenth-century Renaissance, Herman Melville's calls for special notice by virtue of the sheer cogency of the discernment that enables it. As to just how substantially Melville's studied response to the *Essais* informed his own pursuit after such wisdom as he was prepared to find in Holy Writ, this nicely anachronistic text from *Mardi* (1849), the first of his genuine romances spun from the notion that "the world revolves upon an 'I,'" gives a clear enough indication: "St. Paul . . . argues the doubts of Montaigne."[10] The argument productive of that observation goes something like this: if "now" we see *per speculum in aenigmate*, in the words of Melville's cardinal New Testament text (I Cor 13:12), what we read in the mirror of "God's Publications" is the living dubiety that is the world and ourselves.[11] Like book, like author, like reader; like enigmatic God, then, like enigmatic Man, since neither is readable unvaguely, by reason's light. "So man's insanity is heaven's sense"–[12] so Melville would subsequently have the doubtful, riddling narrator of his bible-mimicking *Moby-Dick*, with its prefatory references to St. Paul's darkling glass and a Montaigne text of ships and men swallowed up by a monstrous whale,[13] provocatively conclude from his experience of humanity's questing after godhood bodied forth in a hunt for the Leviathan of Leviathans. What sense the "awful Chaldee" writ on the great Melvillean white whale's brow has to convey is naturally made to dizzy human reason: the divinely "plaited . . . riddles" that *Moby-Dick* itself simulates effectively scribe a "circle . . . impossible to square" (2.83-84). "*Nescio quid sit*," as the author of the great American book of "The

Whale" found ample reason to respond (in company with another close reader of Montaigne, Sir Thomas Browne) to the question of "what the Spermacetti is" (1.xvi).

Speaking in words altogether his own, in Chapter 14 of *The Confidence-Man: His Masquerade*, Melville spells out the grounds for his own radical conjoining of un-knowing and unknowable Man with an unknown since unknowable God:

> Upon the whole, it might rather be thought, that he, who, in view of its inconsistencies, says of human nature *the same* that, in view of its contrasts, is said of divine nature, that it is past finding out, thereby evinces a better appreciation of it than he who, by representing it in a clear light, leaves it to be inferred that he clearly knows all about it.[14]

Reference to the living reality of the "duck-billed beaver" or *ornythorhynchus paradoxus* that many a scientist of his age initially denounced as a fraud–a stuffed rodent with a bill "artificially stuck on" (59)–introduces that text for the genuine conjoining of divine and human nature in mystery. The wondrous platypus of *The Confidence-Man*, like the ManGod *homo paradoxus* (and therefore *ambiguous*) that Melville found modelled in the *Essais*,[15] is made to stand for the hidden, mystic verity of verities in the natural order of things. The ostensibly eccentric is the rule of Creation in the world according to *The Confidence-Man.*

Now, to propose a reading of Melville's ManGod as Montaigne's GodMan cogently discerned and reconfigured might seem somewhat inapt, given the manifold sentences against overreaching that dot and tone the text and spiritual complexion of the *Essais.* Heaven knows, instances of Montaigne's assailing of humankind's inordinate pride in its capacity to think and to articulate–"la folle fierté de langage ayant pour but de ramener Dieu à la mesure de la pensée humaine"–are not hard to find in the "Apologie" (Micha 16). Humbled by the doubt that comes of bona fide self-knowledge, Montaigne in this mood presumes not God to scan; he finds himself more suitably occupied with playing chase-your-tail with brother kitten.[16] Prudence, self-abasement and limitation are his watchwords. Montaigne in this persona can mock the Cicero of *De finibus*, for example, for affirming that "the infinitie of things, the incomprehensible greatnesse of nature, the heavens, the earth, and all the seas of this vast universe, are made known unto us" by the intromission of human science, "the knowledge of Letters" (*FM* 282). Nor does his scoring of the humanist will to knowledge "derive[d] from self-over-weening" ("qui nous conduit à mettre le nez partout") stop there: "Seemeth not this goodly Orator to speake of the Almighties and ever-living Gods condition?" as the text of Montaigne's "Apologie" immediately goes on to indicate the extent of the nosineness and presumption to which the Cicero of *De finibus* attests (*FM* 282). Self-effacing Montaigne would have no truck with any earthly intelligence that would aspire even to begin to seek to approach the condition of God.

But, wily as it is with the wisdom of *ogni medaglia ha il suo riverso*, Montaigne's autobiography in balancing doubt bespeaks a proudfully humble turn of mind. The generation of virtue from vice and vice from virtue proceeds apace and as a matter of course in the unremittingly ironic, vice-versa moral universe according to the *Essais*. Again, "Of Praiers and Orisons" provides a salient example. If the first paragraph of that essay opens with a profession of obedience to "the holy prescriptions of the Catholike, Apostolike, and Romane church," it ends with a confession true to the cosmopolitan worldliness of the whole of autoscopic Montaigne's enterprise as *fol sage*: "And yet . . . do I meddle so rashly, to write of all manner of purposes and discourses, as I do here" (*FM* 172). With "here" he hits the white. For all its sending up of heads ballooned like Protagoras and Cicero's, his book likewise concerns itself with "the infinitie of things." "This goodly Orator," one might ask of the wit disporting itself in the body of the *Essais*, seems he not "to speake of the Almighties and everliving Gods condition?" That question, in "Of Praiers and Orisons" as in the "Apologie," is rhetorical, since "the infinitie of things" and "du *moi*"[17] demonstrably figures as the ruling theme and subject of the *Essais*. Essayist Montaigne's is a wily agency–a frankly covert con-artistry, as it were–in the cause of a wisdom-loving wed to self-divinisation. The presiding genius that "Of Experience" inscribes, certainly, is something of a diabolico-angelical omnivore: "I suffer few things to escape about me. . . . I studiouslie consider all I am to eschew and all I ought to follow" (*FM* 640). Montaigne's confession in "Of Profit and Honestie," that "Verilie (and I feare not to avouch it) I could easilie for a neede, bring a candle to Saint *Michell*, and another to his Dragon" (*FM* 476), rings true to that self.

Melville would aver likewise in his double-speaking *The Confidence-Man: His Masquerade*, which opens with a rewriting of the Pauline sentences immediately preceding "For now we see through a glass, darkly" (2-3). "[There is] something Satanic about irony," according to the enigmatic, devilishly tricky confidence-man Frank Goodman (a.k.a "The Cosmopolitan"), who professes himself "Philanthropos" and a good friend of reason (119, 198). As *The Confidence-Man*'s probing revisitation of Montaigne's theme of the alliance of human with divine nature in ambiguity invites the recollection, the text of the *Essais* is rife with signs of a substantial enigmatism. "Nature," according to the Platonic "divine saying" embraced in the "Apologie," "is nothing but an aenigmaticall poesie of infinite varietie"; all contraries find themselves gathered up and reconciled in "this infinite vaste Ocean" (*FM* 311, 258). Nature, like the greatest poetry, "the good and loftie, the supreme & divine, is beyond rules, and above reason," in the words of Montaigne's essay "Of Cato the Yonger" (*FM* 115). Humankind and its history as meditated in "Of Bookes" constitute a subject the truth of which is no less unfathomable to reason: "a subject . . . so full and large," the history of man "is almost infinit" (*FM* 242). The text of the *Essais* represents a launching out into just such a virtually boundless element, "this infinit altercation, and perpetuall discordance of opinions and reasons," "this infinite confusion of opinions," "this infinit varietie of contrarie reasons," "this . . . huge heap of learning and provision of so infinite different things" such as the author of that book of "infinite irresolution" finds recapitulated in himself (*FM* 321, 326, 320, 325, 288). And Montaigne's own writing, its autobiographical speculation "turning, tossing and floating up and down, in this vaste, troublesome, tempestuous sea," justly figured as "this infinite deepe [of thoughts]" (*FM* 301, 297), spells out with due witty candour and indirection his own epitomizing of the human condition that he would compass, however inconclusively. A Montaigne tongue-in-cheek would prudently leave to others, "the wiser sort," the work of stitching together the bits and pieces of his "articles loose and disjoynted . . . ; [and] to Artists" the task of "rang[ing] into sides . . . the infinite diversitie of visages so double, so ambiguous and partie-coloured" figured in his *Essais* (*FM* 640-41), where contraries meet. "Our life," so Montaigne rehearses his Plato's refrain, is

> composed, as is the harmonie of the World, of contrary things and of divers tunes, some pleasant, some harsh, some sharpe, some flat, some low and some high: What would that Musician say, that should love but some one of them? He ought to know . . . how to intermingle them . . . the contraries consubstantial with our life. (*FM* 648-49)

Who among fellow humans, then, could rationally compass or read with any certainty the design of such a life? What sense that life might have must seem unfathomable, no less deep than that of the God of wondrous obscurity Montaigne had occasion to scan in the pages of *De docta ignorantia*, speculative mystic Nicholas of Cusa's book of "l'ignorance . . . doctorale" (*E* 1.54.370):

> Ubi vedutur in caligine et nescitur, quae substantia aut quae res aut quid entium sit, uti res, in quo coincidunt opposita . . . . Haec visio in tenebra est,

> ubi occultator ipse deus absconditus ab oculis omnium sapientum.[18]

And who, then, it might also be asked, could comprehensively discern the self behind the "infinite diversitie" of Montaigne's "visages"? Strictly or logically speaking, the answer to that question must be no-one: in the words of Alexandre Micha's Introduction to his recent edition of the *Essais*,

> La physionomie [de Montaigne] ne se laisse pas entièrement déchiffrer. Un sourire énigmatique . . . accueille le lecteur. L'enchanteur dont parle Sainte-Beuve éteint sa lampe au cours de la promenade où nous l'accompagnons pour réapparaître là où nous ne l'attendions pas, entre deux ombres, ou dans une lumière vite obscurcie. (1.22-23)

In tenebra, the reader of Montaigne encounters a being *in quo coincidunt opposita* remarkable by virtue of his special, yet characteristically human, "sinuosité artiste" (Micha 1.25). Obscurity answers unto obscurity, darkling human art unto divine artistry–six of one, half-dozen of the other, rhetorically at least. According to the ruling sentence of the "Apologie," "Things most unknown are fittest to bee deified" (*FM* 298).

The most substantive of the questions left up in the air by the *Essais* thus suggests itself: when Montaigne responds to the "so bottomlesse a deapth, and infinit a varietie," "the infinit course of an eternall night" (*FM* 640, 304) that he reads in the mirror of Nature, Man and himself, does he not do so in a voice that bespeaks a self-divining?

Montaigne leaves little doubt in this regard, most notably in the "Apologie," when he observes that "of our Creators works, those beare his marke best, and are most his owne, which we understand least" (*FM* 289). Apparently, it is by virtue of our *bestise* or *ignorance doctorale* that we accede to a wisdom most like God's–or like Montaigne's: "*Cavete, nequit vos decipiat per Philosophiam & inanes seductiones, secundum mundi. Take heed, lest anie man deceive you by Philosophie and vaine seducements, according to the rudiments of the world . . .* ," as he philosophically recontextualizes St. Paul (Col 2:8; *FM* 282).[19] Montaigne's Saints Socrates and Paul–each of whom authorizes the notion that to philosophize is to doubt–"philosopher, c'est doubter" (*E* 2.11.123)–are of a mind on the godliness of human ignorance, uncertainty: in the ironic language of the most apparently candid of Montaigne's essays, "Of Experience," "*Affirmation & selfe-conceit, are manifest signes of foolishness*" (*FM* 640)–that is to say, "signes exprès de bestise" (*E* 3.13.286). If, according to Melville, "St. Paul . . . argues the doubts of Montaigne," Montaigne's St. Paul argues the doubts of his Socrates, "le maistre des maistres" (*E* 3.13.280), the holiest of men. "So sacred an image of humane forme," as Montaigne is disposed repeatedly to acknowledge, "the soule of *Socrates* . . . is absolutely the perfectest that ever came to my knowledge" (*FM* 628, 244).

But, according to Montaigne's own writing for learned ignorance, would not human folly stand as wisdom before God? If humanity is created *in imago Dei* and if godhood is signed by human unknowing, both of which hypotheses the text of the *Essais* seems well designed to advance, the answer to that question is understandably yes. Melville, shrewd reader of Montaigne's *bêtisier* and pursuer after divinity who found himself lost in the unfathomable mystery of a Being beyond measure, answers accordingly, with a rhetorical exaggeration duly rich in joking wit: "man's insanity is heaven's sense." Enigmatic like the ineffable publications of the Creator, the weave of texts that constitute the *Essais* reveals itself a godly work. Of Montaigne's writings, "those beare his marke best, and are most his own, which we understand least." *À bon rat, à bon chat*, as it were.

Now, it might logically be objected that the above purchase on the enigmatism of the *Essais* proceeds from a straw-man style of confounding two very different kinds of mystery, which confounding has then been foisted on Montaigne. Certainly, the affirmation by the author of the "Apologie," that "if there bee any thing" that is his in what he writes, "then is there nothing [in it] that is Divine" (*FM* 300), patently flies in the face of such a proceeding. But Montaigne, it goes without saying, was not very long on the traditional formal logic. There are indications galore of his disposition *à se démentir*, to betray himself: "sans cesse [il] se contredit et se trahit lui-même," as André Gide with good reason has been pleased to recall.[20] It is no less evident a matter of historical record that Montaigne effectively helped prepare the way for the "humanist theology" of the many Victorian sages who read him religiously and were likewise disposed to "conflate the mystery of existence with the mystery of the Bible," by making use of the traditional Christian "language of numinous awe to deify a strictly secular universe."[21] The distinctly *Christian* character of the humanism such as traced by John Spencer Hill's recent *Infinity, Faith and Time*, from Augustine, Anselm and Cusa to modern times,[22] is remarkable for its absence from the writings of Carlyle, Melville and Emerson, for example, as much as it is from those of Montaigne. Reference to the ManGod Christ, to the mysteries of the Incarnation, Resurrection and Ascension, is scarcely to the found in the *Essais.* And if Montaigne, unlike the main body of his nineteenth-century emulators, never sought overtly to diminish the gap between his own folly and divine wisdom, his rhetoric of the infinite belies such a demurring. He retains the vocabulary proper to matters divine, even as he makes it his business not to refer to the mysteries basic to traditional Christian belief: as the Sainte-Beuve of *Port-Royal* pointedly observes, Montaigne was certainly a Catholic, less certainly a Christian (*Port-Royal* 3.13). This is not to suggest, though, that Montaigne's text compasses no wisdom at all. "I helpe my selfe to loose, what I perticularly locke up" (*FM* 378), so he confesses himself in "Of Presumption." Logically invincible as they are, illogicians always have reason on their side.

We are now in a position to retranslate Montaigne's sentence against Protagoras: "Truely *Protagoras* told us prettie tales, when he makes man the measure of all things, who never knew so much as his owne." Protagoras never knew so much as his own because what he could not fail but not know was immeasurable, like the infinity of things, and of God. Thus a Protagoras ignorant of himself told a true story in making man the measure of all things. And it is in this sense that Montaigne's mocking of Protagoras substantially accords with "the quaint inscription wherewith the the Athenians honored the coming of *Pompey* into their Cittie":

> *D'autant est tu Dieu, comme*
> *Tu te recognois homme.*
> So farre a God thou mai'st sccompted be
> As thou a man doost re-acknowledge thee.
> (*FM* 664)

The following lines from Melville's poem "The Conflict of Convictions" inscribe a closely parallel sense of ManGod:

> YEA AND NAY–
> EACH HATH HIS SAY.
> BUT GOD HE KEEPS
> THE MIDDLE WAY.[23]

This unknown God traditional to the sceptical, negative logician's balancing way Melville had found exemplified in bold in the *Essais*. And according to *The Confidence-Man: His Masquerade*, this unknown, ambiguous, infinite God is made in the image of its creator–that is to say, in the image of an artist as sceptic who endlessly reads himself in a mirror. Like his mentor in wisdom-writing Montaigne, Melville the latter-day Renaissance sceptic scales God according to the measure of human ignorance:

> Upon the whole, it might rather be thought, that he, who, in view of its inconsistencies, says of human

> the same that, in view of its contrasts, is said of the divine nature, that it is past finding out. . . .

Pursuant to Montaigne the enchanter's enterprise as *fol sage*, Melville's logically concludes with an extinguishing at once of human science and the positive wisdom of Holy Writ. *The Confidence-Man: His Masquerade*, the last of the prose fictions he saw to press, ends with a "lights out" (217) that brings the curtain down on a mystifying performance of muscular humility consistent with the proposition that "*Deus est anima brutorum*."[24] Darkness calls unto darkness, unknowing unto unknowing, deep unto deep, *bêtise* unto *bêtise*.

ENDNOTES

1. Peter Burke, *Montaigne* (Oxford: Oxford UP, 1981) 11.

2. Cited from Alexandre Micha's critical edition of the *Essais,* 3 vols (Paris: Garnier Flammarion, 1969) 2.12.222; hereafter abbreviated *E*. English translations from Florio, *The Essayes . . . of Michaell de Montaigne* (London, 1603); hereafter abbreviated *FM.*

3. See Burke 11, 75.

4. "Le monde n'est qu'une branloire perenne. Toutes choses y branlent sans cesse" (3.2.220).

5. Walter Pater, *Plato and Platonism* (London and New York: Macmillan, 1893) 174.

6. Charles-Augustin Sainte-Beuve, *Port Royal*, eds. R.L. Doyon and C. Marchesné, 3 vols 9 (Paris: La Connaissance, 1926) 3.13, 59-60.

7. John Sterling, "Montaigne and His Writings," *London and Westminster Review* 29 (1838): 321-52.

8. Ralph Waldo Emerson, *The Complete Works*, ed. Edward Waldo Emerson, 12 vols (Boston: Houghton Mifflin, 1903-04) 4.173, 162.

9. For an account of Montaigne's deep impress on nineteenth-century wisdom-writing in English, see Camille R. La Bossière, *The Victorian* Fol Sage: *Comparative Readings on Carlyle, Emerson, Melville, and Conrad* (Lewisburg: Bucknell UP, 1989).

10. Herman Melville, *Mardi*, 2 vols (New York: Russell & Russell, 1963) 2.279, 54.

11. A standard Melvillean trope, as in all of *Mardi*, *Moby-Dick*, *Pierre*, *The Confidence-Man,* and the Preface to *Israel Potter*.

12. Herman Melville, *Moby-Dick*, 2 vols (New York: Russell & Russell, 1963 2.170.

13. "With full eyes and empty glasses. . . . Here ye strike but splintered hearts together . . . there, ye shall strike unsplinterable glasses!" (*Moby-Dick* xii). "And whereas all the other things, whether beast or vessel, that enter into the dreadful gulf of this monster's mouth, are immediately lost and swallowed up, the sea-gudgeon retires into it in great security, and there sleeps.-Montaigne, *Apologie for Raimond Sebond.*"

14. Herman Melville, *The Confidence-Man*, ed. Hershel Parker (New York: Norton, 1971) 59; emphasis added.

15. See Lawrence Thomson's *Melville's Quarrel with God* (Princeton: Princeton UP, 1952), for a close scanning of Melville's negative theology in the light of Montaigne's in the *Apologie.*

16. See Melville's letter of 5 October 1885 to Mrs. Ellen Gifford: "It is now quite a time since you first asked me for my photo: Well, here it is at last, the veritable face (at least so says your now venerable friend. . . . What the deuce makes him look so serious, I wonder. I thought he was of a gay and frolicsome nature, judging from a little rhyme of his about a Kitten ['Montaigne and His Kitten'], which you once showed me" (Jay Leyda, *The Melville Log: A Documentary Life of Herman Melville, 1819-1891* [New York: Harcourt Brace and World, 1951] 2.793-94). Emerson earlier had evoked the image of the kitten famous for having played with Montaigne: "If you could see with her eyes you would see her surrounded with hundreds of figures performing complex dramas, with tragic & comic issues . . . many

ups & downs, & meantime it is only puss & her own tail" (*The Journals and Miscellaneous Notebooks of Ralph Waldo Emerson*, ed. William Gilman *et al*, 16 vols [Cambridge: Belknap P of Harvard U, 1960-] 8.259).

17. "Je suis moy-mesmes la matiere de mon livre" ("Au lecteur," *E* 1.35).

18. Nicholas of Cusa, *Opera* (Paris, 1514), 1.I.viii.

19. Montaigne stops short of citing Col 2:8 in full: the Pauline verse ends with ". . . and not according to Christ."

20. André Gide, *Les Pages immortelles de Montaigne* (Paris and New York: Éditions Corrêa and Longmans Green, 1939) 37-38.

21. Ronald Hepburn, "A Critique of Humanist Theology." *Objections to Humanism*, ed, H.J. Blackham (Harmondsworth: Penguin, 1963) 32.

22. John Spencer Hill, *Infinity, Faith and Time: Christian Humanism and Renaissance Literature* (Montreal and Kingston: McGill-Queen's UP, 1997). Professor Hill gives full weight to the faith and Christology that underpin and enable Nicholas of Cusa's sense of infinity in *De docta ignorantia* (see chap 3 in particular). When the text of the *Essais* reads "l'ignorance doctorale," it does so in a way that occludes the considerable, substantial difference that sepa-

rates Pauline fideism from Socratic doubt, as in this passage from L. Moulnier's translation of *De docta*:

> C'est là notre docte ignorance, par laquelle saint Paul lui-même s'éleva à l'idée que ce Christ, qu'il ne connut par le savoir que quelque temp, il l'ignorait, quand il se haussa jusqu'à lui. Nous sommes conduits, nous, fidèles du Christ, dans la docte ignorance, jusqu'à cette montagne qu'est le Christ, que la nature de notre animalité nous empêche d'atteindre. (*De la docte ignorance* [Paris: Félix Alcan, 1930] 212)

Justifiably, given Hill's theme of "Christian humanism," Montaigne comes in for only a passing mention, in a note: "Time for Montaigne is time *present*. His subject is himself, and he seeks wholeness and continuity by looking steadily at the flux of his own being" (176-77 n20).

23. Herman Melville, *Poems* (New York: Russell & Russell, 1963) 10.

24. The Latin quotation is from Oliver Goldsmith's poem, "The Logicians Refuted," written in imitation of Montaigne and Jonathan Swift (*The Miscellaneous Works of Oliver Goldsmith*, ed. James Prior, 4 vols [New York: Derby & Jackson, 1857] 4.127). For an account of Goldsmith's impress on *The Confidence-Man*, see M. Izora Costner's pamphlet, "Goldsmith's *Citizen of the World* and Melville's *The Confidence-Man*" (Comanche, Oklahoma, 1963).

X

OF HUXLEY AND DAVIES

[from "Davies Tristram-gistus," Introduction to *Robertson Davies: A Mingling of Contrarieties,* edition from U of Ottawa P, 2001]

"The ANTITHESIS, or SEESAW, whereby Contraries and Oppositions are balanced in such a way, as to cause the reader to remain suspended between them. . . ." Alexander Pope, *Peri Bathous, or the Art of Sinking in Poetry*

"The middle of the day is just like the middle of the night. . . . Indolence, how well I know you." *Amiel's Journal*, translated by Mrs. Humphrey Ward

"The meridian demon was upon him; he was possessed by that . . . post-prandial melancholy which the coenobites of old knew and feared . . . acedia." Aldous Huxley, *Crome Yellow*

"[A] qualified Yes, conditioned by a prudential No. . . . It is [a cast thought] that keeps you constantly alert to every possibility. It is a little understood aspect of the Golden Mean." Robertson Daves, *Murther and Walking Spirits*

Once upon a time, in 1949, Robertson Davies revisited the time of his youth to recall of his first reading in Aldous Huxley that it "lifted" him into "the sunshine world of high comedy" and cast over his life "a summer glory which no conceivable winter could dispel" (*Enthusiasms* 230). The book was *Antic Hay* (1923), taken up at the suggestion of a lad of his own age who aspired to priesthood in the Church of England. "Enthralled" by the "wonderfully amusing people," "easy scholarship" and "witty pedantry" he met with in that novel, the teenaged Davies immediately "knew that this man Huxley stood in a very special relation" to him (229).

Some twenty years later, in "The Conscience of the Writer" (1968), Davies extended his account of that very special relation, from his "surprise" at the appearance of *Eyeless in Gaza* (1936) to his considered understanding of Huxley's mid-life change from neo-Augustan satirist to religious mystic: "What was significant about *Eyeless in Gaza* was that it was written when he was forty-two, and ripe for change. If there had been no change, we should have tired of the old Huxley wearing the young Huxley's intellectual clothes" (*One Half* 127). The Davies of "The Conscience of the Writer" continues to prize the young Huxley's work for "the brilliance of its wit," its "strong satirical edge" and "stringent charm" (126), even as he more or less explicitly acknowledges the persistence of Huxley, "one of the more far-ranging, capacious and powerful intellects of our time" (*Enthusiasms* 141), as *éminence grise* in his own spiritual life: "And from that time [of *Eyeless in Gaza*] to the end of his life . . . [Huxley's] exploration of mystical religion and his discussions of morality were at the root of everything he wrote" (*One Half* 127).

But signs of disenchantment, not long in coming after "The Conscience of the Writer," seem evident enough in the record of Davies' subsequent commentary on Huxley's intellectual clothes, whether new-Restorationly flashy or latter-day monastic in cut. Certainly, both the young Huxley and the old come in for a somewhat circumspect ruffling in *World of Wonders* (1975), where an intermittent discussion of "intellectual fopperies" touches on unwordly "non-attachment" as much on "the Ironic Spirit" of the early 1930s (175, 204). And when the theme of Huxley's shift in garb is revisited in a Davies lecture of November 1976, it is by a critic apparently much altered in his view since 1968: though Huxley "became fascinated with those things which he had formerly derided," according to Davies in "Thunder without Rain," he continued to suffer from his "earlier defect–he thought too much and felt too little" (*One Half* 253, 254). Like the "heatless[ly]" witty proceeding of *Crome Yellow* (1922), *Antic Hay* and *Point Counter Point* (1928), the mystical Huxley's enterprise, as Davies now sees it, was impelled by "a negative and life-diminishing" spirit: his quest for "the Absolute" effectively occluded the "infinitely complex mingling of contrarieties" essential for the generating of "a new and stronger spirit in man" (253, 258, 263). Now altogether privileged over Huxley are Powys, Mann and, of course, Jung, agents for a "Mystical Marriage of Opposites" that results not in a static, deadening "perfection," but in an inspiriting, dynamic "wholeness" (263, 268). The Davies of "Thunder without Rain" leaves little doubt as to the traditional theological import of his critique: Huxley young and old suffered from the cardinal vice of the modern age, "Wanhope" or "Accidie," the "very old sin" attributed in the Middle Ages to "monotony of life" (248, 258).

For all its surface transparency, though, the seasoned Davies' pronouncement of his break with Huxley on the grounds of persistent unfeeling or acedia remains substantially curious, perhaps even mystifying. And the curiosity is this: that Davies, in effect, takes a page from Huxley even as he turns from him. Readers familiar with Huxley's "Accidie" (in his first volume of essays, *On the Margin*, published in the same year as *Antic Hay*) will recall his early recognition of "the meridian demon's triumph" in "the most characteristic modern literature" (22)–and, with duly cogent obliqueness, in his own productions as ambivalent, ironic wit of "The Golden Mean"as well. And the still-young Huxley, in his *Point Counter Point* and *Do What You Will* (1929), surely made explicit enough his adoption of a Blakean model for overcoming the melancholy and indolence in which he found himself more or less (un) happily mired: "in favour of life and wholeness," the "sane, harmonious Greek man" Blake "was civilized . . . *civilized.* Civilization is harmony and completeness. Reason, feeling, instinct, the life of the body. . . . Barbarism is being lopsided. [. . .] Blake strikes a balance of the conscious soul and the unconscious, physical, instinctive part of the total being" (*Point* 123, 141-42); as exemplified by *The Marriage of Heaven and Hell*, the "life-worshipper's aim is to achieve a vital equilibrium, not by drawing in his diversities, not by moderating his exuberances but by giving them reign one against the other. His is the equilibrium of balanced excesses, the safest perhaps of all (is it not between the projecting extremities of a long pole that the tight-rope walker treads his spidery bridge?") (*Do What* 279). Rabelais, Montaigne, Shakespeare and Mozart figure prominently in the genealogy for the Blakean ideal of "moderation in terms of balanced excesses" that *Do What You Will* advances (223).

Nor do Davies readers familiar with *Eyeless in Gaza* (the crucial moral concern of which progressively issues from Huxley's meditating on a wisdom of balance-and-mean rehearsed from such Augustan notables as Dryden, Pope, Johnson, Gibbon and Hume, and developed from his very early *Limbo: Six Stories and a Play* to *Point Counter Point*) have all that much reason to be surprised by the coincidence in spiritual discernment that Huxley's pivotal testament and the text of "Thunder without Rain" inscribe. As the protagonist of *Eyeless in Gaza* comes to recognise with his entry into mid-life, the *daemon meridianus* is upon him: his is "the besetting sin" of that "indifference" or "inner sloth" to which practitioners of "the Higher Life," whether mystical coenobites or savants ironic in the best *dix-huitèmiste* mode, are naturally susceptible (*Eyeless* 13, 617, 171). The central perception of the book that stands at the pivotal point in Huxley's spiritual progress could hardly meet more closely with the moral theology that Davies comes to invoke against the whole of his oeuvre: "Indifference is a form of sloth, and sloth in its turn is one of the symptoms of lovelessness" (*Eyeless* 15). Such an instance of close agreement on what for Davies as for Huxley is the crucial, perennial problem in higher living ("Sloth,"so Davies accordingly emphasizes in a Queen's University convocation address of 1962, is "the deadliest of the sins" [*One Half* 62]) provides some indication of the closeness of their special relation. In 1962, Huxley published his last novel, *Island*, in which the once "indifferent," "nay-saying"

Will Farnaby, heir to Voltaire and Hume (like Theodore Gumbril Jr., bored schoolmaster and main figure of lazy felicity in *Antic Hay*), comes to experience “a marriage between hell and heaven,” of antithetical yet “complementary philosophies,” “the paradox of opposites indissolubly wedded, of light shining out of darkness, of darkness at the very heart of light,” in an uplifting transport accompanied by counterpoint from the composer of *The Well-Tempered Clavier* (27, 130, 129, 274, 288). What, in a sense, could be more substantially agreeing with Davies?

WORKS CITED

Davies, Robertson. *The Enthusiasms of Robertson Davies*. Ed. Judith Skelton Grant. Toronto: M&S, 1979.

----------. *Murther and Walking Spirits*. Toronto: M&S, 1991.

----------. *One Half of Robertson Davies*. Toronto: Macmillan, 1977.

----------. *World of Wonders*. 1975. Harmondsworth: Penguin, 1977.

Huxley, Aldous. *Antic Hay*. London: Chatto & Windus, 1949.

----------. *Crome Yellow*. London: Chatto & Windus, 1952.

----------. *Do What You Will*. London: Chatto & Windus, 1956.

----------. *Island*. New York: Harper & Row, 1962.

----------. *On the Margin*. London: Chatto & Windus, 1971.

XI

PAST AND PRESENT: NEOBAROQUE NOVELS FROM FRENCH CANADA

[*Studies on Canadian Literature,* ed. Arnold E. Davidson, (New York: Modern Language Association, 1990)].

> "Infinis esprits, comme des peuples, se trouvent ruinez par leur propre force et soupplesse."
> Montaigne, *Apologie de Raimond Sebond*

> " [U]ne encyclopédie qui viserait d'abord à l'auto-détermination et à l'autosuffisance de chacun de ses lecteurs." Michel Belair, *Franchir les miroirs*

> "Eux aussi et . . . la croix. . . ." P. Tremblay, *La Terre*

The title of Gérard Tougas' *Destin littéraire du Québec*, a follow-up to his *Puissance littéraire des États-Unis*, is certainly weighty. It seems ironic as well. *Le destin*, in the sense of the necessary succession of events that are independent of the human will, is far from apposite to the future Tougas' history envisions and embraces. In fact, *Destin littéraire* is anything but a call for humility or resignation before the edicts of history and fate, exhorting as it does Québec's *littérateurs* to follow in the American way of cultural self-reliance and independence from imitation. With such critics as Henry S. Canby and F.O. Matthiessen for exemplars, they are retrospectively to invent their great writers by remaking them in their own image (177). The future makes the past, and Québec's history is ripe for creation according to the wills of its writers, so pronounces Tougas: "Ce n'est pas le passé qui nous instruit sur le passé, mais le futur" (147). In this respect, Tougas' *destin* is a principle no less active than the predestination fundamental to the Manifest Destiny informing Walt Whitman's 1856 "Letter to Ralph Waldo Emerson": the poet's reaching to take Montréal and Havana into his and America's embrace is prologue here to a proximate future history of "A Hundred States" (1:2038). And the acted-upon responds to, as it records, the presence and activity of the will to inventiveness. Delivered in a place made pliant to Whitman's visionary imagination, Thomas D'Arcy McGee's exhortation to the members of the Montreal Literary Club in November 1867–that they and the new Dominion resist imitation of a Bostonian literary culture assuming "the American democratic system to be the manifestly destined form of government for all the civilized world, new as well as old" (66)–reaffirms the concept that destiny American-style, like Tougas' *destin*, is a principle for action, of mind over matter and history, and not, ironically, a counsel to piety or respect or resignation before the limitations of time and place.

Understandably, then, *Destin littéraire* tends to privilege the critic as artist in the process of making particular works and national literatures; and so much so, that the disjunction Tougas outlines between American literature in the nineteenth century and the American Renaissance conceived in the twentieth century appears strong. Emerson's *American*

Scholar (1837), for example, a declaration of the need for his country's authors and students to break free of imported books and ideas, fell largely on deaf ears, according to *Destin littéraire* (16). The sovereignty precious to Emerson was to be achieved only in the next century. Similarly, Melville's struggle to give life to "le nouvel homme" proved abortive, since contemporaries greeted his works after *Omoo* (1847) for the most part with rejection, a prelude to neglect. The status of *Moby-Dick* as representative American book and universal work of genius is "une invention de la critique américaine contemporaine" (137). The point is well taken and instructive in what it makes explicit. Tacitly conveyed is a history no less instructive, serving to remind one that American criticism in the autogeneal-autotelic mode has taken important lessons from Emerson and Melville or their likes. For example, *"Moby-Dick" as Doubloon*, edited by Hershel Parker and Harrison Hayford, whose introduction concludes with a celebration of the inviolable privacy of Melville's enterprise and that of his readers–the fiction, like its Spanish coin, is a mirror for self-reflection–testifies as much. Autonomy calls unto autonomy, invention unto invention.

American criticism as creative art has a history of formation, is shaped by a tradition of considerable age. For all the topsy-turvydom, all the twists and turns in Emerson's whimsical reflections, their emphasis on the mind's imperial power is constant enough to be manifest: "Perception makes" (*Journals* 13.51). "What's a book?" Emerson asks himself and gives the answer (by now a cliché) to students of self-consuming artifacts: it is "everything or nothing. The eye that sees it is all" (*Journals* 5.93). In the words of his 1830 sermon "Self-Culture," "The world is but a mirror in which every mind sees it own image reflected" (*Young Emerson Speaks* 101). On that score at least, Melville is of a mind with Emerson. If we see as in a glass darkly, as he relentlessly speculates, what we read there is of our own making. "The world revolves upon an 'I,'" according to *Mardi* (2.279), Melville's eclectic, genuine romance picturing a pursuer pursued over an endless sea; and *Moby-Dick*, his epic invention that readers are advised not to take for veritable gospel cetology or history, logically follows. When set within the context of the literature it reads, the inventiveness of twentieth-century criticism in the U.S.A. seems old hat, as J.C. Rowe's *Through the Custom-House* confirms: contemporary critics follow in the steps of the authors they make, of the autodeconstructed writings they dismantle to reinvent. "Nous nous promenons sur nos pas" 'We walk in our own footsteps,' from Montaigne's *Essais* (3.122), would make a good epigraph for Rowe's charting of the modern critic's progress. If the future writes the past, the past writes the future. If the critic or reader is artist, the artist is critic or reader too.

Emerson and Melville as readers are in a position not substantially at variance with that of the twentieth-century criticism invoked by Tougas. They too have their antecedents and mentors, their time and place and tradition. Both variously respond to and register the transatlantic fluxions of that post-Kantian idealism founded on doubt that feeds on as it stimulates the nineteenth-century's appetite for reviving Renaissance and baroque texts. Among those texts most privileged are Montaigne's *Essais*, Shakespeare's *Tempest* and Calderón's *La Vida es sueño* (*Life Is a Dream*): each proclaims the imagination's power of metamorphosis, affirming that "life and dreams are leaves from the same book," a truth inscrutable to the Aristotelian realism and linear logic of "the dreary Middle Ages" (Schopenhauer 1.22, 62, 463-65). In the readerly world of dreams, relativity, improvisation and uncertainty, where distinctions between illusion and reality, self and other fade in ambiguity, the somnambulist travels not in a straight line but in a circle, the cardinal figure for the baroque logic of unreason that rules life's book. "Les contraires se rejoignent" recapitulates the endlessly reflexive grammar of contradiction governing Montaigne's *Essais* and the literature of "l'âge baroque" that follows in Europe (Rousset 27). The example of the dreamy Renaissance sceptic's private and therefore circular enterprise is efficacious in the United States as well. "Saint Michel de Montaigne"–so "this prince of egotists" is canonized by Emerson's *Representative Men* (1850)–announces the Sage of Concord's perennial wisdom (*Complete Works* 4.162, 173): "Extremes meet: there is no straight line," Emerson repeats time and again (see, for instance, *Journals* 8.397) and figures that logic in "cold fire" (*Complete Works* 3.171). Their presence detected in Shakespeare's "Montaignism" (Leyda 1.291), the *Essais* enact a coincidence of opposites consistent with the syntax described in Melville's retrospective "Art," a poem privately printed a few months after his reading of *The World as Will and Idea*: "What unlike things must meet and mate: / A flame to melt–a wind to freeze" (*Poems* 270). The student of baroque literature is on familiar, if shifting, ground here, in the dizzying roundabout dreamworld of contradiction appropriated by nineteenth-century idealism on both sides of the Atlantic.

Nor does the student of baroque literature (any more than Emerson and Melville before the mirror of Montaigne's oneiric autobiography, or contemporary autoscopic critics before the writings of Emerson and Melville) have reason to feel *dépaysé*, lost in terra incognita, in the presence of the mental infinity-box (de)constructions of the postmodern novel. The inventiveness that contemporary fiction or criticism in the newest manner generates, within itself and in its sympathetic reader, has a history that goes back more than four centuries. In terms of salient speculative underpinnings and artistic practices, writing in the postmodern manner is no less antique than the history of the neobaroque novel in French Canada, which shares in that mode's literary-philosophical provenance. Intellectual genealogy suggests that the rapprochement of contemporary French-Canadian and United States literature is a matter less of future than of past development. If Québec's critics still have some way to go in the American way of autonomic creation, a number of Québec's contemporary novelists have already made the round trip, albeit indirectly at times, and at great expense. Like Emerson and Melville, these writers of fiction precede the van of readerly criticism that takes up their lead. Accordingly, the following commentary on a few of the many contemporary novels from French Canada will suggest their role as critical *éclaireurs*. The selected fictions represent major contributions to the French-Canadian Renaissance and to the instauration of the baroque literature of subjectivity and circular unreason that gives that rebirth its proper expression. With the publication of Gérard Bessette's fourth novel, *L'incubation*, and Hubert Aquin's first, *Prochain épisode*, both in 1965, the age of invention comes to Québec fiction with force. *L'incubation*, a recent literary dictionary records, marks a clean break with the traditional realism Bessette himself had practiced in his earlier novels (Dorion 428).

Life is "*a tale told by an idiot*," Herr Professor Wilhelm Ricard Bartolomeus Weingerter avers to Lagarde, the narrator of *L'incubation* (64). Lagarde's rumination of his own life, in which are entangled the dimly recollected tales of Weingerter and others similarly encoiled in the 'problematic' of remembering their past coherently and giving it finite expression, does not belie the professor's self-confirmed wisdom. No less than theirs, the text of Lagarde's experiences during World War II and the present, in London (England), Montréal, Toronto and a place named Narcotown (shades of Kingston), is rife with indeterminacy. *L'incubation*, like its narrator's life, haltingly dramatizes the unknowing that full privacy makes invincible: "la vida es sueño" (Tougas 42) and its semantic performance a delirious dreaming. The toils of Bessette's noctambulists to allay the torment of their suffocation and to have done with interminable soliloquizing are necessarily vain, trapped as the characters are in a mind-cage without exit, "cette ovoïde boîte crânienne sans issue" (150). Merely one among other visually impaired subterranean wanders and alone in a world conceived as a dark labyrinth of mirrors, Lagard is kin to "the blind moles" babbling their lives in the Melvillean universe (*Pierre* 246) and to the mental prisoner sketched in the grim "Conclusion" of Pater's *Renaissance*:

> Experience . . . is ringed round for each one of us by that thick wall of personality through which no real voice has ever pierced on its way to us. . . . Every one of those impressions is the impression of the individual in his isolation, each mind keeping as a solitary prisoner its own dream of the world. (196)

Neither reason nor the language of sense can penetrate the shell of Lagarde's solitude: "Le monde est ma représentation" (162). What his endlessly sounding tale may *express* is hard to know or tell with any certainty, for Lagarde is snared in the web of words spun out from his own bowels (15, 35), as Bessette repeats Montaigne's figuration of the solipsized interpreter (*Essais* 3.278). Bessette's narrator must consequently rely on obliquity, more on the resonance than the sense of words, to relate what he can of his vague impressions. Written in the manner of "un poème surréaliste" (Lauzière and Bessette 20), *L'incubation* has the eloquence as well of the symbolist's *poème-silence*. Significance is unspeakable in a fiction of invincible ignorance and solitude.

Inherent in the inquisition of the self by the self about the self in *L'incubation* is a logic of the kind remarked in the "Late-Baroque" chapter of Wylie Sypher's *Four Stages of Renaissance Style*: "Every proposition *implies* the existence of its opposite; consequently every affirmation involves a contradiction" (294). It is the logic of the Ouroboros. Always vexing to Melville (see *Mardi* 1.295) and to Emerson sometimes so (see *Journals* 8.246), that Renaissance emblem of the snake with its tail in its mouth graphs the self-contradiction that impels Montaigne's autoscopic dictation (Glauser 152) and aptly gives Louis Lasnier's 1974 article on Bessette its title, "L'Ouroboros est un serpent qui se mord la queue."

L'incubation answers closely to the double sense built into that snaky circle. If the action of paradox is infinitely reflexive, as Rosalie L. Colie's *Paradoxia Epidemica* parses the syntax of the Ouroboros, it is also "self-cancelling" (40). The snake with its tail in its mouth figures at once a never-ending revolution of opposites and their mutual concellation: infinity and zero. In *L'incubation* the wheels of the closed railway car taking Lagarge "nulle part" inscribe the pattern of his mental travelling, "un cercle une spirale sans fin" (72). Necessarily endless, the circular logic of *L'incubation* is self-annihilating as well. An anaconda "wound round and round its own neck" images the God of Suicides in Melville's *Mardi* (2.26-27), and Lagarde's narration analogically pays homage to that deity. One reflection nullifies its opposite, and paralysis follows: "veux pas veux veux pas" 'want not want want not' (103). The only way out of paradoxy's interminable discoursing, so Lagarde ponders to himself in the last pages of *L'incubation*, is suicide. The death of the Englishwoman Néa-Antinéa, by a self-administered overdose of sleeping pills unwittingly provided by Weingerter, enacts the one kind of concluding possible in the world of Bessette's novel. In a fiction begun by a narrator gazing into the stagnant pools of another dizzy narrator's eyes, Néa-Antinéa's suicide frees her of entanglement in paradox, brings her interior circling to term, and stops the decay that the paralysis of contradiction visits on its prey. Her fatal, final lot concludes, redundantly, with such decomposition as comes of suffocation in a world of self-enclosure.

As in *L'incubation*, the opening page of Hubert Aquin's *Prochain épisode* pictures a narrator picturing himself in a watery mirror, sinking in the envelope of his words. From this, his first novel, to *Neige noire* (English title: *Hamlet's Twin*), his last, Aquin does not leave that mirror. It is the instrumental cause of his fictive enterprise and a device the multiple uses of which continally engage his inventiveness. As one commentator summarizes, "His books are ironic melodramas couched in self-reflexive forms of the nouveau roman, complicated in the telling by every baroque device of allusion and illusion, every inner duplication, or outer artifice, every shift from one identity to another, even from 'character' to 'text,' that Aquin's fertile imagination could devise" (Merivale 11). Implicit in that eloquent summary is the subtext of Aquin's oeuvre as a whole: the grammar of the Narcissus mirror. A review of his ingenious, perhaps even thorough, exploitation of the thematic-structural possibilities built into that device provides a way of sketching the dominant lines of neo-modern and baroque speculation that his fiction traces and retraces and to which his thought constantly returns.

Ideologically contextualized by past and present civil wars in Greece, Latin America, Africa and Québec, Aquin's first novel is indeed revolutionary. All things work in circles of self-reflexiveness, of creation and destruction proceeding together in "un cercle prédit" (*Prochain épisode* 59). Actually written in the summer of 1964, when its author was a prisoner of the RCMP, *Prochain épisode* is the composition of a narrator sitting in a prison dreaming his

he young Bérénice. Hers is a readerly philo-
·ance, denying the text of 'the other' any
·r than the one she gives it. Perception makes;
'e outside the mind; the world is a Narcissus
ıilitant idealist's self-reflexiveness ensures her
that full independence which absolute self-
'ers. Her will bent on (de)construction,
ts herself the power to ra(i)se buildings in the
ın eye. The swallower swallowed, she is like
pting itself; and like the maker of self-
tifacts, she is ever at war with herself. The
nnered efforts of Ducharme's text to ensure a
te with Bérénice's make the translator's lot an
ıe. Traducing increases as solitude deepens.
ce's philosophy accords well with an aesthetic
vention. In the absence of external reference
anything goes. Kant's dubitative, anticipated
's Socrates and followed by Carlyle, Emerson
·'s Montaigne, that perhaps we cannot even
know that we know nothing, abridges the
devilling Ducharme's characters (Imbert 233).
ıe je sais?" Ducharme repeats the ancient
'ez qui voque 182); and "un ludisme constant"
's response (Imbert 235). Bérénice plays with
ıs with a bauble, while her author subverts
ntic structures and the conventions of linear
ke a language and a narrative that are sui
ılée des avalés, like its heroine, is Promethean
ns. Exulting in her self-conferred liberty,
;ines herself a new Icarus, free as an eagle
sun at will. Daedalus Ducharme implicitly

his life and the circumstances leading to his incarceration. "My book writes me," as a critic cites from Penny Williams' translation of *Prochain épisode* (Merivale 11), which itself translates from Montaigne's "Du dementir": "mon livre m'a faict" (*Essais* 2.326). Writing the writer is dizzying business, as Borges, Barth, Nabokov and Barthes more recently confirm. Revolution, as Aquin's narrator reflects on his vertiginous creation, is neither rational nor sober: its dialectical proceeding cannot be explained "comme un syllogisme" (125). The spiraling descent into the mirror of the self that *Prochain épisode* narrates, an activity perilously like "une noyade écrite" 'a written drowning' (27), duplicates the endless self-pursuit of Narcissus. Fortunately for the narrator, a Separatist agent assigned to track down and erase a counteragent in Switzerland, he is unsuccessful in his task, for the would-be assassin and his target bear an uncanny resemblance. The suicidal mission remains happily unaccomplished, and *Prochain épisode* ends inconclusively. Revolutionary pursuit and invention can go on indefinitely, in countless episodes.

Aquin's mirror play continues in *Trou de mémoire* (English title: *Blackout*), a tale of textual obsession written "dans le style 'pur baroque'" (25). Diaries and diarists, editors and manuscripts, actors and spectators, persons and characters embrace as they simultaneously read and write each other in a "révolution permanente . . . qui peut se comparer à la rotation terrestre" (58). Paradox abounds and there are high jinks galore in *Trou de mémoire*, to the astonishment, dismay and delight of the fiction's participants. The editor RR, for example, is made pregnant by the narrator in the text she is putting together. But *Trou de mémoire*, for all its high-spirited theatrics, marks an increase in darkness from *Prochain épisode*. Each text inscribed in the novel is a "miroir noir" (82), a mirror for sombre self-reflection and in which, Narcissus-like, one can drown. At the end of *Trou de mémoire*'s story, both the narrator Magnan and his mysterious double, an inverted mirror image of himself, commit suicide. Like the uppers and downers that govern the teller's interior life, he and his opposite cancel each other out: taken together, their effect is reduced "à zéro" (32). Similarly fatal is the identification of reader and read in Aquin's third novel, *L'antiphonaire*, in which the violence in (and of) a Renaissance texts destroys a historian whose life in modern Québec becomes inseparable from the sixteenth-century Italian text she is reconstructing. Her fate signals the peril of being at once the pursuer and the pursued–the condition, coincidentally, of Aquin himself as the prisoner of contradiction who writes the literary-philosophical speculations gathered together in *Point de fuite*.

Neige noire is the story of a director's remaking of *Hamlet* and his own life. "Le monde est un rêve et le rêve est un monde" 'the world is a dream and the dream is a world" (184), speaks the new Hamlet, which text sums up the substance of Aquin's novel, rendered more epigrammatically still in the oxymoron of its title. Recalling Anaxagoras' "black snow" and Montaigne's use of that figure in an extended jeu d'esprit on the paradoxes generated by epistemological perspectivism (*Essais* 2.169), *Neige noire* embodies the dreamer's logic, the *coincidentia oppositorum* also dramatized in Shakespeare and Calderón (Cope 126; Smart). In the dreamworld of Aquin's novel, everything is

inseparable from its in
death, love and hate, pl
illusion and reality, fr
with its opposite by t
circularité" that makes u
and "la structure voilé
another life (138). "At
(Merivale 16), Aquin adv
of that logic. If "une
oeuvres humaines sont en
which all human enterpr
last novel writes a sent
mirrorings. What surcea
exhausting and intermina
but one way. As Aquin
written in 1962, double ag
of endless self-contradicti
dily drawn to seek the p
dissolution" ("Cultural Fati
neobaroque inventions, hi
tragically logical.

Labyrinthine as Aq
they seem almost straightfo
formance of radical subjecti
first novel, *L'Avalée des aval*
Like a hermetic poem in its
condite allusiveness and co
the book resists anything a
lation. That resistance, in
avalés is "about." "Je sui
constant avowal and plaint of

protagonist
sophy *à o*
existence o
there is no
mirror. Th
solitude ar
reliance c
Bérénice g
twinkling
a statue
consumin
complexly
privacy co
unenviabl
Bé
of limitle
or knowle
by Monta
and Niet
know tha
conundru
"Qu'est-
question
gives the
the univ
received
history
generis.
in its ar
Bérénice
flying in

claims a prerogative no less categorical.

But the liberty conferred by Promethean self-reliance comes at a cost, for creature and artist alike. Bérénice is free to do as she pleases, but at the price, ironically, of self-entrapment. A penned wolf, a trapped rat, sardines in a can and a caged squirrel figure the lot of Bérénice in "le cul-de-sac" of her mind (230). And with solitude comes inanition. Left with only herself to feed on, she starves. Bérénice knows from experience the truth of the couplet heading Emerson's essay "Heroism":

> The hero is not fed on sweets,
> Daily his own heart he eats.
>
> (*Complete Works* 2.249)

The inhabitant of a world in which linear logic and realism have no place is bound to endless self-consumption and self-contradiction, forever to travel in circles, "à tourner en rond" in a hell of fire and ice (165). As Bérérnice repeatedly entertains, only suicide would bring the infernal whirligig to a stop and give her (and Ducharme's) narration a concluding. But she wills to soldier on, knowing full well the consequences of pronouncing the mind its own place. Unlike Marlowe's Faustus, the extravagantly learned Bérénice (Renaissance travel books are all her delight) squarely faces the torment that boundless audacity exacts.

Ducharme goes on as well, with *Le Nez qui voque*, *L'Océantume*, *La Fille de Christophe Colomb* and *Les Enfantômes*. The diary of egocentricity's travails begun with *L'Avalée des avalés* continues through these novels, the principal characters of which unite in themselves the beloved and the lover, "l'amoureux et l'amoureuse," in the words of the masturbating teenager Mille Milles (*Le Nez qui voque* 261). But the luxuriant mannerism seems pro forma after *L'Avalée des avalés*. Ducharme repeats and caricatures himself, returning always to the "literary recipes" that produced his initial work, as Tougas observes in *Destin littéraire* (31). Why so? Robbe-Grillet, Ducharme's familiar and an éminence grise for Bessette and Aquin as well, suggests an answer: if the world is a labyrinth of mirrors, duplication and reduplication are unavoidable. And repetition induces ennui, which itself can become a subject for neobaroque jesting. "Etc . . . . etc . . . etc . . . ," Robbe-Grillet responds to his own killing reduplication in *Maison de rendez-vous* and so spares himself the task of rewriting and his public of rereading once again the novel's repeated single episode (La Bossière 30). The life of Iode Ssouvie, the youthful heroine trotting the globe of her mind in Ducharme's *L'Océantume*, writes in small the larger cultural history of which Robbe-Grillet's joking is a part: hers, she reckons, is an age of ennui and vanity, "des voyageurs immobiles" (96). Iode has cause to agree with the prescient Emerson too, when, glossing Montaigne's "Des coches"– "we travel round and round, in our own footsteps" (*Essais* 3.122)–he avers that the quest of "the new Narcissus" leads nowhere: "The world is a treadmill" (*Journals* 7.22). Infinite as it is, then, and as Ducharme concurs, the inventiveness that unremitting reflexiveness permits also consigns the self-reliant to poverty of invention. Self-repetition, like running on (the spot) without end, must prove exhausting and cramping. Melville confirms the diagnosis. The plaint of Ishmael, that "Such is the endlessness, yea, the intolerableness of all earthly effort" (*Moby-Dick* 1.73), issues from a condition familiar to the self-styled drunken sailor spinning the universe and his life out of his own mind in Ducharme's *Les Enfantômes*. Alone in an attic room lit by a single candle, Vincent Falardeau finds himself lost in the words of his diary and log, going round and round "au fond de mon trou . . . de l'enfer" 'at the bottom of my hole . . . of hell' (280). Ducharme's solitary peripatetic sees that he is effectively "immobile": advance as he will, Vincent always arrives "à la même place" (232). Like creature, like author. Narrated by dreamers immobile in their abyss of unrest, Ducharme's fictions are hermetic diaries composed with magic monotony.

The rapprochement of the French-Canadian and the United States Renaissance explicitly informs the novels of Victory-Lévy Beaulieu, the author of book-length treatments of Kerouac (1972) and Melville (1978). And in no Québec novel are the problems attendant on *la renaissance* more prominently and poignantly put on display than in Beaulieu's 1974 poignantly metafictional *Don Quichotte de la Démanche*. Abel Beauchemin, its author-narrator, owns dozens of copies of *Moby-Dick*, none of which he can translate. The inscrutability of Melville's book is confirmed by Abel's inarticulate response: he babbles his way through it, sometimes from end to beginning. So cognate are the two solitudes, of reader and text, that Abel can claim he knows *Moby-Dick* by heart. The joke is in deadly earnest, for Abel's 'reading' of Melville's epic of communal narcissism exemplifies the cardinal paradox that persistently vexes Beaulieu and drives the writing of *Don Quichotte*. Beaulieu and his novel about writing that novel aim to create new life, but the work itself is a solitary's production: the inventiveness generated by the identification of reader and text, conceiver and conceived, comes at the price of infecundity. So snared in a contradiction of ends and means, the artist is bound ever to work at cross-purposes. The wrenchings undergone by Beaulieu as an autogeneal-autotelic artist who would make something other than himself correspond to "the difficult and painful birth-pangs of a nation on the verge of creating and inventing itself" (Mezei 44). Like Beaulieu's many other novels (no French-Canadian author has added more to neobaroque fiction's population of uneasy spectral dreamers), *Don Quichotte* enacts an artist's toiling to cut himself free of the trammels of self-enclosure and to express what his inviolable privacy makes inexpressible.

Don Quichotte narrates the story of its own gestation by an author who sees himself as a prey "au monde baroque de ses images" (25). Set to paper by a somnambulist lost in a subterranean world ruled by "l'impérieux pouvoir de l'imagination" (157), the novel reads like an encyclopaedia of neobaroque perplexities: Abel's writing is "un acte créateur abolissant toute réalité" (157). Like masturbating before a mirror (128), it is an act performed in perfect self-enclosure. His words he likens to black snakes on a field of white, their configuration the perfectly circular field of his anguish, "un champ d'angoisse parfaitement circulaire" (13); and his sentences remind him of hundreds of boot laces each knotted end to end. Kin to Ducharme's Bérénice, Abel is a swallower swallowed, and his self-consuming act of self-creation finds its logical term in death. The author-narrator of *Don Quichotte* sees himself spiralling down to hell with the PEQUOD, an effect of Promethean narcissism; and the book-child of his invention is stillborn, the product of a solitary's self-conception. As his narration ends, the feverish Abel imagines himself freezing, stock-still as he spirals in the innermost circle of his mind, trapped in his solitude. Like Melville's Ishmael, Beaulieu's Abel effectively finishes his tale a solitary "orphan," himself his own mother and father.

If the work is a veritable exemplum of self-creation postmodern-style, its disposing causes and their effects, *Don Quichotte* does not augur well for the rebirth by self-invention awaited by *Destin littéraire du Québec*. The novelist lights the way for the critic, and the future looms dark. Bessette, Aquin and Ducharme likewise serve as *éclaireurs*, providing obcure yet revealing illumination to those who would follow in the way of boundless autonomy. The solipsistic entrapment, sterility, inanition, ennui and suicide variously featured in their neobaroque novels sign French Canada's belated entry into the age of rebirth and invention.

Such gloom is not as inevitable as destiny, though, at least for those who find themselves closer to home in a literary culture prizing liberty of a less cramping kind. It is worth remembering that inventiveness in the contemporary French-Canadian novel is not limited to its neobaroque practitioners. There is another tradition, popular, older and nowhere near as sombre, of a narrative literature made for reading in community. It continues, for example, in Antonine Maillet's *Crache à Pic* (English title: *The Devil Is Loose!*). This imaginary chronicle of Acadian bootlegging during Prohibition, of seafaring thaumaturges practising their dizzying improvisations, sets out to rebuild the world in a carousal of fabulation. But the inventiveness that *Crache à Pic* celebrates is held in community, and the skills of improvisation that Maillet puts to use, like the stories she imagines, are ancestral. Working in the spirit of Albert the Great's *Liber de alchima*, she shares in the power to transform passed on from narrator to narrator in *Crache à Pic*, from generation to generation. The spirit blows where it lists, and Maillet follows its life-giving inspiration, an eau-de-vie, wherever it takes her, just as she sees her people to have done from their very beginning. Sociability and inventiveness go hand in hand in *Crache à Pic*, which near its end narrates the witnessing of an Acadian community before a judge who cannot understand their language nor follow their sprightly logic. Blessed with the vigour of the medieval *homo ludens*, each witness performs ably, to the delight and profit of the collectivity. Each teller is part of a whole, *Crache à Pic* emphasizes: "Chacun se sentait bien dans la peau de l'autre, et n'aspirait pas à l'autonomie" 'Each felt at home in the other, and did not aspire to autonomy' (333)–a condition alien to the restless solitaries as sea in the neobaroque novel of French Canada. Maillet, according to Tougas in 1982, can but repeat herself ("ne peut rigoureusement que se répéter"), tied as she is "à la langue folklorisante des Acadiens" (*Destin littéraire* 32). *Crache à Pic*, published two years later, argues otherwise. The past has gifts for the future; and, in this case, it promises to be a lively one made possible by the renewal of an ancient and unifying faith.

WORKS CITED

Aquin, Hubert. *L'Antiphonaire*. Montréal: Cercle du Livre de France. 1969.

----------. "The Cultural Fatigue of French Canada." *Contemporary Quebec Criticism*. Ed. and trans. Larry Shouldice. Toronto: U of Toronto P, 1979. 55-82.

----------. *Neige noire*. Montréal: Cercle du Livre de France, 1974.

----------. *Point de fuite*. Montréal: Cercle du Livre de France, 1971.

----------. *Prochain épisode*. Montréal: Cercle du Livre de France, 1965.

----------. *Trou de mémoire*. Montréal: Cercle du Livre de France. *Blackout*. Trans. Alan Brown. Toronto: Anansi, 1974.

Beaulieu, Victor-Lévy. *Don Quichotte de la Démanche*. Montréal: L'Aurore, 1974.

----------. *Jack Kérouac*. Montréal: Jour, 1972.

----------. *Monsieur Melville*. 3 vols. Montréal: VLB, 1978.

Bélair, Michel. *Franchir les miroirs*. Montréal: Parti Pris, 1977.

Bessette, Gérard. *L'Incubation.* Montréal: Déom, 1965.

Colie, Rosalie L. *Paradoxia Epidemica: The Renaissance Tradition of Paradox.* Princeton: Princeton UP, 1966.

Cope, Jackson I. *The Theater and the Dream.* Baltimore: Johns Hopkins UP, 1973.

Dorion, Gilles. "*L'Incubation.*" *Dictionnaire des oeuvres littéraires du Québec.* Ed. Maurice Lemire et al. Montréal: Fides, 1984. 4.428-30.

Ducharme, Réjean. *L'Avalée des avalés.* Paris: Gallimard, 1966.

----------. *Les Enfantômes.* Paris: Gallimard, 1976.

----------. *La Fille de Christophe Colomb.* Paris: Gallimard, 1969.

----------. *Le Nez qui voque.* Paris: Gallimard, 1967.

----------. *L'Océantume.* Paris: Gallimard, 1968.

Emerson, Ralph Waldo. *Complete Works.* Ed. Edward Waldo Emerson. 12 vols. Boston: Houghton, 1903-04.

----------. *Journals and Miscellaneous Notebooks.* Ed. W.H. Gilman *et al.* 16 vols. Cambridge: Belknap-Harvard UP, 1960-82.

----------. *Young Emerson Speaks.* Ed. A.C. McGiffert Jr.

Port Washington: Kennikat, 1968.

Glauser, Alfred. *Montaigne paradoxal.* Paris: Nizet, 1972.

Imbert, Patrick. "Révolution culturelle et clichés chez Réjean Ducharme." *Journal of Canadian Fiction* 25/26 (1979): 227-36.

La Bossière, "'En sens inverse': The Traditional Imagery of Alain Robbe-Grillet's New Art." *Selecta* (*PNCFL*) 1 (1980): 29-31.

Lasnier, Louis. "L'Ouroboros est un serpent qui se mord la queue." *Le Québec littéraire* 1 (1974): 92-116.

Lauzière, Arsène, and Gérard Bessette. "Gérard Bessette: l'art de préciser pour (s') (m') (l') expliquer." *Journal of Canadian Fiction* 25/26 (1979): 11- 25.

Leyda, Jay. *The Melville Log: A Documentary Life of Herman Melville (1819-1891).* 2 vols. New York: Harcourt, 1951.

Maillet, Antonine. *Crache à Pic.* Montréal: Leméac, 1984. *The Devil Is Loose!* Trans. Philip Stratford. Toronto: Lester and Orpen Dennys, 1986.

McGee, Thomas D'Arcy. "The Mental Outfit of the New Dominion." *Canadian Anthology.* Ed. Carl F. Klinck and Reginald E. Watters. 3rd ed., rev. and enl. Toronto: Gage, 1974. 63-66.

Melville, Herman. *Mardi.* 1849. 2 vols. New York: Russell & Russell, 1963.

----------. *Moby-Dick.* 2 vols. New York: Russell & Russell, 1963.

----------. *Pierre.* New York: Russell & Russell, 1963.

----------. *Poems.* New York: Russell & Russell, 1963.

Merivale, Patricia. "Hubert Aquin." *Dictionary of Literary Biography: Canadian Writers since 1960: First Series.* Ed. W.H. New. Detroit: Gale, 1986. 53: 8-17.

Mezei, Kathy. "The Literature of Quebec in Revolution." *The Human Elements.* Ed. David Helwig. Ottawa: Oberon, 1978. 31-51.

Montaigne, Michel de. *Essais.* Ed. Alexandre Micha. 3 vols. Paris: Garnier-Flammarion, 1969.

Parker, Hershel, and Harrison Hayford, eds. *"Moby-Dick" as Doubloon: Essays and Extracts, 1851-1970.* New York: Norton, 1970.

Pater, Walter. *The Renaissance.* New York: Modern Library, 1899.

Rousset, Jean. *Circé et le paon: la littérature de l'âge baroque en France.* Paris: Corti, 1954.

Rowe, J.C. *Through the Custom-House: Nineteenth-Century American Fiction and Modern Theory.* Baltimore: Johns Hopkins UP, 1982.

Schopenhauer, Arthur. *The World as Will and Idea.* Trans. R.B. Haldane. 3 vols. London: Routledge, 1883-86.

Smart, Patricia. "*Neige noire:* Hamlet and Coinciding Opposites." *Essays on Canadian Writing* 11 (1978): 97-103.

Sypher, Wylie. *Four Stages of Renaissance Style.* New York: Doubleday, 1955.

Tougas, Gérard. *Destin littéraire du Québec.* Montréal: Québec/Amérique, 1982.

----------. *Puissance littéraire des Etats-Unis.* Lausanne: L'Age d'Homme, 1979.

Whitman, Walt. "Letter to Ralph Waldo Emerson." *Norton Anthology of American Literature.* 2nd ed. New York: Norton, 1979. 1:2032-41.

XII

OF MONTAIGNE, DOSTOEVSKY AND GIDE: A *SOTIE*

[*'Living Record': Essays in Memory of Constantine Bida*, ed. Irena R. Makaryk (U of Ottawa P, 1991)]

Where there is life, there is contradiction,
and whever there is contradiction,
the comical is present.
Kierkegaard, *Concluding Unscientific Postcript*

Gide the Lucid. . . . Nabokov, *Pale Fire*

Before getting Robert Browning to pose with the subject centring his *Dostoïevsky* (1923), André Gide warns that the combining portraiture may prove too startling, be too "choquant" by its incongruity.[1] Why this advisory to contemporaries whose familiarity with *The Ring and the Book* and *Crime and Punishment* might reasonably be presumed, he does not expressly say. The silence tantalizes. Perhaps Gide is playing on his own reputation as professional *inquiéteur*, sounding a false alarm of the kind that signals self-parody. Such a speculation is inviting, since even those readers taxed to the limit by the relatively unperplexing Browning of *Dramatic Idyls: First Series* and with access to Dostoevsky criticism limited to what was readily available in the early twenties need not range out of soundings to discover affinities between Browning the author of "Ivan Ivanovitch" (the tale of a carpenter dispensed from the law when found holy in an axe-murder),[2] for example, and the *narodnik* sketched in the 1916 translation of Evgeny Soloviev's critical biography: for Dostoevsky as for the Russian peasant, "'Life according to Truth' (as distinguished from life according to rule and doctrine)."[3] As Bernard Grugière serves more recently to remind us, Gide does little to disturb a venerable commonplace in the English poet's reception at home and abroad: Browning is a defender of "l'esprit contre la loi."[4]

Nor is it evident that conventional critical wisdom in the twenties would have enjoined a great distancing of Browning from Dostoevsky on the fundamental and much-debated question of the end(s) proper to art. When, in his Introduction to the 1925 English edition of Gide's *Dostoïevsky*, Arnold Bennett avers that the book's subject is "made for its author"–like Dostoevsky, Gide is "a publicist of genius" who never slights "aesthetic concerns"–he repeats Soloviev's characterization of Dostoevsky as an "artist . . . in the publicist business,"[5] even as he engages, in principle, an issue debated as a matter of course among Browning's early-twentieth-century readers. "A publicist of exalted and impassioned temperament" had summarized Browning, although pejoratively, for the argumentative popular generalist John M. Robertson in 1903.[6] What to shock in Gide's combining portraiture? Not so very much at bottom, it would seem.

This is not to suggest for a moment, though, that Gide's performance as comparatist in *Dostoeïvsky* falls short of the standard of unconventionality normally expected of him. Quite the contrary. His actually complaisant invitation to consider Browning with Dostoevsky shows the celebrated wily gadfly in good form: it is an act of rhetorical misdirection well designed to draw attention away from the really subversive business at hand. Potentially more resistant to dating from an easy compliance with convention and continuing to retain power enough to jolt slumberers into thought is the meeting of minds that arguably constitutes the subtext of the book as a whole. And that quiet communion is all the more efficaciously subversive for being covertly advanced, lulling readers into dropping their defences. Only near the end of *Dostoïevsky*, as though saving for the last an almost frank disclosure of his study's single *bona fide* provocation, does Gide allow the secret conversation that it narrates to become less muted. He opens the final chapter with the confession that Dostoevsky is more often than not but "un prétexte" for his own thoughts, and immediately passes to an analogy from Montaigne's self-portrait: he is like the bees, who make honey from their preferred flowers. Then, in the best manner of the paradoxical old essayist of "De l'utilite et de l'honneste," who *says* he much prefers frankness to duplicity,[7] the adept counterfeiter Gide professes his horror of contradiction. "J'ai grande horreur des paradoxes, et ne cherche jamais à étonner," so he reads himself, and thereby makes it plain enough that he and Montaigne share more than just one turn of thought (*D* 252).

There is nothing new or striking, of course, in remarking Gide's predilection for Montaigne. Each, as commentators have repeated, is a Proteus vaunting his uncertainties and contradictions.[8] What does carry a considerable punch in Gide's Montaigne-like reading of Dostoevsky is the barely concealed notion which that action incorporates: that, like Dostoevsky and Gide, Montaigne and Dostoevsky are "made for each other."[9] That analogical extension jars in significant ways, calling up as it does a harmonious imaginary conversation of Dostoevsky with a Renaissance Roman Catholic whose writings never suffer mystical oracles or latter-day prophets gladly and which make no mention of Christ or the Synoptic Gospels. Ecclesiastes is Montaigne's ruling biblical text. More readily conjured is a Montaigne nodding in sympathy with the Grand Inquisitor of *The Brothers Karamazov*, whose convictions are normally taken to clash with Dostoevsky's. Seeing himself paralyzed by the limitless freedom that the endless contradictions of the private self confer, Montaigne frequently has recourse to the authority of ecclesiastical and civil laws to resolve his impasse. "Elles m'ont choisy party et donné un maistre," as he writes in "De l'utilite et de l'honneste" (*E* 3.10). John Cowper Powys' ardently oracular *Dostoïevsky* (1946)–ironically enough a work demonstrably indebted and sympathetic to Gide's reading–puts the matter with uncharacteristic economy: "the sagacious, philosophical, cool-blooded pragmatism" of Montaigne is alien to the flamboyant Russian prostrate "in demonic worship of Christ."[10] Not for Dostoevsky, certainly, the middling way of prudence, of a balancing actor intent on getting through the absurd hurly-burly of life with a minimum of suffering–or, less exaltedly, of fuss. The spectacle of Montaigne and Dostoevsky in concert has in it contradiction enough to induce bafflement or to provoke laughter.

But Gide is also true to his word in *Dostoïevsky* when he

says that he does not look to astonish, since the concordance which that study obliquely narrates has a positive foundation and is therefore only apparently paradoxical. What Gide's reading of Dostoevsky hints at, his *Essai sur Montaigne* (1929) posts in plain view, explicitly marking off the ground that he takes Montaigne and Dostoevsky to share. *L'inconstance*, the word abridging Montaigne's constant theme, brings Gide to pause, to reflect on "l'instabilité du moi"–and Dostoevsky is immediately summoned for confirmation: "Je crois que, à l'abri de ce mot, se cache précisément la vraie question, laquelle ne sera abordée que beaucoup plus tard par Dostoïevski."[11] No writer in the intervening three centuries has engaged the one substantive question, of humanity as fluxion incarnate. The character of the statement is as eloquent as the sentencc it pronounces. Gide's dogmatism here gives a measure of the importance he attaches to what is coincidental in their enterprise, while the violence his statement does to intellectual history (Gide's own knowledge of Pascal, Hume, Schopenhauer and Emerson, for example, must have risen in protest) suggests the depth of his need to reconcile the two writers. What, then, is at stake for Gide in his reading of Dostoevsky and Montaigne that he should go so far to bring them together? A comparison of his Dostoevsky with his Montaigne, focusing on the large consequences that "l'instabilité du moi" has for Gide's conception and practice of the artist's vocation, offers an answer.

The Gidean Dostoevsky and Montaigne are impartial tellers of unitary reality. Extraordinarily rich in those antagonisms and contradictions that for Gide constitute the essential grammar of existence, they are disinterested artists painting the dark and the bright with equal vividness: their synthetic vision faithfully renders the coincidence of opposites in a world of radical indeterminacy. Montaigne's equanimity before the Cimmerian ambiguity of the world he sees reflected in himself compels him to carry "une chandelle à Saint-Michel, l'autre à son serpent" (*E* 3.7), as the *Essai sur Montaigne* seems pleased to recall (38). The comparable double allegiance in Dostoevsky brings Gide to think of Rembrandt's *chiaroscuro* (*D* 61, 63, 75, 165), which pictures the integrating logic of Blake's *Marriage of Heaven and Hell*: "tout art est un lieu de contact . . . un anneau du ciel et de l'enfer" (*D* 247). Like the chameleon poet true to the "orbic rondure"[12] of the reality he pictures, the artist who would render truth whole must part ways with and be a "shock" to "the virtuous philosopher" intent on unambiguously disguishing right from wrong.[13] "Les autres [les moralistes] forment l'homme, je le récite," Gide cites from "Du Repentir" (*E* 3.20), which choice of vocation follows from the truth of things as they are, of "le perpétuel écoulement de toutes choses" (*ESM* 17). No ethical absolutes and therefore no moralizing for Montaigne, a creature of inveterate inconstancy swinging true to the come-and-go of the universal pendulum. No affirmation can hold for more than a moment; every proposition implies the existence of its opposite; everything is relative. Gide's Dostoevsky practises an art no less conceptually indeterminate:

> Ses idées sont presque jamais absolues; elles restent presque toujours relatives aux personnages qui les expriment, et je dirai plus: non seulement relatives à ces personnages, mais à un moment précis dans la

> vie de ses personnages. (*D* 154)

And when Gide remarks of Dostoevsky that he is "[un] homme d'aucun parti, craignant l'esprit qui divise," "éclairant équitablement une idée sur toutes ses faces" (*D* 40, 51), he in effect rehearses the ruling ideology of his *Essai sur Montaigne*.

Montaigne's essays and Dostoevsky's novels are model readerly texts for Gide. They enact that reflexiveness and relativity which mark the genuine work of art: "A Truth in art is that whose contradictory is also true."[14] Unconstrained by the logic of non-contradiction, the creative artist frees up his readers in return, liberating them for the creation of autonomous works of art by unfettered interpretation. Unreason calls unto unreason. Montaigne is exemplary in this regard, his inconsequence a stimulus to conflicting readings. "Il nous donne l'exemple et sans cesse se contredit et se trahit lui-même," according to Gide's portrait of the ideal critic (*ESM* 37-38). Dostoevsky's fictions are said to liberate in much the same way. "La cohabitation des sentiments contradictoires" gives Gide warrant to take from the works whatever meaning he will, to interpret them in the way he perceives Dostoevsky to have read the New Testament, by his private lights only (*D* 171, 226). As Gide's autocritical *Characters* (1925) confirms, he sees in the mirror of Montaigne and Dostoevsky the lineaments of his own activity as artist. Having likened himself to an indifferent spectator of "the conflict of ideas" in "the theatre within," he goes on to explain of his own method as a tutor of liberation aesthetics: "Each of my book turns against the *enthusiasts* of the preceding one. This ought to teach them to applaud me only for the right reason, to take each of my books solely for what it is: a work of art."[15] Gide would have no followers or writerly readers, only fellow artists. He would be interpreted as his Montaigne and his Dostoevsky interpret–impartially, integrally, autonomously.

It is not surprising, then, that Gide should break with these exemplary anti-dogmatists whenever they appear to him to break with the artist's creed. The image of the doctrinaire philosopher that *The Diary of a Writer* returns is understandably repugnant: "Dès que Dostoïevsky théorise, il nous déçoit" (*D* 154). As Gide acknowledges, there are times when Dostoevsky is something of a scandal to the faithful among beauty's devotees. Although a novelist above all, he is also social reformer, prophet, sage, preacher and moralist (*D* 78). The incongruity in that alliance of callings is a scandal to reason as well. And since bad faith among artists is at least as serious a matter as unreason in the virtuous philosopher, the conundrum that Dostoevsky sets for Gide is not one that he can take altogether lightly. The 'problematic' built into the conjunction of incompatible vocations seems to elude Bennett (Gide's "Dostoevsky in the end stands out not simply as a supreme psychologist and narrator, but also as a publicist of genius endowed with a prophet's view");[16] but it does altogether escape Gide, who on occasion makes quite explicit his view in the book so introduced that Dostoevsky has no real value as a dogmatist, that his social prophecies are inaccurate and his political teachings unenlightened when not downright pernicious (*D* 78). Dostoevsky the publicist is no impartial truth-teller and therefore no insightful artist. Not for Gide the smiling detachment of a Soloviev before the whimsies of "an artist with a consistent leaning towards propaganda."[17]

For all its earnestness, though, there is something inherently comical in Gide's separation of himself from Dostoevsky on the grounds of temporary anti-aestheticism. Bennett, so his performance on this occasion suggests, is unwitting straight man to the antic comedian when he celebrates the alliance of Dostoevsky with Gide, declaring as the "outstanding characteristic" of each "that he is equally interested in the aesthetic and in the moral aspect of literature."[18] If that is so, Gide's quarrel with the preaching partialist in Dostoevsky has a distinctly internecine aspect. Bearing as it does a striking resemblance to "the constant conflict . . . between the propagandist and creative artist" that centres Dostoevsky studies,[19] the scholarly combat over Gide's status corroborates that he, too, is a writer "at war with himself."[20] The dual entry for Gide in the enlarged edition (1980) of *The Columbia Dictionary of Modern European Literature* reports on as it repeats that war in microcosm.[21] His "position as a moral philosopher," so Justin O'Brien ends the first half of the article (reprinted from the 1947 edition), "has only grown with time." Anne L. Martin, of another mind in the second half, offers a 1980 recessional for the reading of Gide as "a great moral philosopher." "It is rather his position as one of the major *literary* figures of the century that has grown with time"; and this in accordance with Gide's stated wishes: as he repeatedly insisted, it is from "the point of view of art and not of morality that he ought to be judged." And that insistence, Martin recalls, "bore fruit in the years following his death [in 1951]." History, so she implies, has settled the conflict.

But the line of opposition bisecting the main body of Gide's faithful admirers (and dividing him against himself) is not so readily erased. Although unlisted in Martin's bibliography, it is O'Brien himself, in his *Portrait of André Gide* (1953), who fully confirms her recollection of Gide's "proper" reception after 1951, even as he annuls the division she logically pronounces between morality and art in the adjudication of Gide's works. Having established the principle that "all considerations other than the aesthetic" are to be "excluded," O'Brien subsequently charts Gide's progress as a moral thinker and concludes that his author had "ideas" to "convey," many of which "have already gained acceptance." Like subject, like painter: working as cross-purposes, O'Brien replicates the conflict in Gide, whom he sees "contradicting himself." Appropriately, the biographer takes Gide's "capital book on Dostoevsky" for his model.[22] As O'Brien is to his portrait of Gide, so is Gide to his Dostoevsky–a mirror for faithful reduplication by self-reflection.

Gide's autoscopic reading of Montaigne, on the other hand, offers a portrait in serenity. And the relaxation of tensions between the propagandist and artist evident in the *Essai sur Montaigne* is proportionate to the distance separating its subject from Dostoevsky. As Montaigne brings Gide to reflect, "les oeuvres . . . les plus belles" are those composed with an easy indifference: "En art, il n'y a pas de *sérieux* qui tienne" (*ESM* 19). Dostoevsky's, by contrast, are works of hard labour, dramatize "de si dures luttes" (*D* 23). If, as the Russian novelist's example suggests, the pages most rife with struggle, "les plus ardues, sont les plus belles" (*D* 60), it would seem to follow from the principle that Montaigne illustrates that theirs is a beauty purchased at the expense of the relaxed playfulness essential to art. Gide does have his differences with Montaigne as well, but they present no diriment impediment to a happy marriage of minds. He can critize the "Apologie de Raimond Sebond" for advancing "une sorte de doctrine" (*ESM* 19), but the work's argument is so manifestly suicidal (the apology is actually an attack) that it can hardly be taken *au sérieux* as philosophy. As for Montaigne's bending of the knee before ecclesiastical and civil authority, it can be dismissed without much thought as an act of prudence before the thought-police (*ESM* 28). Nor does the Roman Catholic's undisguised hostility to the Protestant reformers of his time cause the Protestant-raised Gide much serious difficulty. What his Montaigne objects to is their dogmatism, their confounding of private lights with public truth (*ESM* 34). The conviction that "une privée fantaisie . . . n'a qu'une jurisdiction privée" (*E* 1.168) is one that Gide as artist can endorse without the least reservation. As Montaigne repeatedly insists and confirms by his practice (much to Gide's approval), he is no wisdom trafficker but a fool, a player adept at flipping coins, seeing both sides of the medal. What teaching Montaigne does impart is a lesson easy for the anti-dogmatist to swallow, "le *libéralisme*" (*E* 39): *à chaque pied son soulier*, in literature as in politics and morality.

Unlike Gide's Dostoevsky, his Montaigne never seriously compromises the artist's calling, which is "not to nourish but to intoxicate," according to Gide's own distinction in "The Importance of the Public" (1903). The danger for artists in times when "the old doctrines no longer suffice," he goes on to warn in that lecture before the Court at Weimar, is that they may be tempted to feed the public's "hunger" for new answers. Those who succumb falsify their art, become *ersatz* moralists, "providers of substitutes."[23] Although he means it for praise in *Dostoïevsky* (no irony seems entended in the figuration of the novelist's works as "une source, où les nouvelles soifs de l'Europe se peuvent abreuver aujourd'hui" [*D* 1-2]), Gide in fact gives his readers good reason to number Dostoevsky among those who have so sinned against the craft. Montaigne is similarly recommended and thereby indirectly accused of wandering from the true path: his essays provide "un aliment susceptible de rassasier les faims divers" (*ESM* 12). But true to the artist's creed on this occasion, and no less to Montaigne, Gide goes on correct himself, picturing the old actor not as a provider of substantial nourishment, but as a distiller of whisky (*ESM* 32-33). Unlike the Gide of *Dostoïesky*, a double to his subject entangled in self-contradiction on the question of the end(s) proper to art, Montaigne sins against truth and beauty only venially, if at all.

There are, then, two salient points that emerge from a comparison of Gide's Dostoevsky with his Montaigne: that they are (not) made for each other, and that Gide's narration of their relationship has much to tell about the conflict at the centre of his own calling. He is able to bring them together to the extent that each is an impartial and playful teller of unitary reality who returns to Gide a picture of himself as an artist faithful to his own creed of anti-dogmatism. But his self-reading is not always so serene. Like the pleasure-loving Montaigne he pictures, Gide has his differences with Dostoevsky; and these quietly register the antagonism in his own dual activity and role as "great moral philosopher" and "major *literary* figure." "Se concilient les antagonismes [dans l'oeuvre de Dostoïevsky]," he writes, holding out the promise of that peace to come for those who take the Dostoevskian way (*D* 40). That reconciling power has at least one limitation, however, as Gide's criticism of Dostoevsky itself testifies: the doctrinaire prophet remains at odds with the indifferent artist.

And that antagonism of incompatible vocations is as poignant for the author of *Dostoïevsky* as it is comical for his disinterested reader, since Gide's repudiation of the dogmatic element in Dostoevsky effectively figures a break with himself, an indirect confessing of his own infidelity to the true aesthetic faith. A Dostoevsky fully in concert with Montaigne would have represented a resolution to the Gidean internecine conflict. But the creed that compels Gide to separate himself from the dogmatist in Dostoevsky and so sign the fundamental incongruity in his own double function as feeder and intoxicator guarantees irresolution. As close to Montaigne in artistic principle as Gide is, he seems closer yet in practice to the Dostoevsky he pictures with Browning, an artist in the publicist business or a publicist of exalted and impassioned temperament.

ENDNOTES

1. André Gide, *Dostoïevsky* (Paris: Plon-Nourrit, 1923) 237-38. Browning joins Blake, Doestoevsky, and Nietzsche to

form "une constellation." Abbreviated as *D* in the body of the essay.

2. Robert Browning, *The Poems and Plays* (New York: Modern Library, 1934) 1057-64.

3. Evgeny Soloviev, *Dostoïevsky: His Life and Literary Activity*, trans. C.J. Hogarth (London: George Allen and Unwin, 1916) 231.

4. Bernard Grugière, *L'Univers imaginaire de Robert Browning* (Paris: Klinskieck, 1979) 20.

5. Soloviev 213.

6. John M. Robertson, *Browning and Tennyson as Teachers* (London: A. and H.B. Bonner, 1903) 85.

7. Michel de Montaigne, *Essais*, edited and with an introduction by Alexandre Micha, 3 vols (Paris: Garner-Flammarion, 1965).

8. See, for example, Christopher Bettinson, "André-Paul-Guillaume Gide," in *Makers of Modern Culture*, ed. Justin Wintle (London: Routledge & Kegan Paul, 1981): 194-95.

9. Arnold Bennett, Introduction to Gide's *Dostoïevsky* (1925; repr. London: Secker and Warburg, 1952) 8.

10. John Cowper Powys, *Dostoïevsky* (1946; repr. New York: Haskell House, 1973) 148-49, 202. Like Gide, Powys is frequently reminded of Blake's *Marriage of Heaven and*

Hell as he considers "the most prolific compound of contradictory elements" in Dostoevsky (58).

11. André Gide, *Essai sur Montaigne* (1929; reprint, Paris: Corrêa, 1939) 22-23. Abbreviated *ESM* in the body of the essay.

12. Powys 93.

13. See W.C. Booth's Introduction to Mikhail Bakhtin's *Problems of Dostoevsky's Poetics*, trans. Caryl Emerson (Minneapolis: U of Minnesota P, 1984) xix-xx, which refers to Keats' figure for Shakespeare as it moves towards a consideration of "the essential, irreducible multicenteredness, or 'polyphony,'" of human life in Dostoevsky's fiction. Powys similarly likens Dostoevsky to Keats, a favourite for Gide among the English poets: both are concerned with "real reality" in the "*multi*verse" (69).

14. Oscar Wilde, "The Critic as Artist," in *The Artist as Critic*, ed. Richard Ellmann (1969; repr. Chicago: U of Chicago P, 1982) 432. References to Wilde are not difficult to find in Gide's *Dostoïevsky*.

15. André Gide, *Pretexts: Reflections on Literature and Morality* (London: Secker and Warburg, 1959) 308-09.

16. Bennett 9.

17. Soloviev 224.

18. Bennett 7.

19. David Magarshak, *Dostoevsky* (1963; repr. Westport: Greenwood, 1975) 311. Nikolai Berdyaev's *L'Esprit de Dostoïevsky* (1921), trans. Alexis Neville (Paris: Stock, 1945), attempts to resolve the conflict by arguing that Dostoevsky should be considered "non du point de vue moral, mais du point de vue ontologique" (155). Robert Lord's *Dostoevsky: Essays & Perspectives* (Berkeley and Los Angeles: U of California P, 1970) dismisses Berdyaev's reading and yet has recourse to a cognate solution: "The only possible remedy is Beauty, the aesthetic sense, which alone can heal and make whole" (234). Lord, Todorov and many other commentators are of mind on this score, especially as it pertains to *The Underground Man* and that Dostoevskian masterpiece of negative theology, *The Idiot.*

20. Magarshack 3.

21. "André Gide," in *The Columbia Dictionary of Modern European Literature*, 2nd ed. Jean-Albert Bédé and W. B. Edgerton (New York: Columbia UP, 1980): 304-06.

22. Justin O'Brien, *Portrait of André Gide: A Critical Biography* (1953; repr. New York: Octagon, 1977) 5, 14, 353.

23. Gide, *Pretexts* 56-58.

XIII

OF MACLENNAN OR CONRAD

[excerpt from "'Endlessly Rocking': MacLennan's Archaic Sedations," in *Hugh MacLennan*, ed. Frank M Tierney (Ottawa: U of Ottawa P, 1994)]

The bard so sage and staid . . . as if transformed to stone / Marvelled the [Wizard's] song could with such sweet art unite / The lights and shades of manners, wrong and right. James Thomson, *The Castle of Indolence*

We had better, perhaps, content ourselves with a kind of sad moderation. Rilke, *Duino Elelgies* 2

. . . the sage's indolence . . . .
Pope, *An Essay on Man*, Epistle II

"Opium is not so stupifying to many persons as an Afternoon Sermon," Dean Swift once taunted the "lukewarm" among his congregation, who had prudently chosen "safe and convenient Stations and Postures for taking their Repose" (*Sermons* 210, 211, 212). The preacher's humbling sarcasm in "Upon Sleeping in Church" accords well with the Socratic wit of *Gulliver's Travels*: the wry satirist satirizes himself and thereby avoids seeming "as violent for truth as the most passionate exponent of divinity" (Carnochan 342). Swift's habitual pose is familiar to Hugh MacLennan, a student and teacher of *Gulliver's Travels* (Kroetsch 138; cf. *Voices in Time* 123) whose fiction shows signs of a similarly driven self-relexiveness.[1] In *Return of the Sphinx*, for example, the portrait of an officious master of a doomed ship that looks "like something out of a Conrad novel" (32) bears some resemblance to sketches of MacLennan by some of his critics: "The captain . . . smelled sourly of opium and he punctuated the day by unnecessary announcements delivered from the bridge by megaphone" (32-33).

There is irony here more than enough to induce immediate laughter, with some in reserve for the spectacle of another master-teacher busy with forging "the Canadian conscience" (Buitenhuis 80) in tales the "hazy," "indecisive finales" of which have left many a reader suspended in ambiguity (Cockburn 148). Just as the increasingly sceptical Dr. Conrad Dehmel of *Voices in Time* can be brought to smile not only at the vanity of his own sustained effort to achieve a universal "Moral Philosophy" (166), but also at the ingenuousness of his romantic father, who once acted on "a divine revelation" from a Conrad novel (137), so MacLennan can join with his critics to poke fun at the inconsequence built into his own double function as aesthete for sedation and earnest life-guide, even as he serves a witty Socratic caution to readers immoderate enough to invest his announcements with an authority only slightly below Holy Writ's.

There is poetic and critical justice in MacLennan's choice of a Conradian text for an artless romantic's sacred reading, for if there is one posture that Conrad abjures, it is that of the artist as trustworthy pilot. As Conrad warns in "A Familiar Preface" to *A Personal Record*, he is never to be mistaken for "a sage": that is, "a moralist" concerned with teaching others how they should live (xii-xiii). The business proper to the artist, so he professes in the Preface to *The Nigger of the* NARCISSUS, is to bear true testimony to the enigmatic spectacle of things as they are. That and no more. Striving to render the least possible injustice to the ethically ambiguous truth–"the incapacity to achieve anything distinctly good or evil is inherent to our earthly condition. Mediocrity is our mark," "indolent" Marlow is made to reflect in *Chance* (23, 253)–the Conradian artist aspires to the achievement of music, "the art of arts" (Preface, *NoN*), since best attuned to the darkling grammar of the world as it is. And, like the chant of the worker bees in *Heart of Darkness*, the art of the novelist faithful to that grammar of ethical indeterminacy naturally works to sedate: the sound that comes out from "the black, flat wall of the woods" has "a strange narcotic effect" upon the temperamentally lazy Marlow's "half-awake senses" (141). Given a choice of two nightmares, the seer into the heart of the human enigma takes neither.[2] He is disposed, rather, to finish his tale as he began it, seated "in the pose of a meditating Buddha" sans lotus-flower (50, 162), perhaps only slightly more elegant in his indolence than the protagonist of Conrad's first novel, an *homme moyen sensuel* who comes to find lasting refuge from conflict and pain in an opiate haze and death in a "House of Heavenly Delight" (*Almayer's Folly* 205).

"To choose is painful," the sedate MacLennan agrees

in principle (*Thirty* 249). On this score at least, the musical thinkers MacLennan and Conrad see eye to eye. In practice, though, MacLennan takes his balancing act one step farther, into a region studiously avoided by Conrad. Given a choice of the artist's way or the moralist's, Conrad takes the former; MacLennan, on the other, chooses both. And nowhere is that difference more sharply indicated than in the responses assigned to their seers as they reflect on the ultimate experience of human ambiguity. "I have wrestled with death," Marlow recounts in *Heart of Darkness*, and goes on to meditate with a scrupulous scepticism:

> It is the most unexciting contest you can imagine. It takes place in an impalpable grayness, with nothing underfoot . . . without clamour, without glory, without the great desire of victory, without the great fear of defeat, in a sickly atmosphere of tepid scepticism, without much belief in your own right, and still less in that of your adversary. If such is the form of ultimate wisdom, then life is a greater riddle than some of us think it to be. (150-51)

Doubt answers unto doubt, darkness unto darkness in Conrad's perdurably ambiguous tale of a blindfolded Enlightenment sage's mission to the unilluminated. The wisely passive hero of *The Watch That Ends the Night* also looks on the enigma of the final human struggle, but with a distinctly unMarlovian eye, to preaching. "Go to the musicians," George Stewart enjoins the reader who would fully experience the last truth in art:

> In the work of a few musicians you can hear every aspect of this conflict between light and dark within the soul. You can hear all the contradictory fears, hopes, desires of Everyman fissioning and fusing into new harmonies out of the dead ones.

What follows from the happy *discordia concors* comprehensively rendered by Bach and Beethoven is the injunction (appropriated from 1 Corinthians 13:7) "to endure all things, suffer all things, hope all things, believe all things" (343-44). Self-confessed agnostic theologian George Stewart has faith enough to infer *ought* and *ought not* from *is* and *is not*, to draw para-biblical authority from distinterested art. It is a form of inconsequence alien to the Conradian sense, in practice as in principle, of the end proper to the artist's craft: "the aim of creation cannot be ethical at all . . . ; its object is purely spectacular" (*Personal Record* 93).

The moralizing difference between *Heart of Darkness* and *The Watch That Ends the Night* gives a measure, then, of MacLennan's straying from the strict aesthetic way and his fidelity, at bottom, to the example set by eighteenth-century preachers of balance-and-mean.[3] As Barrie Davies suggestively remarks, "MacLennan felt obliged to teach as thoroughly and representatively as Samuel Johnson did in 'The Vanity of Human Wishes'" (110)– and, to extend the comparison, as did Tolstoy in *War and Peace*.[4] Written "for and about a people that lived spiritually in the eighteenth century" (O'Connor 127-28),[5] Tolstoy's epic antithesis enshrines indolence as the highest philosophic virtue, the spiritual mode of wise passiveness.[6] The same might be said of the oeuvre left by melancholic McLennan, representative Canadian sage committed to the task of disseminating, for better or for worse, the lulling musical wisdom of the *Deus prudens*, the divine principle of (neo)classical equipoise.

ENDNOTES

1. There are times, clearly, when the high ferocity in Swift's assailing of human vanity suggests a lapse into zeal. But as the opening of his "Brotherly Love" serves to illustrate, the intent of Swiftian aggression is finally defensive, to incite readers to a prudential moderation by driving them to take cover on the middle ground:

> This Nation of ours hath been for an Hundred Years past, been infested by two Enemies, the Papists and the Fanaticks, who each,in their Turns, filled it with Blood and Slaughter, and for a time destroyed the Church and Government. The Memory of these Events hath put all true Protestants on their Guard against both these Adversaries, who, by Consequence, do equally hate us. . . . (*Sermons* 172)

L.K. Barnett detects other (and related) "strategies for self-defense" in Swift's poems of self-portraiture: "The characteristic structure of his poetry is a dialectical clash between opposing versions of Swift, one of which embodies the principle of unity" (48). For "unity" I would substitute "balance." MacLennan's philosophical auto-reflection evinces a similar dialectical structure: "his argument was for wholeness," Eslpeth Cameron remarks of MacLennan's defining of himself in the 1930s, against British writers or those with no thought "on the one hand" and American writers or those with no feeling "on the other" (108).

2. In MacLennan's fiction as in Swift's satires and sermons, the notion of balance-and-mean is itself subject to a moderating irony. One should be moderate even in one's moderation, lest it become mere temporizing or something else even less virtuous, as the portrait of Polycarpe Drouin in *Two Solitudes* would seem to suggest: "'The trouble with the English is they got no moderation,' Drouin said. 'Now me, I'm behind the war all right, only not too much'" (63). Three faded flags hang from his shop-front: "One was the Red Ensign of the British Mercantile Marine with a Canadian crest in the corner. Another was a square white cross on an azure field with a fleur-de-lis in each corner which had come to be accepted as the flag of Quebec. The third and middle one was the white and yellow ensign of the Pope" (58). MacLennan has additional fun with the golden mean in *Two Solitudes*, in the portrayal of a financier gifted with "the sense of balance": Huntley McQueen's Montreal is located at "the exact centre of the country's heart . . . at the precise point where the interlocking directorates of Canada found their balance" (107, 105).

3. Cameron draws this likeness between George Stewart in *The Watch That Ends the Night* and the Marlow of *Heart of Darkness*: each "travels down into his soul to find only the

perversion of human energy" (286). See La Bossière, *The Progress of Indolence,* for a reading of MacLennan's oeuvre in the light of neo-Augustan Huxley's early essays on the virtue of the "*Deus prudens*" as the vice of "Accidie" transvaluated by moderns into "a lyrical emotion."

4. MacLennan writes in his Introduction to *The Time Gatherers*: "I have long ago learned that it is impossible to persuade anyone to change his attitudes by telling him to change them. Conrad was right when he said that the writer's task is to make you hear, to make you feel, above all to make you see" (4). T.D. MacLulich judges that, in *Voices in Time* at least, MacLennan "ignores his own warning" (117). Cameron recalls of MacLennan's students at McGill in the 1950s: indisposed to "false optimism," they found Conrad the writer whose "mood" most appealed to them (271).

5. R.F. Christian comments on Tolstoy's tidying up of General Kutuzov in the process of composing *War and Peace*: the military hero of "wise passiveness" is "stripped in the novel of his more unprepossessing characteristics (some of which appear the the drafts but not in the final version) and his lechery and sloth are played down" (1458). What "Tolstoy and Dostoevsky" together provide, according to the presiding spirit of *The Watch That Ends the Night*, "is not a literature of understanding. You couldn't pin it down. That's why it broke all the limits and was true, because the truth couldn't be pinned down" (287). In *Under Western Eyes*, the practical wisdom that flows from that mystic, ambiguous truth is summarized by "a good-natured

man" who, diffident like MacLennan's George Stewart, shrinks "from taking definite sides in a violent family quarrel" (11): immediately following his encounter with the drunken hostler Ziemianitch and the inspired bomber Haldin, the philosophic Razumov reads in "the sacred inertia" of the Russian soul "a guarantee of duration, of safety, while the travail of maturing destiny went on - a work not of revolutions with their passionate levity of action and their shifting impulses - but of peace" (33). Douglas Spettigue, reading *Return of the Sphinx* and *The Watch That Ends the Night* in the context of modern "wise hopelessness," sees reflected in those novels "a Dostoevskian faith in the power to endure" (160). *Gulliver's Travels* and Dostoevsky's *The Idiot* sit side by side on a bookshelf in *Voices in Time* (123).

6. As George Woodcock observes, "*War and Peace* is the novel and Tolstoy the novelist whom MacLennan admires most of all" (38). Cameron agrees (269, 272).

WORKS CITED

Barnett, Louise K. *Swift's Poetic Worlds*. Newark: U of Delaware P, 1981.

Buitenuis, Peter. *Hugh MacLennan*. Toronto: Forum House, 1969.

Cameron, Elspeth. *Hugh MacLennan: A Writer's Life*. Toronto: U of Toronto P, 1981.

Carnochan, W.B. "Gulliver: The Satirist on Himself." In Norton Critical Edition of *Gulliver's Travels*. Ed. Robert A. Greenberg. 2nd ed. New York: W.W. Norton, 1971. 338-50.

Christian, R.F. "The Theme and Art of *War and Peace*." In Norton Critical Edition of *War and Peace*. Trans. Louise and Aylmer Maude. Ed. George Gibian. New York: W.W. Norton, 1966. 1456-80.

Cockburn, Robert. *The Novels of Hugh MacLennan*. Montreal: Harvest House, 1969.

Conrad, Joseph. *The Works of Joseph Conrad*. 21 vols. London: Dent, 1946-54.

Davies, Barry. "Commentary on Eli Mandel." *Hugh MacLennan*: 1982. Ed. Elspeth Cameron. Toronto: Canadian Studies Programme, University College, U of Toronto, 1982. 109-13.

Kroetsch, Robert. "Hugh MacLennan: An Appreciation." In *Hugh MacLennan: 1982.* Ed. Elspeth Camerson. 135-39.

La Bossière, Camille R. *Joseph Conrad and the Science of Unknowing*. Fredericton: York P, 1979.

----------. *The Progress of Indolence.* Toronto: York P, 1997.

MacLennan, Hugh. "Introduction," *The Time Gatherers*. Ed. Gertrude Katz. Montreal: Harvest House, 1970. 1-5.

----------. *Return of the Sphinx*. New York: Charles Scribner's Sons, 1967.

----------. *Thirty and Three*. Ed. Dorothy Duncan. London: Macmillan, 1955.

----------. *Two Solitudes*. Toronto: Macmillan, 1945.

----------. *Voices in Time*. Toronto: Macmillan, 1980.

MacLulich, T.D. *Hugh MacLennan.* Boston: Twaye, 1983.

O'Connor, Frank. *Mirror in the Roadway: A Study of the Modern Novel*. New York: Knopf, 1956.

Spettigue, D. "Beauty and the Beast." In *Hugh MacLennan.* Ed. Paul Goetsch. Toronto: MHR, 1973. 157-61.

Swift, Jonathan. *Irish Tracts (1720-1723) and Sermons*. Vol. 9 of *The Prose Writings of Jonathan Swift*. Ed. Herbert David and Louis Landa. New York: New York UP, 1968.

Woodcock, George. *Hugh MacLennan*. Toronto: Copp Clark, 1969.

XIV

POP CONRAD AND CHILD'S PLAY

(à Gilbert Joseph, Lise Marie et Marie-Loranda-Yolande)

[*The Dalhousie Review* 71 (1991)]

> "We are the creatures of our light literature more than is generally suspected. . . .". Conrad, *Chance*
>
> "Behold the boy." Conrad, "A Preface to Thomas Beer's *Stephen Crane*"
>
> "I made play in this world of dust. . . ." Proverbs 8:31, as translated by David Jones in *Epoch & Artist*

1

In February 1921, the diplomat Alexis Saint-Leger Leger (who would come to sign his poems Saint-John Perse) wrote to Conrad from Beijing: "Je vous écoute encore me réciter les premières laisses des *Jumblies* d'Edward Lear, où vous m'assuriez trouver 'l'esprit des grandes aventures' plus que dans les meilleurs auteurs de mer, comme Melville" (*Oeuvres complètes* 886; cited as *O*).[1] That encounter, remembered from their long nightly conversations at the novelist's home in Kent some nine years before, had made a deep impression on a Perse then in his mid-twenties. His letter to André Gide dated 7 December 1912 registers the force of the effect: "Si je pouvais me permettre jamais de citer mon plaisir ou mon goût, je ne recommenderais [qu'Edward] Lear, seul poète d'une race qui me semble la race même poétique" (*O* 781).[2] The impression was to be a lasting one. In September 1947, shortly after the publication of his prose-poem *Vents*, with its reprise of the spirit animating Lear's crew of a sieve bound for the Western Sea and the Hills of the Chankly Bore,[3] Perse recalled (for G. Jean-Aubry) Conrad's sallying into the "nonsense lyrics ('The Jumblies'!) brought down from the the children's room" in the summer of 1912 (Little, "Letter" 264). As to how perdurably alive the memory and effect of that reading remained for Perse, his letter of 9 September 1958 to the American writer Mina Curtiss leaves little doubt: especially remarked among the genial spectres haunting the seventy-one-year-old poet's new home on the Giens Peninsula are "Stevenson, et Conrad, et le cher Edward Lear" (*O* 1062).

Given the constancy of Perse's commitment to "la pleine liberté d'esprit" epitomized by *The Jumblies* (*O* 889, 1005), Lear's exclusion from Perse criticism is remarkable, even mystifying. Given the leaning of Perse's commentators to high gravity, on the other hand, that absence is understandable. Hugo von Hofmannsthal, for one, in his 1929 preface to *Anabase*, places its author at the head of "les saints nouveaux" to be born out of France (*O*, "Notices et notes" 1108). Avers another follower, "Saint-John Perse est bien le poète qui satisfait en nous l'incoercible et redoutable *besoin d'absolu*" (*Honneur* 236). The complete book of Perse, according to a recent monograph, is a palimpsest bible, "un texte sacré qu'on vénère" (Favre 110-11). Recognition of the funny Lear in a poet so solemnified would seem out of place, as Roger Little implies in his one-sentence response to Perse's venturing into *The Jumblies* with Conrad: Lear is a "surprising point of reference for two essentially serious-minded writers" ("Letter" 263).[4] Even in Erika Ostrovsky's *Under the Sign of Ambiguity*, where the design is to upend Perse's "idolizers" in the name of the comic unreason that animates his oeuvre, Lear's place is outside the margins. The merriment of *The Jumblies* is displaced by Nietzsche's (Ostrovsky 52), and this in spite of "le mécanisme d'esprit" Perse found and rejected in the autobiographer of *Ecce Homo*: "Ce n'est pas la contradiction en elle-même qui me déçoit chez lui," as he explains in a letter of February 1909 to Gabriel Frizeau, "mais son impuissance à en poursuivre le train jusqu'à sa libre exploitation" (*O* 742-43). Nietzschean unreason is a dead end, for adults only (*O* 927). It should come as no surprise that some of the youngest students at the Lycée de Marseille shared with Guillaume Apollinaire and Rainer Maria Rilke an enthusiasm for Perse's *Eloges* and its "Images à Crusoé."[5]

On the face of it, the main record of Conrad's reception among sober adult students has a very different story to tell. Unlike Perse's commentators, Conrad's have tended (and with good reason) to be anything but silent on their author's reading of popular "juvenile" literature. And yet, the manner Conrad criticism has generally found suitable for the treatment of that literature suggests a substantial accord with the solemnizing readers of Perse. In compliance with the invitation extended by Conrad's fictions that have come to be especially prized for their riddling of the conventional, the narratives of adventure popular with Victorian and Edwardian readers enter modern Conrad studies but to have their value and conventions undermined, contrasted with high art's. Reference to Stevenson and other "boyish" questers after "a pure dispassionate adventure" (Stevenson, *Travels* 148) serves to gauge the maturity of Conrad's achievement: he better understood "the temptations which beset the romantic dreamer" (Kiely 103). For those readers who, like Gary Geddes, would raise the stock of the often devalued "later novels," Conrad never relinquished the art of "the ironic romance" (6). As Geddes intimates, the refiguring of Conrad in Lowry's *Under the Volcano* affords a model for a properly bifocal reading of the Conradian corpus as a whole.[6] "Having stopped growing when seventeen," Lowry's greying protagonist continues to take inspiration from Edward Lear and *Peter Rabbit*, now bottled with mescal (*UTV* 22, 39, 44, 138,213).[7] "A kind of more lachrymose 'Lord Jim'" unable to distinguish his life from "a quixotic oral fiction" (39), Consul Geoffrey Firmin has his quest for love and light and honour ended at the bottom of a hell-pit with a dead dog for a compañero. What role juvenile literature finds itself assigned in comparably discerning critical responses to Conrad at his darkling best is to install the superior realism and value of an art mirroring the peripeties of (dis)enchantment in a world of unremitting ambiguity. The high seriousness served by the silence of Perseans on Lear, Conrad criticism achieves by ironic contrast. In each case, the greater the writer's distancing from popular light reading, the weightier or more adult his achievement.

By the same token, of course, any apparent reduction in that distancing invites devaluation, affords a measure of artistic decline. According to the now institutionalized charting of achievement-and-decline, Conrad's irregular slide downward after *Under Western Eyes* hit bottom in his last completed romances. In *The Rescue*, finds one critic, Conrad created a hero like those of Fenimore Cooper and Captain Frederick Marryat, "long on pragmatic energy, short on both brains and moral intention." Captain Tom Lingard of the LIGHTNING is a juvenile hero in a book for boys (Gurko 13, 230). Old Conrad's reach in his tale of Master-Gunner Peyrol suffers a similar abbreviation. "At best a true adventure story for boys," pronounces Albert Guerard, *The Rover* "is at its worst a coarse-grained study of feeble-minded and inarticulate people"; to consider it otherwise would be "to take simple matters very seriously" (284, 285). Far from inviting comparison with Schopenhauer or Nietzsche, as the "major" Conrad does (Said 65-76, Bonney 3-11, Land 192-94), the Conrad in full swansong brings light Stevenson and company to mind (Schwarz 140-43), which comparative declining recalls, in its turn, the history of reader-reception built into Timothy Findley's *The Wars*: Conrad's association is with the *Boy's Own Annual*, *Chums* and Charles Kingsley's *Water-Babies* (65, 95, 107). Modern comparative readings unfriendly to *The Rescue* and *The Rover* prolong the history of that association, though to sheerly reductive effect: Conrad's last romances are not to be taken much more seriously than the juvenile works they are seen to resemble. Lear's exclusion from Perse criticism effectively spares the poet-priest-metaphysician of *Anabase*,

Vents and *Amers* from any potential lowering or indignity of the kind.

2

"I was never one of those wonderful fellows that would go afloat in a wash-tub for the sake of the fun," Conrad confesses in *A Personal Record* (18-19). And no sage, it goes without saying, would go to sea in a bowl. His literary craftsmanship has been no less sober. The verity Conrad would share with his readers, in the words of his essay "Books," extends beyond "the truth of a childish theatrical ardour in the game of life" such as one finds in fiction "the least worthy of the name"; his chronicling of "the adventures of mankind amongst the dangers of the kingdom of the earth" has a more "serious intention" (*Notes on Life and Letters* 6-7). In private correspondence Conrad's reaction to readers suspected of taking him for an improvident lover of adventure could be less composed, altogether direct. He protests in a letter of January 1902 to the literary agent James Brand Pinker: "Am I a confounded boy? I have had to look death in the eye once or twice. It was nothing. I had not then a wife and child. It was nothing to what I have to go through now pen in hand before what to *me* spells failure. I am no sort of airy R.L. Stevenson. . ." (cited from Karl 491). The intensity of that more personal response lends authority to Frederick R. Karl's assessment of the comparisons often made by Conrad's reviewers, with writers of popular romance: they were "superficial," "inept" (546).

Conrad, though, did not entirely lack for discriminating readers adept in the literature of adventure and able to understand, like Perse, that the Conradian craft of fiction was no mere “jeu littéraire” for the entertainment of bored tourists or pure aesthetes (*O* 888).[8] In Pierre MacOrlan’s *Petit Manuel du parfait aventurier* (completed 1920), for instance, the distinguishing of “l’aventurier passif” (“un sportsman documenté” in fairyland, exemplified by Stevenson) from “l’aventurier actif” (a responsible professional, disciplined in confronting unimaginary hazards), prepares a reading of Conrad as ironist, “un écrivain à ce genre infiniment rare et précieux qui comprend les aventuriers à la fois passifs et actifs” (193, 195, 200). No less studied than MacOrlan in the ways of paradox and adventure, G.K. Chesterton locates the Polish romancer, with “his record of hard or violent adventure at sea,” in the company of those “who introduced a sort of irony into [the Stevensonian] fairyland”: Conrad’s fiction connects the “fantastic element” with “the more realistic” in a brilliantly individual way (*Common Man* 89-90).

The comparative readings by ironists MacOrlan and Chesterton certainly accord with Conrad’s own sense of his relation to “airy R.L. Stevenson,” even as the disjunction they describe is weak rather than strong. Just as certainly, those readings do nothing to infirm the thinking comparatist’s perennial rule, *simile non est idem*. As their example shows, similarity and sameness are not quite the same thing: no comparison without difference, and without difference no irony.

Nor do those readings gainsay the recent observation from John Coates, that the division between “high-brow” and “low-brow,” “juvenile” and “adult” in Edwardian literary culture was “in some ways less marked than it has subsequently become” (279, 281). That division could be ambiguous, as in the Conrad recognized by MacOrlan and Chesterton. For MacOrlan, Conrad's is a rare comprehension, encompassing as it does the boyish Stevensonian adventurer and the adult active adventurer in such a way as to make impossible a clear separating out of the boy from the man. The Chestertonian reading concurs, but with a difference suggestive of a closer attention to the collocation of past and present, the juvenile and the adult in Stevenson's own romancing as well. To Chesterton's way of reading, the Conradian vision of (dis)enchantment represents a development in "what may be called the Stevensonian stereoscopic view; the looking at the same object in a double fashion, with the eye of the adult and of the child" (*Common Man* 89-90). Chesterton need adduce no narrative by name in the presence of a public au fait. The grown-up Jim Hawkins, as readers of Stevenson's first and least complex romance will recall, can reflect on the impercipience of the fanciful lad who (among other follies) once went to sea in a bowl of hides–"But I was only a boy, and I had made up my mind" (*Treasure Island* 148)–even as his storytelling testifies that he has not altogether changed his mind. And so it is for the not quite sober(ed) Captain Marlow of *Youth*, for example, sadder but not much wiser than the second mate who sailed for the East, romantically, in the do-or-die old JUDEA. The old salt has seen a thing or two since those days, but he still prefers the soldier Burnaby to the philosopher Carlyle (*Youth* 7). If "stereoscopy" is not the *mot juste* for the Conradian seeing of past and present, it does not miss by much.

Criticism that would sharply distinguish the highbrow and the adult from the lowbrow and the juvenile in the writings of Conrad has a lesson to take, then, from Mac Orlan and Chesterton. Attuned to the writing of the epoch out of which Conrad fashioned his chronicles of humanity's adventures amongst the dangers of the earth, they were in an ideal position to appreciate that the line separating "child's play" (*Youth* 11) from "man's play" (*Rescue* 121) can be devilishly hard to draw in a storied universe where all enterprise, however grave, recalls as it partakes of "a child's game in a nursery" (*Victory* 213). There is, in addition, room enough in MacOrlan and Chesterton to accommodate the grimly democratic conviction that "every age is fed on illusions" (*Victory* 94), a principle set aside by a grown-up Conrad criticism secure in its scaling of value according to time of life. The child is father to the Conradian man of (dis)enchantment, for better or for worse. Conrad, it is worth remembering, did come to figure the serious professional undertakings of his own "literary childhood" as "but paper boats, freighted with a grown-up child's dreams and launched innocently upon that terrible sea [of human life]" (*Last Essays* 143).

3

"The simple sense of wonder at the shapes of things . . . is the basis of spirituality as it is of nonsense," so Chesterton gives the riposte to the nineteenth-century solemnities of utility and positivist science in his "A Defence of Nonsense" (1901). Against that orthodoxy well designed for the drabbing or unmarrowing of things, he sets the comic paradoxy of Lear and "the huge and undecipherable unreason" of the Book of Job (*Stories, Essays & Poems* 127). For Perse, too, the topsy-turvydom, joking and jumbling of "le cher Edward Lear" keep faith with the substantial reality of the Creation, a vast nonsense syllabary enigmatic "comme une Bible," rife with wonders and terrors "qui passent l'entendement" (*O* 199, 306). "L'absurde," by Perse's reckoning in a letter of September 1917 to Paul Valéry, "est une incitation légitime de l'esprit," a justified flying in the face of those killing restrictions imposed on the spirit by "le lamentable positivisme" of the prolonged Victorian Age (*O* 823-24).

Early in that age, the often grotesquely funny fictions of Captain Marryat, prankster and punster extraordinaire, had evinced a similar commitment to the spirit of great adventures sapped by the solemn among the savants of his time. "The Creation," Marryat has the hero of his *Masterman Ready* consider, is "odd" in the sense that is is "fearfully and wonderfully fashioned" (193). Partaking as it does of "this strange world" big with jest, "a riddle," as the text of his *Japhet in Search of a Father* repeatedly signs, humankind is no less an abode of mystery: "we are odd mixtures" (234, 82, 68). What is life but a "wandering in mystery, and awe, and doubt," do-or-die Philip Vanderdecken is given cause to wonder in *The Phantom Ship* (200), a tale of "the agony of suspense" suffered by a humanity in the midst of endless contradictions (8, 127, 142, 206, 329).

James Fenimore Cooper, one of Stevenson's (and Conrad's) masters, is of a mind with his contemporary on that score. In *The Sea Lions*, for example, where all things "are to be taken by their opposites," Cooper provides this gloss on the moral universe of the Antarctic wanderers Daggett and Roswell: "It is all a mystery, as is the creation itself" (231, 56). To "those unbelievers in the marvelous" the 1849 preface of *The Pilot* recommends that they look again and see: "It is probable that a large proportion of our acts are more the result of sudden impulses and accident than of that reason of which we so much boast" (3). The field of unreason that is the physical and moral universe (typically co-figured as "the deep" in Cooper) constitutes "a marvel, or a downright mystification"; in the words of his tragicomic romance *Homeward Bound; or, The Chase*: "*c'est une équivoque*" (509, 482). The "funny cosmogony" spelled by Lear, who saw himself as a wanderer in "the dusty twilight of the incomprehensible" (Holbrook x, xxiii), bespeaks just that kind of awe.

Conrad's response to the dogmatics of a practical and scientific reason taken with its own gravity is likewise "spiritual." "Life and the arts follow dark courses, and will not turn aside to the brilliant arc-lights of science," he gives the twitting reply to the argument of an author who would marry the lastest scientific learning with poetics (*Notes on Life and Letters* 74). In another review from 1910, of a book of religious belief based on and assured by reason, Conrad's conviction is as clear as his irony is telling: "Science, having in its infinite wanderings run up against various wonders and mysteries, is apparently willing now to allow a spiritual quality to man and, I conclude, to all his works as well" (*Notes on Life and Letters* 67). Composed early in his literary childhood, within a year of his tribute to Marryat and Cooper, the preface to Conrad's first deepsea novel had claimed just such a spiritual quality or intention for his own work: unlike "the thinker or the scientist," the artist speaks to what is "more permanently enduring" in humanity, "to our capacity for delight and wonder, to the sense of mystery surrounding our lives. . ." (Preface to *The Nigger of the* NARCISSUS).

That conviction remained fixed in Conrad. "The aim of creation," he would propose in *A Personal Record*, " . . . is purely spectacular: a spectacle for awe, love, adoration, or hate, if you like, but in this view–and in this view alone –never for despair!" The task that falls to humanity is "to bear true testimony to the visible wonder, the haunting terror, the infinite passion and illimitable serenity; to the supreme law and the abiding mystery of the sublime spectacle," which sight "may move us to laughter" or (as in the case of the Walrus and the Carpenter before "such quantities of sand") to "tears" (92-93).

Guided by his sympathetic imagination, the Conradian artist strives to render the least possible injustice to "the mystic nature of material things" (13), "the mystic ordering of common events" (141). It is this sense of mystery that "professors of intense gravity" would deny or rule out of court and that the "solemnly mystifying" prose of their unwittingly funny science would work to deaden (*Last Essays* 86, 40). Their "lamentable essays in seriousness" (86) are of a piece with those of the no-nonsence Captain H.C. Jörgenson of *The Rescue*, that wreck of an old adventurer whose experiments in the timing of fuses are undertaken so very seriously ("He was playing very gravely indeed with those bits of string" [368]), and whose very presence "robs life of all heat and mystery" (369); "really nothing in the world could astonish or startle old Jörgeson" (334). "No child's play" for this walking cadaver (100, 366).

4

The mystic ordering-of-things indicated in Conrad's prose of statement coordinates nicely with the way of enlightenment plotted by his narratives. Conrad's fiction introduces a host of characters sure of themselves in their ignorance of life and its dark courses: from Jim, son of a parson possessed of "certain knowledge of the Unknowable" (*Lord Jim* 5), and Harry Whalley, blind master of the SOFALA and erstwhile daredevil purveyor of knowledge, like Kurtz, to dark places (*End of the Tether* 176-77, 285-86); to M. George, tyro gentleman-sailor ignorant, like Razumov, of "the dreadful order" in "the darkest shadows of life" (*Arrow of Gold* 283) and Captain Tom Lingard of the LIGHTNING, "a man ready for the obvious" but "blind to the mysterious aspects of the world" (*Rescue* 11). The tale of this last's enlightenment traces in bold the way to such science as Conrad's art is empowered to reveal (La Bossière, *Joseph Conrad* 33, 63-66). Like the many protagonists of Conrad's earlier finished fictions, "Red-Eyed" Tom has his eyes opened by way of immersion in a bedlam element, a nonsense world featuring, in this instance, a march hare, a white rabbit, a watch with hands that have stopped, a ticking watch without hands, an animated mushroom and at least one earnest and proper dodo. Plunged into a universe "so painful with all sorts of wonders" (*Notes on Life and Letters* 11), Lingard and his antecedents come to see, more or less acutely, something of the enigma at the heart of things and themselves.

The protagonist of *The Rover* is joined to their company, the last full figure in the Conradian fellowship of impaired vision and ignorant hearts. Led down the Giens

Peninsula by an intelligent mule, Master Gunner Peyrol in his fifty-eighth year is introduced as a man of "gravity" (16), "serious as a judge" (17), calm in his indifference, "having learned from childhood to suppress any sign of wonder before all extraordinary sights and events, all strange people, all strange customs, and the most alarming phenomena of nature" (24).[9] No child or "man to lose time in idle wonder," as he is quick to remind anyone who would even suggest otherwise (46, 48, 114, 117), the rover who would retire to a quiet, ordered life in the vicinity of his childhood appears the very image of sound and sober adulthood: "All Peyrol had ever done was to behave rationally" (34). The homecomer ripe for enlightenment is in for a few surprises. In a dreamy, fabulous world, of "bizarre sights" (50), "the veriest nonsense" (218), the "perfectly absurd" (257), of "incomprehensible signs" (164) or facts of "no visible, conceivable or probable reason" (204), where all happens "as if by enchantment" (119), Peyrol comes to feel increasingly "funny" (9, 252), to experience "mingled curiosity and awe" (88) before the enigma he inhabits and finds in himself. "Dream left astern. Dream straight ahead," he is brought to "wonder" (233) before a mirror and the contradictory impulses, to indifference and engagement, that he glimpses there. Peyrol's gradually intensified tuition in perplexity concludes in the recognition that "strange things do happen" (249), not the least surprising of which is the act of love and deception, from impulse and cunning, that is his last. "A look or ironic gaiety" (239) responds to manifold wonders as the seeker after repose and rational order sees himself drawn in from the sidelines of "the field of nonsense . . . a playground for games of so high and mysterious a nature, as well as being so normal and commonplace," in the words of Elizabeth Sewell on Carroll and Lear, there to put his "lovely skills" fully to work (183-84).[10]

If the plotting of enlightenment to mystery in *The Rover* runs true to the nonsense logic normal to the Conradian imagination, however, it does so with a difference. In a way peculiar to *The Rover* among Conrad's fictions, the ordering of crucial events here (from Peyrol's surprising of his old shipmate "Testa Dura" Symons to his last tricky move in decoying the English) seems to have been worked out with at least two specific games in mind. The first, favoured in Renaissance and Victorian times, by adults and children alike, and still played by Mediterranean seamen, is Blind Man's Buff (Fr.: "La Main chaude"), or "the sport of giving a person a clout and having him guess who did it" (Opie 293-94). "Who are you? (*Rover* 128, 138), Symons gropes after the identity of the agile white-haired trickster who, "stealthily like an Indian" (122), had knocked him on the head from behind. Peyrol's immediate response to the improbable discovery of his secreted tartane and the subsequent failure of "Testa Dura" to discover in his assailant his old Brother of the Coast "Poigne-de-Fer" lead to the improvising of the "inspired fib" that prepares a complex series of moves in the "game" the French will play with the English (135, 127, e.g.).

And the plotting of those moves suggests, in turn, a scaled-up and witty reworking of the most popular and baroque of catching or capturing games, Prisoners' Base (Fr.: "Le Jeu de barres"):

> Two captains pick up sides . . . and each side takes

> possession of a base, but the prison in which they hope to place their captives is the one diagonally opposite, not the one nearest them. . . . When one captain sends a player to rescue a captive, his opponent sends a player to intercept the rescuer. Then one after another, players are sent to rescue rescuers and intercept interceptors. . . . Each player will be both chasing and being chased. . . . (Opie 143)

The patterning of manoeuvres in the contest between Peyrol and the AMELIA's master simulates the design of that game, but with an added twist, to increased baroque effect. For the fib of the tartane as a courier boat to come into play, the captive Symons must be allowed to report it to Captain Vincent. Having taken precautions to prevent any interference in his plan–"having, so to speak, guarded his base" 190)–Peyrol oversees the *escape* of his prisoner and old friend: "No nurse could have watched with more anxiety the adventure of a little boy than Peyrol the progress of his former prisoner" (199). The deceiving rescue so lovingly and playfully engineered readies the deceiving capture of Peyrol and his "plaything" tartane as couriers of authentic intelligence (268). "It isn't going to be child's play" (207), the old rover has warned of the landlubberly Gallic officialdom's airy game plan.

Events bear his words out, and in more ways than one. Like the playing of Blind Man's Buff and Prisoners' Base by spirited children of all ages in a world of quotidian nonsense and wonder (so the Conradian ordering of things leaves it understood), the deft, expert working of a craft in an element of unreason is no *jeu d'enfant*. In *The Rover* Conrad produced a popular book. He did not produce an easy one.

ENDNOTES

1. Conrad read this letter shortly after his return from Corsica in April of that year (Najder 460).

2. Perse had just returned to Paris after a six-month stay in England, during which time he had also visited with Chesterton.

3. Compare, for example, the first stanza of *The Jumblies:*

> They went to sea in a Sieve, they did,
> In a Sieve they went to sea:
> In spite of all their friends could say,
> On a winter's morn, on a stormy day,
> In a Sieve they went to sea!
>
> And when the Sieve turned round and round,
> And every one cried, "You'll all be drowned!"
> They called aloud, "Our Sieve ain't big,
> But we don't care a button, we don't care a fig!
> In a Sieve we'll go to sea!"

> Far and few, far and few,
> Are the lands where the Jumblies live;
> Their heads are green, and their hands are blue,
> And they went to sea in a Sieve. . . .

with this passage from *Vents*:

> Ces vols d'insectes par nuées qui s'en allaient se perdre au large. . . . On leur a dit, on leur a dit - ah! que ne leur disait-on pas? - qu'ils s'allaient perdre sur les mers, et qu'il fallait virer de bord; on leur criait, on leur criait - ah! Que ne leur criait-on pas? - qu'ils s'en revinssent parmi nous. . . . Mais non! Ils s'en allaient plutôt par là, où c'est se perdre avec le vent! (*O* 208)

4. Little elsewhere observes: "La beauté sonore de 'Saint-John Perse', poésie affranchie de toute signification, invite le lecteur à l'aventure" (*Etudes* 203). Again, though, Perse's reading of Lear is given but a passing mention (148).

5. Perse's reception at the Lycée de Marseille in the twenties is recalled from Pierre Guerre's *Le Carnet de Moleskine*. Rilke's translation of "Images à Crusoé" appeared in 1925.

6. Malcolm Lowry's poem "Joseph Conrad" provides the epigraph of Geddes' *Conrad's Later Novels.*

7. Consul Geoffrey Firmin even composes his own nonsense alphabet (305-06). Ironically enough, Beatrix Potter's tales,

like Lear's nonsense creations, do not make altogether light of the hazards of adventure. For all their daring, the Jumblies at sea in a sieve know enough to keep their feet dry (st. 3); and the very prudent Flopsy, Mopsy, and Cotton-Tail of *Peter Rabbit* have bread and milk and blackberries for supper, while the venturesome hero of the tale, having barely escaped (and that, empty-handed) from the garden of Mr. McGregor, must content himself with the fruits of his audacity and sup on one tablespoon of camomile tea.

8. In the period of his first contacts with Conrad, Perse wrote to Jacques Rivière: " Il ne doit y avoir de plus agaçant que de jouer du piano sur un pont de paquebot" (*O* 676).

9. Conrad's reading here of "the affectation common to seamen of never being surprised at anything that sea or land can produce" (*Rover* 24) accords closely with Cooper's. For example:

> This *sang froid* of seamen is always a matter of surprise to landsmen; but adventurers who have been rocked in the tempests for years, whose utmost security is a great hazard and who safety constantly depends on the command of faculties, come in time to experience an apathy on the subject of all the minor terrors and excitements of life that none can acquire unless by habit and similar, daily risks. (*Homeward Bound* 499)

And again, in *Afloat and Ashore*:

> Sailors, as a class, are very philosophical, so far as

> the peculiarities and habits of strangers are concerned, appearing to think it beneath the dignity of those who visit all lands, to betray wonder at the novelties of any. . . . (262)

In his 1848 preface to *The Sea Lions*, Cooper spells out his response to such a philosophical turn of mind:

> If anything connected with the hardness of the human heart could surprise us, it surely would be the indifference with which men live on, engrossed by their worldly objects, amid the sublime natural phenomena that so eloquently and increasingly speak to their imaginations, affections, and judgments. (3)

For Cooper as for Conrad, "this is a life of mysteries . . . though its incidents seem so vulgar and of everyday occurrence. There is mystery in its beginning and its end; in its impulses, its sympathies, and all its discordant passions" (*Water-Witch* 548).

10. Najder suggestively recalls of Conrad in the 1920s that he would wake up his son John in the middle of the night to play chess; then, after a few moves, he would return to his writing (462). Evidently, Conrad also enjoyed sailing toy boats with the lad in the privacy of his garden.

WORKS CITED

Bonney, William W. *Thorns & Arabesques: Contexts for Conrad's Fiction*. Baltimore: Johns Hopkins UP, 1980.

Byrom, Thomas. *Nonsense and Wonder: The Poems and Cartoons of Edward Lear*. New York: Dutton, 1977.

Chesterton, G.K. *The Common Man*. New York: Sheed & Ward, 1950.

----------. *Stories, Essays & Poems*. London: Dent, 1935.

Conrad, Joseph. *The Works of Joseph Conrad.* 21 vols. London: Dent, 1946-55.

Coates, John. "Chesterton and the Meaning of Adventure." *The Chesterton Review* 5 (1979); 278-99.

Cooper, James Fenimore. *The Works of James Fenimore Cooper*. 5 vols. New York: Collier, 1892.

Favre, Yves-Alain. *Saint-John Perse: le language et le sacré.* Paris: Corti, 1977.

Findley, Timothy. *The Wars*. Toronto: Clarke, Irwin, 1977.

Geddes, Gary. *Conrad's Later Novels*. Kingston: McGill-Queen's UP, 1980.

Guerre, Pierre. *Le Carnet de moleskine.* Cahiers du Sud, 1954.

Holbrook, Jackson. "Introduction." *The Complete Nonsense of Edward Lear.* London: Faber, 1947. I-xxiii.

Honneur à Saint-John Perse. Comp. Jean Paulhan. Paris: Gallimard, 1965.

Karl, Frederick. *Joseph Conrad: The Three Lives.* New York: Farrar, 1979.

Kiely, Robert. *Robert Louis Stevenson and the Fiction of Adventure.* Cambridge: Harvard UP, 1964.

La Bossière, Camille R. *Joseph Conrad and the Science of Unknowing.* Fredericton: York P, 1979.

----------. "The Monumental Nonsense of Saint-John Perse." *Folio* 18 (1990):25-37.

Land, Stephen K. *Paradox and Polarity in the Fiction of Joseph Conrad.* New York: St. Martin's, 1984.

Lear, Edward. "The Jumblies." *Anthology of Children's Literature.* Ed. Edna Johnson, Evelyn Sickels and Francis Clarke Sayers. 3rd ed. Boston: Houghton, 1959. 55-56.

Little, Roger. *Etudes sur Saint-John Perse.* Paris: Klincksieck, 1984.

----------. "A Letter about Conrad by Saint-John Perse." *Conradiana* 8 (1976):263-64.

Lowry, Malcolm. *Under the Volcano*. 1946. Harmondsworth: Penguin, 1963.

Mac Orlan, Pierre. *'La clique du Café Brebis', suivi de 'Petit Manuel du parfait aventurier.'* 5th ed. Paris: Gallimard: 1951.

Marryat, Frederick. *Japhet in Search of a Father*. 1836. Boston: Colonial, 1898.

----------. *Mr. Midshipman Easy*. 1836. London: Foulsham, n.d.

----------. *The Phantom Ship*. 1839. London: Routledge, 1874.

Najder, Z. *Joseph Conrad: A Chronicle*. New Brunswick: Rutgers UP, 1984.

Opie, Iona and Peter. *Children's Games in Street and Playground*. Oxford: Clarendon, 1969.

Ostrovsky, Erika. *Under the Sign of Ambiguity: Saint-John Perse/Alexis Leger*. Washington Square: New York UP, 1985.

Perse, Saint-John. *Oeuvres complètes*. Paris: Gallimard, 1972.

Said, Edward. "Conrad and Nietzsche." *Joseph Conrad: A*

Commemoration. Ed. N. Sherry. London: Macmillan, 1976. 65-76.

Schwarz, Daniel R. *Joseph Conrad: The Later Fiction*. London: Macmillan, 1982.

Sewell, Elizabeth. *The Field of Nonsense*. London: Chatto, 1952.

Stevenson, Robert Louis. *Travels with a Donkey in the Cévennes*. 1879. New York: National Library, 1906.

----------. *Treasure Island*. 1881. New York: Grosset & Dunlap, n.d.

XV

OF BELLS, WORDS, NONSENSE, NURSERIES AND TREES: A NOTE ON *THE ROVER*

[from a paper read at the Conrad International Conference, Texas Tech University, Lubbock, August 2000]

Preface

> "Nothing can stop him. [. . .] What are these tricks?"
> Conrad, *The Rover*

First, apologies from this *personne* for the accidental shift in topic and slant, though the gist of the thing promised, "Of Wedding Bells and Desert Regions," remains pretty much unchanged. A case of indigestion, catachresis . . . or having *les yeux plus gros que le ventre*, as said Montaigne. *Mea culpa*. Did give it a try, though.

Some time ago (it seems like only yesterday), this commentator promised himself that he would not *do* Conrad again. (Would that he kept to that promise, you might be brought to reflect.) Not the wonderful subject's fault, of course, but a blurby Minim's: a genuinely attentive reading of Conrad's oeuvre, as we know, requires not a little energy, keen concentration, a fund of (con)textual experience and at least a modicum of active intelligence and imagination. Tedium from fatigue or indolence just will not do. And repetition, at times the mother of unbridled ennui, can be both funny and killing.

But the prospect of rejoining in spirit energetic *vieux copains* Gerald Morgan and Steve Brodsky at Texas Tech University enticed this Conradian laddie now all-too-long-in-the-tooth away from keeping to the letter of his promise. Promise never to do such a thing again, after this.

Avertissement

This is not a piece of finished work. It represents nothing much more than one of the very many possible drafts of a *rigolade*, a quizzical, risky *jeu d'esprit en macaronique*, this one composed "half in jest" with a "half-puzzled smile."[1] Risky business, since the jesting entertains the possibility of falling flat. *On verra.* At bottom, even adamantly in matter and method, it involves or recalls the need for forgiveness, from beginning to end.

*　　　*　　　*

"'Qu'est-ce que je vous sers pour arroser le sanglier boulli? De l'eau chaude, de la cervoise tiède, ou du vin rouge glacé?'
'C'est ma tournée, bien sûr.'
'A propos, quel genre de monnaie utilizez-vous, ici?'
'Aoh, c'est très simple vraiment. . . . Nous avons des lingots de fer qui pèsent une livre et qui valent trois sesterces et demi, plus quatre pièces de zinc qui valent une pièce et demi de cuivre chacune. Les sesterces valent douzes pièces de bronze et . . . .'
'Ils sont [fous, ces Bretons]. . . .'

> ‘Bois ta cervoise, elle va refroidir. . . .’” *Astérix chez les Bretons*

> “Agnomination, or paranomasia. . . . The liveliness is due to the meaning not being just what the words say. . . . Well constructed riddles are attractive for the same reason. This effect is produced even by jokes depending upon a twist to the word used. . . . Here again is the use of one word in different senses [as in this verse]: ‘Death is most fit before you do / Deeds that would make death fit for you’.”
> Aristotle, *Rhetoric*

“**NOTHING**,” so P.L. Heath has observed, “is an awe-inspiring . . . concept highly esteemed by writers of a mystical or existentialist tendency, but by most others regarded with anxiety, nausea, or panic.” As though by force of *agere sequitur esse*, “Nobody seems to know how to deal with it (he would, of course) and plain serious persons generally are reported to have little difficulty in saying, seeing, hearing, and doing nothing.”[2] Savvy as they are with the wisdom of daily living in the visible universe, those serious plain persons know well enough to leave to airy seminarians the all-too-sissy game of parsing “nothing” as a participle of the verb “to noth.” As A.C. Baier’s earnest “Nonsense”(an essay twinned to Heath’s “Nothing” in its engagement with Martin Heidegger’s “The Nothing itself nothings”)[3] likewise works incidentally to demonstrate, the venerable *via negativa* continues to branch out in directions towards *mysterium*, beyond reason. But even human non-sense has its limitations, of course: like nothing, it matters. The fact remains that muscular *volk* and deep grammarians of the world as will and idea do seem to come to some understanding in the shared experience that "*there is nothing to worry about.*"[4] "*Sanfaryan,*"[5] so to speak, for quotidian trenchers and ethereal speculators alike.

And so it is that I am (not) worried about this paper, which must be made to float, soberly as it were, be respectable, *comme il faut*. Must somehow make a fist of it. A matter of honour, always, but especially so when someone else, and a grand old chum at that,[6] is volunteered to serve up to a company of fellow seasoned Conradians *un tout petit discours* something very much like an alphabet soup. Tennyson illustrator and nightly reader of Pascal Edward Lear once cooked up a jumbly regale in twenty-six courses for nursery feeding at Yuletide, and young dog Dylan Thomas, so legend has it, pleasured a convention of distinguished Dadaists by passing round a cup filled to the brim with bits of string–which all goes to show the abiding pertinence of "a place for everything, and everything in its place." *Toujours les bienséances. . . ..*

There must, then, be at least an inkling of a motif to string together the bits of this text into something like an intelligible whole. Much to my relief, one did introduce itself in the action of giving Conrad's swansong yet another listen, in the shape of a venturesome hypothesis. And it is this: that *The Rover* is a very "funny," "jumbled up" book, arguably the "funniest thing" he ever wrote, "an immense joke" (*Rover* 8, 237, 188). ("Funny" here as in Iris Mudoch's definition in "Speaking of Writing": "there is so much that is funny in life; especially if we extend our definition of 'funny' a little to include strange, incongruous, bizarre, ironic. . . . ")[7] A joke is a joke, of course, though some jokes are better than others, as folk are generally agreed. And, again it goes without saying, a joke that *needs* explanation is no joke at all.

"So to speak," "as it were," "in a manner of speaking," "one might say," Conrad's last completed novel, in which "nothing [can] . . . be taken as positive proof" and "nothing could mean anything," signs a reading of the human condition in which, "strictly speaking, nobody is safe," "nobody can be sure," there is "nobody at your back," "nothing to fear" (8, 9, 21, 117, 156, 28, 110, 170, 166, 208). By its very language an act of translation in "ambiguous circumstances" of "endless sinuosities" (like *Under Western Eyes*?), *The Rover* seems designed to make its appeal, again in its own words, to a readership "acutely aware of every syllable" (60, 261, 181). As for the syntax of Conrad's syllabary in this case, it bespeaks a keen sense of the absurd nicely confirmed by readings of *The Rover* as "an easy . . . book,"[8] one "more suited to teenage tastes than to those of the seasoned readers of Conrad,"[9] and therefore "not to be taken very seriously";[10] it represents, so it has been said, "a falling off" from the "humor" characteristic of "Conrad's best work."[11] Indeed, "Strange things *do* happen" (*Rover* 249; emphasis added). "Confounded nonsense" calls unto confounded nonsense (228), or so it would seem; and in that there is at least a modicum of poetic justice or mental consolation. Commentary referring to "the husband Scevola,"[12] for instance, effectively rehearses the wit of the "incensed faithful" of the church at Almanarre: decoyed by "appearances" and "reputation," they mistake Citizen Bron–who mistakes himself–for "the master" of Escampobar Farm and its mistress Arlette (25, 144). Thus even inspired imitations of a "craft concealed under some sort of straight-forward action" (143) by sub-cooks and sub-sub-librarians can sometimes yield a tasty, even piquant mix. *Bonne soupe*, I hope.

Now, *The Rover* makes manifest enough Conrad's abiding fidelity to the art of *le mot juste,* to "that creative task" of bringing "to play" the "light of magic sugges-tiveness . . . over the commonplace surface of words: of the old, old words, worn thin by ages of careless usage" (Preface to *The Nigger of the* NARCISSUS xxv). Moonshine, *ça va de soi*, can spiritualize. In this regard, the sly *de-quoi*/coying artist of *The Rover* is more than a match for Captain Marryat, the coiner of "flapdoodle" (see *OED*), aficionado "du grotesque . . . de l'humour rose et noir"[13] and inveterate wit of "a kind of bright hardness" (in the words of Virginia Woolf's "The Captain's Death-Bed")[14] whose rattling good yarn of *Mr. Midshipman Easy* opens with a take-off on names and naming inspired by *Tristram Shandy*, features the practical, fruitful genius of young Jack's henchman "Mesty" or "Mephistopheles Faust," and comes to a happy ending with the death of difficult philosopher Pater Easy at the hands of a mechanical contraption of his own invention designed to assure the full realization of his *idée fixe*, that "all men are equal." *Vive l'égalité!* There are puns on "un/easy" in *The Rover*, too (see 121-22, in particular), perhaps even in "*Ease after warre.*"[15]

But there are very many others as well, each of which, it goes without saying *encore une fois*, is at least bilingual (as in speaking French in English, for instance); and most obviously featured in playing with "strange," "stony," "marvel," "wonder," "mind," "frank," "change," "gravity," "curious," "slippery," "start," "arrest," "blessed," "incensed," "disappoint," "lodge," "dodge," "penitents," "hair-shirts," "devil," "rove," "fishy," "idle," "upset," "shut up," "tinker," "confidence," "dog," "goat," "pigeon," "crow," "tug," "accident," "phenomenon," "crazy," "utter," "barbarous," "confounded," "lunatic," "bird," "chicken," "yellow," "spy," "sanguinary," "pass," "suspect," "blind," "mystery," "watch," "composed" and "deliberate," to name just a few *qui sautent aux yeux*. If the craft of word-play must figure or count for something in any serious assessment of productions from "the worker in prose" (Preface to *NoN* xxv), indications are that Pop Conrad has lost little or nothing of his wits or sense of humour.

Yet again going beyond the admirably serviceable Marryat, Conrad more resolutely sticks to the task of literalizing metaphors. And he does so in a way less constrained that Swift's (as in the Dean's funny business of spinning a project from the figure that "the English are eating the Irish"). Certainly, *The Rover* shows references galore to "running on all fours," to mules, dogs, cats, lions, panthers, donkeys, cows, goats, wolves, hares, mice, nannies, nurseries and earnest adults still scuttling about on all fours, so often repeated as to hint at a sphinx's riddling. The extravaganza of literal precision gains even more expansion with a run of jokes on "child's play," "worth its weight in gold," "thick skull," "bloody wine," "breaking bread," "curiosity killed the cat," "out of sight, out of mind," "hat in hand," "come to pass," "how on earth," "still as the grave" and "bolt from the blue." No lack of fun here.

Envoy

"Whom could that man be after but him, himself" (*Rover* 196).

The Rover tells the story of an old sea-dog's return to the place of his birth. With more than just poetic justice, the text of that funny story also signs something of a return to "pardon," in the shape of hints of Pop Conrad's at least partial "reconciliation" with the Christianity he took in as a boy (*Rover* 282). Here again, this commentator justifiably relies on co-ordinates provided by Gerald Morgan, Master Mariner, poet and *Docteur de l'Université de Montréal*, who introduced me to Conrad's oeuvre. His comprehensive 1991 essay, "Quixotic Sail: Conrad's Prison World," which opens with "the implicit theme of forgiveness," ends in this way:

> Conrad's declared tribute to seamen, *The Nigger of the* NARCISSUS, tells not of doom but of a saving of a ship, by a crew depicted "in attitudes of crucifixion," led by a clear-minded captain despite themselves, and given the author's valediction. "Haven't we, together, and upon the immortal sea, wrung out a meaning from out sinful lives?" / Which bears at least a hint of forgiveness, from some indefinite quarter. Like mankind's "mysterious origin" and "uncertain fate" in the Preface to the novel, it needed

only a name to signify forgiveness and home.[16]

I would add nothing much more than a footnote, consistent with Master Gunner Peyrol's observation that "temples . . . never look quite empty" (*Rover* 140). Protagonist Peyrol, "man of mystery and power" and "messenger from the unknown," asks "forgiveness" of the simple Michel and is granted it (247, 219, 253); Catherine forgives her God of the Aristocrats and is subsequently forgiven by the orphaned Arlette for a wounding still deep enough to rankle; Arlette forgives Lieutenant Réal for his somewhat prissy, inept legalism; and he, in turn, forgives Arlette for drawing him away to a love long desired. The list of absolutions and benedictions could go on. Arlette prays to her God, is granted "a terrestrial revelation" (160), and gets what she wants; Réal prays to his God and gets a lovely surprise; Catherine prays to her God and is granted re-entry into the fold; fisherman Michel sits at the foot of a cross, at his master's knee, and is fed; and Peyrol, praying to Nobody, gets what he needs, "a gift" (249). Only nasty little old juvenile sansculotte Scevola, in whom the sound of "the church bell" (which "had only lately recovered its voice") rankles "like poison," is left out in the cold, only temporarily "somewhat soothed by the assurance that he would not die by drowning" (40, 147, 265). At the end, *en fin de compte*, wedding and cow bells ring, and masses are said at Toulon's "church of Ste Marie Majeure" for "the soul" of proud old sea-dog Peyrol, now christened "Jean" (283).

Trees and "sign[s] of the cross" figure large in that progress towards celebration in a world of humanly "incomprehensible signs" (232, 164). Between the time of his first encounter (while astride a prescient mule) with simple fisherman Michel seated next to a devoted dog on a stone at the foot of a wooden cross, and his praises being sung by a manly hunchback, wedding musician and community messenger bearing two crutches on a donkey savvy enough to know where to go, Peyrol is repeatedly afforded occasions to "throw his arms affectionately over the trunk" of a "pine" (144, 255, 258). "*Sacré nom d'un chien!* (a heavenly hound?)[17]– so Jean Peyrol is nonsensically brought to swear; and perhaps, even ironically, as in Péguy's famous last words "*Tirez, tirez, nom de Dieu!*," in a sense to pray. Old Józef did not fail to watch his language(s), mind his manners, *à faire comme il faut*.

"A défaut du pardon, laisse venir l'oubli," so romantic ironist and satirist Alfred de Musset consigned his cardinal principle to paper ("La Nuit d'octobre"). . Pop Conrad did not forget. Like the epic old crouchbacks *au Canada, il se souvient.*

postscript

Du vin rouge glacé?
Oui, s'il vous plaît. Merci.
"It's nothing" (*Rover* 214).
"*Je vous en prie.*"
"Plutôt. Quoi."
Pardon?
Mési, simèktédbin.
Tanni.

ENDNOTES

1. Joseph Conrad, *The Rover* 174, 266. All references to Conrad's works are cited from the Dent Collected Edition.

2. P.L. Heath, "Nothing," in *The Encyclopedia of Philosophy*, ed. Paul Edwards (New York and London: Collier Macmillan, 1972) 5.524, 525.

3. A.C. Baier, "Nonsense," in *The Encyclopedia of Philosophy,* ed. Paul Edwards (New York and London: Collier Macmillan, 1972) 5.522.

4. Heath 526.

5. G.W. Stephen Brodsky, *Gentlemen of the Blade: A Social and Literary History of the British Army since 1660* (New York: Greenwood, 1988) 172.

6. This paper was delivered by G.W. Stephen Brodsky, frère de la Côte at the bilingual Royal Roads Military College, Victoria, British Columbia.

7. Iris Murdoch, "Speaking of Writing," *The Times* [of London], 13 Feb 1964, p. 14, col. 2.

8. Z. Najder, *Joseph Conrad: A Chronicle* (New Brunswick NJ: Rutgers UP, 1984) 485.

9. Adam Gillon, *Joseph Conrad* (Boston: Twayne, 1982) 168.

10. Albert J. Guerard, *Conrad the Novelist* (Cambridge: Harvard UP, 1966) 284-85.

11. H.F. Lippincott, "Sense of Place in Conrad's *The Rover*," *Conradiana* 6 (1974) 111.

12. Guerard 285.

13. Maurice-Paul Gautier, *Captain Frederick Marryat: l'homme et l'oeuvre* (Paris: Didier, 1971) 411-12.

14. Virginia Woolf, *The Captain's Death Bed & Other Essays* (New York: HBJ, 1950) 44.

15. See G.W. Stephen Brodsky and Camille R. La Bossière, "*The Rover* and *The Faerie Queene*," *Joseph Conrad Today* 2 (1977) 58-59, for an account of the irony of *The Rover*'s epigraph (and Conrad's epitaph).

16. Gerald Morgan, "Quixotic Sail: Conrad's Prison World," in *Living Record: Essays in Memory of Constantine Bida*, ed. Irena Rima Makaryk (Ottawa: U of Ottawa P, 1991) 311, 321.

17. See Morgan 321: "In the widespread tradition of such common men [as exemplified by Chaucer's pilgrims], the figure of Christ crucified (so vehemently denied by Conrad) is the supreme figure of exile: from Infinity, no less, and betrayed. Conrad could have heard as much in London, from the poet Francis Thompson of 'The Hound of Heaven': 'All things betray thee, who betrayest me'."

XVI

PÉGUY

[*Dictionary of Literary Biography: Modern French Poets*. Ed. Jean-François Leroux (Detroit: Bruccoli-Clark, 2000)]

in memoriam Léon Mainguy, *soldat*
franc-tireur Uncle Bert
et la belle Tante Jacqueline

Seclected Books

Jeanne d'Arc (Paris: Georges Bellais, 1897; Paris: Gallimard, 1948).

Notre Patrie (Paris: Cahiers de la Quinzaine, 1905; Paris: Gallimard, 1915).

Le Mystère de la Charité de Jeanne d'Arc (Paris: Cahiers de la Quinzaine, 1910; Paris: Gallimard, 1918).

Notre Jeunesse (Paris: Cahiers de la Quinzaine, 1910; Paris: Gallimard, 1933).

Victor-Marie comte Hugo (Paris: Cahiers de la Quinzaine, 1910; Paris: Gallimard, 1934).

Un Nouveau Théologien M. Laudet (Paris: Cahiers de la

Quinzaine, 1911; Paris: Gallimard, 1937).

Le Porche du Mystère de la deuxième vertu (Paris: Cahiers de la Quinzaine, 1911; Paris: Gallimard, 1929).

Le Mystère des Saints Innocents (Paris: Cahiers de la Quinzaine, 1911; Paris: Gallimard, 1929).

Oeuvres choisies de Charles Péguy, 1900-1910 (Paris: Grasset, 1911).

L'Argent, suivi de *l'Argent (suite)* (Paris: Cahiers de la Quinzaine, 1913; Paris: Gallimard, 1932).

Les Tapisseries (Paris: Cahiers de la Quinzaine, 1912-1913; Paris: Gallimard, 1936).

Ève (Paris: Cahiers de la Quinzaine, 1913; Paris: Gallimard, 1927).

Note conjointe sur M. Descartes, suivie de *Note sur M. Bergson* (Paris: Cahiers de la Quinzaine, 1914; Paris: Gallimard, 1935).

Oeuvres complètes de Charles Péguy, 1873-1914, 20 vols. (Paris: Gallimard, 1916-1955).

Oeuvres poétiques complètes de Charles Péguy (Paris: Gallimard, Bibliothèque de la Pléiade, 1941; revised eds. 1948, 1954, 1957).

Back to Sources

La République . . . Notre Royaûme de France, ed. Denise Mayer (Paris: Gallimard, 1946).

Oeuvres en prose 1909-1914, ed. Marcel Péguy (Paris: Gallimard, Bibliothèque de la Pléiade, 1947.

Le Choix de Péguy (Paris: Gallimard, 1952).

Notes politiques et sociales, ed. André Boisserie (Paris: Cahiers de l'Amitié Charles Péguy, 1957).

Oeuvres en prose 1898-1908, ed. Marcel Péguy (Paris: Gallimard, Bibliothéque de la Pléiade, 1959).

Les Oeuvres posthumes de Charles Péguy, ed. Jacques Viard (Paris: Cahiers de l'Amitié Charles Péguy, 1969).

The generously inclusive achievement of poet, editor, dramatist, philosopher, editor, pamphleteer, amateur medievalist, revolutionary socialist and pious mystic Charles Péguy bespeaks an integrity that understandably remains difficult to identify in conventional political terms. A heretic among Marxists, a "half-rebellious son" to the Roman Catholic Church and an ardent patriot who kept his distance from nationalism of the kind preached by Maurice Barrès and Charles Maurras, he achieved in his life and writings a coherence and independence of spiritual action based on faith, hope and charity, which virtues he understood to be inherently consistent with the secular ideals of liberty, equality and fraternity. The examples of Joan of Arc and St. Vincent de Paul helped inspire Péguy's own apostolate in service to the oppressed, the suffering, the destitute; and, in sympathy with the toilers of the world, he made his own the Benedictine principle that "to work is to pray." The 229 volumes of his Cahiers de la Quinzaine, published from January 1900 to July 1914, and the more than eight thousand items in the collection of his correspondence housed at the Centre Charles Péguy d'Orléans provide some indication as to just how resolutely he worked to share his thoughts with others. But the writer Péguy is most often remembered for his poetry–*Le Mystère de la Charité de Jeanne d'Arc*, in particular–the oral style of which, with its "phrases simples et touchantes" like those of the Synoptic Gospels, in the words of mayor of Orléans René Thinat, makes it naturally suitable for popular, communal dissemination. Péguy's Christian sense of *mysterium* invites comparison with existential philosopher Gabriel Marcel's.

Charles Pierre Péguy was born at Orléans in January 1873, to Cécile Péguy (née Quéré), a chair-seat mender from a line of impoversished Bourbonnais farm labourers, and to her husband Désiré, a cabinet-maker often unable to work because of poor health. Widowed within a year of her only child's birth, some six months after his baptism at the Church of St. Aignan in the Val de Loire, Cécile eked out a living by working sixteen hours a day while her mother, Étienette Quéré, attended to the boy. From the vivid stories he heard from his analphabetic grandmother, who had never married, Charles learned something of "the Devil, Hell, and Damnation" (as he puts it in his *Pierre, commencement d'une vie bourgeoise*); and from the tireless efforts of his mother, who taught him his letters in what little free time she had, the virtue of perseverance in a task. Though not churchgoers themselves, Madame Quéré and Cécile also took care to encourage a sense of religious observance in their charge by regularly sending him to Sunday Mass with a neighbouring family.

The lessons in "concentration, seriousness and industry" that Charles learned at home encouraged the development of his talents at school. Outstanding achievement at the primary school annexed to the local École Normale (1879-1884), then at the École Municipale Professionnelle d'Orléans (1884-1885), earned him a municipal government scholarship to the Lycée d'Orléans. The assiduity of youngster Charles likewise showed itself in his quick mastering of catechism lessons from the curate of St. Aignan. And youth Péguy continued to work hard during his years at the Lycée d'Orléans (1895-1891), where he soon came to establish himself as the school's most promising student. He won prizes in all academic subjects, most notably in Latin, philosophy and French composition, and gained further recognition for his leadership in athletics and army cadet exercises ("bon soldat" Péguy served as founding president of the Société de Jeux et Exercices de Plein Air at the Lycée in 1891). Other memorable events from Péguy's early youth include the making of his First Communion, in June 1885, and his reading of Victor Hugo's *Les Misérables*, in a copy provided by blacksmith and home-spun philosopher Louis Boitier. With his *bachelier ès lettres* in hand, he garnered another scholarship, to the Lycée Lakanal at Sceaux, a boarding school in the suburbs of Paris for aspirants to admission to the École Normale Supérieure.

The promise of impending professional success held out by that scholarship was not to be realized. Péguy continued to practice due discipline in his year at Lakanal, winning a prize for Latin and continuing to attend Sunday Mass. But, much to Cécile's disappointment, her son failed his entrance examinations for the École Normale Supérieure in 1892. Putting that failure behind him, Péguy withdrew from Lakanal to enlist in the 131st Régiment d'Orléans. His decision to do so would affect more than just his prospects in academe. He returned from his year of military service an apparently changed man, a self-professed "atheist" committed to the spirit of "brotherhood in humanity" that he had come to deem irreconcilable with official Catholic dogma regarding damnation. In *Toujours de la Grippe,* published in the 5 April 1900 number of *Cahiers de la Quinzaine,* as he would later explain the grounds for his conversion in the year after Lakanal, "For Christianity to be able to accept, side by side, a Church Triumphant and a Hell, a vision of beatitude and a house of death . . . there must be in the roots of Christian feeling some monstrous partnership with death and disease" (translated by Margaret Villiers). Now devoted more to soldiering for practical brotherhood than to maintaining his place in good standing with academic or ecclesiastical authority, Péguy again came up short in his bid to qualify for the École Normale Supérieure in September 1893, two weeks after his discharge from the 131st at the rank of corporal.

Another moving experience of fellowship in action almost immediately followed. A group of his Lakanal schoolmates from well-to-do families afforded Péguy yet another chance to prepare for the Normale's entrance examinations by using their influence discreetly to advance his name for a scholarship to the prestigious Sainte-Barbe, a residential college located in the heart of Paris which numbered John Calvin and St. Ignatius Loyola among its distinguished alumni. Péguy's year at Sainte-Barbe was in many ways a happy one: it saw the beginning of his intimate and enduring frienship with Louis Baillet (soon to enter the Benedictine Order); the first stages in his outlining of a socialist utopia–"the Harmonious City"–in collaboration with Marcel Baudouin; his election (his policy of absenting himself from "prayers" notwithstanding) to the presidency of the student branch of the St. Vincent de Paul Society chaplained by the Abbé Battifol; his completion of a "dissertation française en philosophie" titled *Instinct et Intelligence*; and, in July 1894, his admission to the École Normale Supérieure. Péguy's mother was more pleased with her son's official progress than she was with his newfound disposition to give away what little pocket money and winter clothing he had to the poor he sought out, "pour l'amour de l'humanité," on the streets of Paris.

Enroled as a philosophy major at the École Normale Supérieure in November 1894, Péguy chose to study in company with the *anti-talas* (*talas* from "ceux qui von*t à la* messe"), whose *mot d'ordre* was "Utopia," and began preparing a formal academic thesis on Immanuel Kant and social duty. But the appeal of regular scholarly progress soon waned as he came to concern himself more with writing a life of the mystic-in-action Joan of Arc and with such immediately practical matters as the strike at Carmaux and the case of Captain Alfred Dreyfus. Cognizant though he was of the vagaries and problems that must attend any effort to put the ideal of a perfectly just society into practice, Péguy was able unambiguously to distinguish the principle of "la mystique" (of action in accordance with a disinterested ethic) from the ostensible practicality of "la politique" (of action from mere expediency, in accordance with *raisons d'état*): "A single dishonorable action is sufficient to dishonor a nation," as he rigorously maintains in *Notre Jeunesse.* Convinced of the need for fidelity to the truth of "la mystique," Péguy was granted a yearlong leave of absence from the École Normale Supérieure that he requested in the fall of 1895. He would use the time of that leave to found a socialist cell in Orléans, advance his work on the life of Joan of Arc, learn the craft of typsetting and help his mother mend chairs. Again, Cécile was chagrined by her son's want of worldly prudence and ambition.

Apparently still not all that much concerned with career advancement, Péguy requested a second leave of absence only a few months after his return to the Normale in November 1896. He needed the time to prepare for his marriage to Charlotte Françoise Baudouin, who had stipulated that their wedding be sanctioned by civil authority only and that any children born of their union not be baptized. If Péguy retreated from the prospect of acquiring a teaching certificate that still remained open to him during the year leading up to his marriage with Charlotte in October 1897, he did so to the benefit of his own intellectual and spiritual advancement, by using the occasion of the leave to undertake readings in Alfred de Vigny, Blaise Pascal and Henri Bergson, and to bring the manuscript of his first book to virtual completion. Nor did his spotty attendance at university lectures in the last months of 1897 indicate a lapse in attention to matters of basic import; in their Introduction to *Basic Verities: Prose and Poetry* (1943), translators Anne and Julian Green record Bergson's recollections of Péguy as his student at the Ecole Normale Supérieure: "he had a marvelous gift for stepping beyond the materiality of beings, going beyond it and penetrating to the soul. Thus it is that he knew my most secret thought, such I have never expressed it, such as I would have wished to express it." That "capacity for stepping beyond" in sympathetic spiritual discernment found further expression in Péguy's *Jeanne d'Arc*, published in December of that year.

The resistance to rationalist materialism–and, concomitantly, to "l'esprit capitaliste"– that Péguy found so congenial in the teachings of Bergson is amply reflected in *Jeanne d'Arc*, a play in three acts ("Domrémy," "Les Batailles," "Rouen") dedicated to "all those women and men who have lived . . . and died trying to find a cure for our universal ill [of oppression, poverty, destitution]" (translated by Villiers). Designed to evoke the abiding vitality of a patriotism in service to all of downtrodden humanity, *Jeanne d'Arc* opens with a scene of unsentimental alms-giving–with its heroine in the act of feeding two starving children, even as she remains acutely aware of the limits of her charity, humbled by the "thought of all the other hungry people in this world who have nothing to eat . . . of all the unhappy people who have no one to comfort them" (translated by Villiers). The very production of *Jeanne d'Arc* as an *objet d'artisanat* matched the communal, radically democratic character of its ideal conception. A contribution of two-thousand francs from fellow students at the Normale provided necessary assistance; and Péguy appended to the octavo of seven hundred and fifty-two pages (unnumbered, with some left blank so as to invite creative reader participation) a list of the compositors, printers, proofreaders and bookbinders to whose collective craftsmanship the beautifully finished product as a whole tacitly attested. Proceeding in a way again consistent with socialism as he understood it, Péguy refused to have the book advertised elsewhere but on neighborhood streets, and then only in person, *viva voce*. *Jeanne d'Arc* accordingly received little market response indeed: it sold but one copy within the first month of its publication, and garnered but one printed notice, in the *Revue Socialiste*, which limited itself to remarking the book's adherence to "party" doctrine. Louis Gillet's long commentary, written for *Le Sillon* but which went unprinted, characterized the author of *Jeanne d'Arc* as "a brother to *all* who suffer."

In May 1898, with what little money remained from his wife's dowry, Péguy purchased a lease to the Librairie Georges Bellais, a Parisian bookshop on the corner of the rue Cujas. His aim was to launch a truly communal publishing enterprise respectful of individual liberty ("un coup de révolte de publier ce que ses amis sentaient, disaient, pensaient, voulaient, croyaient"), in which he would participate not only as author on occasion, but also as editor, typesetter, printer and proofreader. Books published within the first year of the Librairie's operation included his own *Marcel: Dialogue de la Cité Harmonieuse*, a poetic dream-vision of complete earthly felicity subsequent to the triumph of universal socialism, and Romain Rolland's *Les Loups*, an allegory of conflict between justice and patriotism based on the Dreyfus controversy. The inherently Christian sense of the socialism that subtends *Marcel* is reiterated in *Pierre, commencement d'une vie bourgeoise*, a recollection of his boyhood years composed in the same year as *Marcel*: "la dignité du travail est le plus beau de tous les honneurs, le plus chrétien."

Péguy's commitment to an apostolate of writing for "the people" involved a choice, of course, and one that in several respects cost him dearly. His preoccupation with the work of the Librairie virtually closed off the possibility of achieving his *agrégation*, even as his unconcern with actually making money from booksales made for one financial crisis after another: "Ce sont des idées [que Péguy] . . . vend dans sa boutique, des idées qui . . . le ruinent"–so Alain-Fournier observed. In August 1899, alarmed at the prospect of impending bankruptcy faced by his Librairie, Georges Bellais arranged for a takeover of the bookshop by a company of socialists, the Société Nouvelle de Librairie et d'Éditions, managed by a board of directors that included Lucien Herr, Léon Blum, Mario Roques, Henri Boivin and François Simiand. The directors, committed as they were to the principle of class warfare in accordance with official party doctrine, and Péguy, convinced as he was that the coming of the Harmonious City depended not on strict adherence to party discipline but on individual spiritual conversion, soon came to a parting of ways. In the words of Romain Rolland, Péguy found "the tyrannical and sectarian point of view of his colleagues . . . intolerable," only too much like the position from which "a Minister of the Empire" would be expected to "operate" (quoted and translated by Villiers). The very idea of class warfare, Péguy had come to conclude, was inherently "bourgeois": "Nous voulons la Révolution, mais nous ne voulons pas la haine éternelle," as he puts it in the eighth issue of *Cahiers de la Quinzaine* (20 April 1900). Late in 1899, he resigned from his editorship with the Librairie and established his periodical *Cahiers,* with its office on the rue des Fossés-Saint-Jacques. Two works published in the second issue (20 January 1900), *Lettre du Provincial* and *Préparation du Congrès Socialiste Nationale*, made clear at once his opposition to the edict of the Congress that "the press will refrain from all communications which might damage the organisation," and his conviction that the materialist division of society into warring classes does "not represent a classification of hearts and consciences." He found the Party's edicts entirely "too despotic," in contravention of the principle of genuine justice. The purpose of the *Cahiers*, as he envisioned it, was to tell the unvarnished truth, whole and unembellished: in the words of his *Lettre du Provincial,* "à dire la vérité, toute la vérité, rien que la vérité, dire bêtement la vérité bête, ennuyeusement la vérité ennuyeuse, tristement la vérité triste."

In the fall of 1901, confident that "tout ce qu'il y avait de mystique, de fidèle, de croyant, dans le Dreyfusisme s'est refugié dans les Cahiers" (*Notre Jeunesse),* Péguy moved his entire publishing enterprise to 8 rue de la Sorbonne, which would prove to be its last home. Once again, his disregard for established commercial practices had its natural effect. For all their limited circulation, though, the first issues of the Cahiers de la Quinzaine succeeded in attracting a number of distinguished and influential subscribers, among them Jean Jaurès, Raymond Poincaré, Étienne Millerand, Anatole France, Gide, the Library of the Senate and the *Bulletin de l'Union pour l'Action.* The considerable minatory criticism that various numbers of the Cahiers met with, even from subscribers, normally had to do with apparent lapses from the *bienséances* dear to Gallic high literary culture. Rolland's response to that line of criticism, as reported by Villiers, remains telling: "You can criticise . . . the authors, the editor, anything except the production. You may say that we don't know French, that we lack common sense, that we are bores, but to say that the paper of the *Cahiers* is poor and the printing is bad shows poor judgment." And Péguy prized judgment as much as practical beauty. If analysis by reason, as he explained in his *De la raison* (December 1901), neither exhausts nor represents the best of life ("nous savons que la raison n'épuise pas la vie et même le meilleur de la vie"), the life of reasoned discipline stands as a necessary condition for all genuine, humane craftsmanship.

Péguy subsequently distanced himself from "the Socialist hunger" for "pure fame" that he was saddened to detect in the political maneouvering of his friend Jean Jaurès, for example, since such a hunger, in his view, signed a disposition to "dictatorship," augured the triumph of the bourgeois spirit resentful of difference and genuine independence: "It is slaves who do not differ, or who differ less." "A *politique* cannot replace a religion, nor can a *politique* displace a *mystique,*" as he averred in his *avertissement* to the M.M. Mangasarian *Cahier* of March 1904. In a series of four formidably titled works–*De la Situation Faite à l'Histoire et à la Sociologie dans les Temps Modernes* (November 1906), *De la Situation Faite au Parti Intellectuel dans le Monde Moderne* (December 1906), *De la Situation Faite à l'Histoire et à la Sociologie et de la Situation Faite au Parti Intellectuel dans le Monde Moderne* (February 1907) and *De la Situation Faite au Parti Intellectuel dans le Monde Moderne devant les Accidents de la Gloire Temporelle* (October 1907)– Péguy characterized the École Normale Supérieure as a "seminary" for the training a new clergy inimical to intellectual freedom. His assailing of "the Socialist Church" had an ironic double effect: Socialist Party members suspected him of being a Catholic and closet anarchist, while the Catholic establishment regarded him as something of an atheistic revolutionary.

Péguy suffered intensely during the years that immediately followed. A crushing workload left him exhausted, prone to illness; and his parting from old friends and cohorts in the cause of social justice left him very much isolated. But with suffering came a blessing: in the autumn of 1908, while recovering from a bout of influenza, Péguy announced to Joseph Lotte that he had come to discover himself "un Catholique." As Villiers records his description of his "conversion," it represented not so much "a return" as a moving forward: "We did not find the high road of Christianity by turning back . . . ; we found it at the end." The news of Péguy's conversion was spread by Raïssa and Jacques Maritain, recent converts to Roman Catholicism who did all that they could to induce him to return to the fold of institutional orthodoxy. But Péguy's fidelity to the promises he had made to his wife Charlotte made it impossible for him to go to confession, attend weekly Mass, have his marriage "blessed" and his children baptized. Nor did he turn away from the Maritains, whose sometimes meddling actions on his behalf he magnanimously understood as prompted by charity.

Three prose *mystères* were to register some of the genuinely theological effects attendant on Péguy's recognition of himself as a traveller along "the high road of Christianity." The first, a poetic drama titled *Le Mystére de la Charité de Jeanne d'Arc* (October 1909), opens with a scene of Joan beset by anxiety and inspired by hope as she prays to "Notre Père" for the coming of His kingdom:

> Notre Père, notre père qui êtes aux cieux, de combien il s'en faut que votre volonté soit faite; de combien il s'en faut que nous ayons notre pain de chaque jour. De combien il s'en faut que nous pardonnions nos offenses; et que nous ne succombions pas à la tentation; et que nous soyons délivrés du mal. Ainsi soit-il.

What consolation Joan finds is in working towards an actualizing of that kingdom: "*orare est laborare.*" *Le Mystère de la Charité* found an enthusiastic reader in André Gide, who wrote a review in praise of Péguy's style (which minded him of "very old litanies") and who sent copies of the book to Francis Jammes, Emile Verhaeren and Paul Claudel. The two subseqent *mystères–Le Porche du Mystère de la Deuxième Vertu* (October 1911), on the virtue of hope as encouraged by the parables of the Lost Sheep and the Prodigal Son; and *Le Mystère des Saints Innocents* (March 1912), a paean to a child-like spirituality reckoned dearer to God than a spirituality born of the complexities of experience–met with little or no immediate reader response. Their very simplicity and homely tenor seem have left such sophisticated sympathizers as Claudel, Maritain and Gide at sixes and sevens, leaving them very much behind, with nothing much to say.

The poet in Péguy also came very much alive with his renewed sense of Christian allegiance. In the period 1910-1912, he composed 1500 sets of quatrains centred on a comparison of the theological virtues (of faith, hope and charity) with the cardinal virtues (of prudence, justice, fortitude and temperance): "Les quatre Cardinales / Viennent des dieux, / Les trois Théologales / Viennent du Dieu." Péguy's substantial concern in these quatrains is with the corruption of the "Theologicals" when the authority of these is derived from the "Cardinals," virtues only too attractive to the worldliness of a politicized spirituality. His conviction of the abidingly mystical, theological character of the human condition is further indicated in his *Tapisseries de Sainte Geneviève et de Jeanne d'Arc* (December 1912), a series of poems in nine parts inspired by his several pilgrimages to Chartres in the summer of 1912:

> Mais c'est l'esprit qui mène et l'esprit qui nourrit

Et la lettre n'est là que comme un mot écrit;
Et la lettre n'a jamains fait qu'un peut de bruit,
C'est elle qui séduit et c'est elle qui nuit.
Et la lettre et l'esprit, c'est le jour et la nuit.

But such a disjoining of "the letter" from "the spirit" hardly accorded with Péguy's own practice. He abidingly kept to the letter of his word. In the first months of 1913, Péguy prayed to Our Lady for the deliverance of his son afflicted with typhoid, promising that he would make yet another pilgrimage to Chartres should his prayer be answered. The boy recovered, and Peguy kept his promise, making a number of pilgrimages (on foot) to that cathedral during the following summer. *La Tapisserie de Notre Dame de Chartres* (1913; initially published in *Le Figaro*), a prayerful testimony in the form of a sequence of poems, bespeaks its author's coming to peace and reconciliation in a place and a spirit of veneration, simplicity, blessing, understanding:

Voici le lieu du monde où tout devient facile,
Le regret, le départ, même l'évènement,
Et l'adieu temporaire et le détournement,
Le seul coin de la terre où tout devient docile. . . .
Voici le lieu du monde où tout est revenu
Après tant de départs, après tant d'arrivées. . . .
Voici le lieu du monde où tout rentre et se tait,
Et le silence et l'ombre et la charnelle absence,
Et le commencement d'éternelle présence,
Le seul réduit où l'âme est tout ce qu'elle était.

For all of the piety and respect for Christian tradition that it evinces, though, the poem failed to convince the Catholic establishment of its author's full orthodoxy. The Benedictine monk Louis Baillet, an old friend from his days at Sainte-Barbe, expressed his fear that the writer of *La Tapisserie de Notre Dame de Chartres* "would make a heretic."

And Father Baillet, attentive as he was to the politics of ecclesiastical thinking, had reason to be so concerned. The anticlericalism of *Véronique: Dialogue de l'Histoire de l'Âme Charnelle* and *Clio: Dialogue de l'Histoire et de l'Âme Païenne*, works from Péguy's last years, was anything but oblique. Since "it is the ligature of the eternal and the temporal . . . which constitutes Christianity," as he observed in *Véronique*, the effects produced by the "lay-curés who deny the eternal aspect of the temporal" and by the "ecclesiastical curés who deny the temporal in the eternal" have been equally disastrous for genuine Christianity. That critique is extended in *Clio*, which stresses the "inorganic," dissociative character of a modern culture founded on a Cartesian-style "dualism" and an economy of "money" (translated by Villiers).

With *Eve* (December 1913), a poem of some two-thousand quatrains, Péguy's belief in the coincidence of the temporal and the eternal in bona fide Christianity found explicitly constructive expression. In his 1970 anthology of critical responses to Péguy's writing, Fraisse includes Jean Onimus's description of the story that *Eve* tells is one of "life confronted by the forces of destruction and placing its ultimate hope in grace." The mystery of the Incarnation essential to Christian belief in grace and reconciliation naturally provides the poem's basic point of reference:

> Car le surnaturel est lui-même charnel
> Et l'arbre de la grâce est racine profonde,
> Et plonge dans le sol et cherche jusqu'au fond
> Et l'arbre de la race est lui-même éternel.

A Péguy rooted in such a faith could hardly help but continue to sympathize, at least in part, with the Bergsonian resistance to any philosophy that would radically sever matter from spirit, "idea" from "extension."

But politically speaking, Peguy's anticipation, shared with Baillet, that he would come to be deemed by the Church as something of "a heretic," was only too well founded. His *Note sur M. Bergson et la Philosophie Bergsonienne* (April 1914) was clearly anti-Cartesian, but was also taken to be anti-Thomist by Catholic critics of Bergson, most notably Peguy's good friend Jacques Maritain. When Bergson's books were placed on the Index of Forbidden Books in the early summer of 1914, Maritain implored Péguy to turn his back on his old teacher. Peguy declined to do so, on the grounds that such an action would betray his own conscience and violate his commitment to "la mystique."

Peguy's Bergsonianism seems also to have played a role in his decision, at age forty-one, to volunteer for army service in August 1914. Yet again, his position was as much philosophical as practical in its justification: the war against Germany was "une juste guerre" since it represented, in his view, a struggle against the forces of scientism and industrialism, ever enemies at once to the principle of *élan vital*, the justice of Christian socialism and the humane ideals of liberty, equality, fraternity. In the late summer of 1914, on the Feast of the Assumption of the Blessed Virgin Mary, Lieutenant Charles Péguy of the 276th Regiment attended Mass for the first and last time since his "conversion." And true to his commitment to the spirit of *élan vital* that he shared with his commanding officers, he urged his troops to move forward whenever the occasion to do so presented itself. According to several accounts, he died suddenly, standing up, from a single shot in the forehead, as he led an attack against retreating German troops in the neighbourhood of Villeroy, on the river Marne. His last words, heard on 5 September 1914, were "Tirez, tirez, nom de Dieu," an oath or an imprecation or a prayer directed to the men under his command, who prudently continued to lie low and keep their heads down. Not long after hearing the news of her husband's death, Charlotte became a Catholic and had her children baptized. In 1920, after much official hesitation, Peguy was made a Chevalier de la Légion d'Honneur and was awarded the Croix de Guerre.

Many other signs of Péguy's recognition were to follow. His writings and the example of his life inspired French prisoners of war and members of the Resistance during the years of Vichy; and the society l'Amitié Charles Péguy was founded in 1946. *Feuillets*, a bio-bibliographical newsletter published by that society, dates from 1948. Commemorations of the fiftieth anniversary of his death included the establishment of the Centre Charles Péguy d'Orléans and the holding of an international symposium in honour of his achievement, also at Orléans. Auguste Martin and Georges Dalgues' 1973 exhibition catalogue presenting

Péguy's manuscripts, and Simone Fraisse's edition of *Les Critiques de notre temps et Péguy* figure among the many still highly useful scholarly works published in celebration of the centenary of Péguy's birth. The long list of writers influenced by his oeuvre includes Rolland, Gide, Louis Aragon, Julian Green, Georges Bernanos and May Sarton. Radical Christian theologians since the Second Vatican Council have increasingly come to value Péguy's achievement. Urs von Balthasar, for one, has ranked the author of *Le Mystère de la Charité de Jeanne d'Arc* among the "ten essential Christians since Jesus."

REFERENCES

Boudon, Victor. *Avec Charles Péguy de la Lorraine à la Marne, août-septembre 1914*. Preface by Maurice Barrès. Paris: Hachette, 1916.

Christophe, Lucien. *Les Grandes Heures de Charles Péguy, du fleuve à la mer*. (Brussels: Renaissance du Livre, 1964.

Fraisse, Simone, ed. *Les Critiques de notre temps et Péguy.* Paris: Garnier, 1973).

Martin, Auguste and Georges Dalgues, eds. *Manuscrits de Péguy*. Introduction by René Thinat. Orléans: Centre Charles Péguy, 1973.

Onimus, Jean. *Introduction aux Quatrains de Péguy.* Paris: L'Amitié Charles Péguy, 1952.

Viard, Jacques. *Philosophie de l'art littéraire et le socialisme selon Péguy*. Paris: Klincksieck, 1970.

Villiers, Marjorie. *Charles Péguy: A Study in Integrity*. London: Collins, 1965; New York: Harper & Row, 1966.

Excursus/Recursus: Parlons d'amour

Lettre d'Albert Jean-Marie Mainguy
à Marie Herminie Moyon.

Haute Silésie [1920]

Mon chérie,
je m'empresse a t'envoyer cette petit foto a vec des copins dela 46e de Chasseurs qui on volue que je ne fasse oublier avec heut et je t'assure qu'au jour d'huit je suis aller les conduire au train avec une grande choie, mais au font je t'assure j'aurais bien voulue partir avec heut alors mon chérie bien aimée je ne peut faire autrements, je suis obligée de restés avec un grand cafard alors mon petit chérie les deux camarade que j'ais conduit au train celui qui a une petit croit au dessue et s'était un bon copain mais pas de chez moi, un de Paris et l'autre du Finistère alors mon chérie je t'aime. ma lettre en transport de tout mon coeur resoie milles et milles bises de ton petit
Albert

Lettre de Malvina Orphilia Grenon La Bossière
to Camille René La Bossière

Hospice Taché, Saint-Boniface [1967]

Appel of my eye,
. . . Bonne cibishes et canne de tomates. . . . Di le rosaire pour toi shaque jour. . . .
Gramma

Québec, Canada
2003